Animals and Christianity

DATE DUE

ANIMALS
and
CHRISTIANITY

A Book of Readings

◆

Edited by ANDREW LINZEY
and TOM REGAN

CROSSROAD ◆ NEW YORK

1988
The Crossroad Publishing Company
370 Lexington Avenue, New York, N.Y. 10017

Library of Congress Cataloging-in-Publication Data

Animals and Christianity : a book of readings / edited by Andrew
  Linzey and Tom Regan.
      p. cm.
    Bibliography: p.
    ISBN 0-8245-0902-1 (pbk.)
    1. Animals—Religious aspects—Christianity. I. Linzey, Andrew.
II. Regan, Tom.
BT746.A55 1988
241'.693—dc19   88-16181
                                                   CIP

Contents

Introduction: 'A Great Ethic'

ANDREW LINZEY and TOM REGAN

> I believe that pity is a law like justice, and that kindness is a duty like uprightness. That which is weak has a right to the kindness and pity of that which is strong.
>
> In the relations of man with the animals, with the flowers, with all the objects of creation, there is a great ethic, scarcely perceived as yet, which will at length break through into the light, and which will be the corollary and the complement to human ethics.
>
> Are there not here unsounded depths for the thinker? Is one to think oneself mad because one has the sentiment of universal pity in one's heart?
>
> VICTOR HUGO

> It is necessary and urgent that following the example of the poor man (St Francis) one decides to abandon inconsiderate forms of domination, capture and custody with respect to all creatures.
>
> POPE JOHN PAUL II

A century separates the words of Victor Hugo and Pope John Paul II. Within the institutionalized church it has been largely a hundred years of neglect of all the objects of creation Hugo mentions, the animals in particular. Indifference has been the dominant response to 'inconsiderate forms of domination,' with few church leaders speaking out or acting boldly in the name of that 'great ethic' Hugo envisaged.

It has not always been so. When the Victoria Street Society was formed in London, in November 1875, it counted the Archbishop of York among its four original members, and by early 1876 the progressive

Roman Catholic thinker, Cardinal Manning, had joined. The Society's objectives were ambitious: to regulate vivisection, then only in its infancy, with a view to bringing about its total abolition. Agreement on the desirability of these goals superceded whatever theological and other differences there might have been, so that even so unlikely a pair as Cardinal Manning and Lord Shaftesbury, the latter being one of the founding members and an unyielding evangelical, were able to work harmoniously in the name of animal protection.

In this effort they were joined by the major writers and poets of the day—Tennyson, Browning, Carlyle and Ruskin, for example. More than fifty years earlier, in 1824, the Royal Society for the Protection of Animals (RSPCA) had been founded, again with Christian leadership, this time in the person of the Reverend Arthur Broome. It was Broome, moreover, who had overseen the reprinting of what was then the definitive work on issues relating to animal abuse: *The Duty of Mercy and the Sin of Cruelty to Brute Animals,* by the Reverend Dr Humphry Primatt, first published in 1776. Religious involvement in animal-protection efforts was a matter of course in the eighteenth and nineteenth centuries, as was the active participation of those who had achieved fame in their own lifetime. In those hopeful days it was not unusual that so renowned a figure as Victor Hugo, already recognized as a remarkable writer, would be asked to be the first president of the *Societé française contra la vivisection,* formally constitued in June 1883, or that when he accepted he is reported to have said, 'My name is nothing. It is in the name of the whole human race that you make your appeal.' It was in this same spirit, 'in the name of the whole human race,' that Cardinal Manning, the Archbishop of York, Arthur Broome and the other Christian members of the respective Societies spoke.

Thus do we have a paradox certain to challenge every thoughtful Christian: On the one hand, we find vital, visionary Christian involvement in the creation of animal-protection organizations during the past century; on the other hand, we witness a century of all but official silence and neglect on the part of almost all Christians, including, most conspicuously, those in positions of power and authority. How might we explain this ascendency of Christian indifference over Christian compassion?

A variety of possible answers comes to mind. To begin with, it cannot be irrelevant that during the more than one hundred years since the formation of the Victoria Street Society (now the National

Anti-vivisection Society, UK) we have seen the slow but steady advance of secular humanism in the Western world. The enormous power and influence of this philosophy, embodying as it does the Protagorian maxim that 'Man is the measure of all things,' has not been kind to the 'great ethic' glimpsed by Hugo. The plain fact is, most humans don't place much value on the nonhuman world, animals included; those 'inconsiderate forms of domination' of which Pope John Paul II speaks are easy to defend when the creatures who are exploited are denied all, or allowed little, independent value. Because a boastful, arrogant humanism has become such a powerful force in the contemporary world, one might view Christian indifference to the many 'inconsiderate forms of domination' animals are made to endure as one among a number of tangible signs of the triumph of secular humanism.

But this explanation, correct though it is in noting the rise of secular humanism during the past hundred years, is incorrect at deeper levels. It is incorrect, first, in underestimating the staying-power of committed Christian belief. For Christians do not surrender articles of considered faith merely because powerful voices speak against them. Just the opposite. The history of the Christian experience teaches us this if it teaches us anything.

The preceding explanation also is incorrect in supposing that Christian neglect of the nonhuman created order is to be attributed to the triumph of forces outside Christianity. In point of fact Christian faith is a house divided against itself on the most fundamental issues arising in this context. The ascension of Christian indifference over Christian compassion is far more likely due to sources from within, rather than those from without, the community of Christian believers.

The materials collected in the present volume more than confirm this judgment. Among the thinkers represented here, some believe that the proper relationship between humans and the rest of the created order is fundamentally the same as the relationship favored by secular humanism: The world and all its nonhuman inhabitants, on this view, because they lack independent value, are to be regarded and treated as so many resources to be used by human beings; what value the rest of nature has, in other words, is to be determined by how well it meets or advances human needs and interests. In practice, therefore, 'Christian humanism' (if we may use this expression thus) yields results that coincide with those sanctioned by any form of 'secular humanism' worthy of the name.

There is, however, a quite different way to read the sacred Christian texts and interpret the Christian experience. Roughly speaking, this involves viewing the animals, the flowers and the other objects of creation, as having independent value—value in their own right, apart from human needs and interests. On this reading, therefore, any exclusively 'humanistic' ethic must fall short of prescribing the kind of life to which Christians are called and in which they are to find (and live) the Truth. A 'greater ethic,' one that is at once more demanding and encompassing, one that speaks directly to those 'inconsiderate forms of domination' of which the Pope reminds us that we are capable, must be found. Whatever the letter of its principles, the renunciation of all forms of humanism captures its spirit.

The resolution of that paradox noted earlier, therefore—the paradox of passionate Christian concern for animals at an earlier time, on the one hand, and, on the other, the more recent triumph of Christian indifference regarding the ill-treatment of these creatures—the resolution of this paradox most likely is to be found inside our Christian traditions, not outside them. In the days of Cardinal Manning, the Archbishop of York, Lord Shaftesbury and the other Christians who in the nineteenth century demanded justice even for the animals, we see discernible hints of a more encompassing ethic, one that would have us protect the interests and integrity of nonhuman animals; and it would have us do this in the name of Christian duty, independently of our measuring how human needs and interests will be affected. In the years since, by contrast, we witness the increasing dominance of a second strand of Christian thought, the one that fixes the value and integrity of nonhuman creation, animals included, by asking what advances our species or our individual needs and interests. Arguably, in short, those pioneering Christians of the nineteenth century, as well as those others, like Primatt, who pre-dated them, glimpsed 'the great ethic' Hugo imagined, while their successors for the most part have seen things differently, which is why they have acted differently. Not for them the cause of 'animal rights,' whether in the pulpit or in the streets.

Which one of these interpretations of the Christian ethic, if either, is closest to the truth cannot be settled in this Introduction. Which, if either, is to be preferred, one might say, is *the* central question to be answered *after, not before* the selections collected here have been read. What is clear, and what can be asserted confidently even in advance of coming to terms with the central question, is that to read these selections is to be reminded again and again that there are alternative, initially plausible and yet mutually inconsistent ways of interpreting the holy scriptures, some of which support humanistic interpretations of the values nature holds, others, not. And thus it is that the apparently minor debate over what, if anything, we owe the animals, in the end obliges us to face the most fundamental questions Christians must ask: Who are we? Why are we? The lesson to be learned, paradoxical enough in its own right, is that the path to self-understanding must proceed through an understanding of 'the other,' even when that other is not human.

But while the moral question, the one that asks 'What do we owe the animals?' arguably is the central question in this context, it is by no means the only one. To see this we have only to remind ourselves of the other theological problems in which animals traditionally have played a role. Theodicy, for example. Were humans the only creatures who suffered, then the quest for an adequate explanation of evil (an adequate theodicy) could limit its scope to the suffering that befalls humanity. But we are not the only creatures who suffer. Indeed, the natural system of predator-prey relationships, as they exist in the world, ensure that many animals—literally billions and billions of them, over time—suffer enormously. Because these animal victims are not plausibly viewed as having done something wrong, we cannot explain their suffering by invoking their guilt. And because their suffering is a brute fact (so to speak), one cannot make the challenge to theodicy easier by denying the reality of animal pain.

What one can do is deny that animal pain or suffering *are evil.* This would certainly be an alternative that proponents of 'Christian humanism' might find attractive. Not so in the case of those who are enamored of that 'great ethic,' the main outlines of which Hugo sets before us. Which of these views, if either, is correct, again remains to be decided on the basis of a close reading of the selections that follow. What is clear even at this point, is that animals are quite capable of making messes in Christian thought.

How much this is true can be seen by considering a different, related matter, that of animal redemption. Some religious opponents of animal rights maintain that humans alone among all God's creatures have immortal souls, and conclude that redemption is possible for humans only. Coupled with this is the belief that whatever has an immortal soul is of inestimably greater value than whatever lacks one, from which it is a short step to the conclusion that the latter exists for the sake of the former. The belief that nonhuman animals lack souls, in short, often is used to bolster a 'Christian humanism' of the sort described earlier.

However, not all Christians speak with one voice on this matter. Some find what they regard as compelling biblical evidence for the view that redemption is not reserved for Man alone. This finding, if valid, is certain to have far reaching consequences regarding the moral status of the created order in general and of animals in particular. Of course, the validity of this reading of the scriptures cannot be decided here. What can and should be said at this juncture, is that there is a *serious question* to be asked in this quarter. We are not likely to behave appropriately toward that which we fail to understand, which is why it is morally incumbent on us to struggle to understand not only our own place in the grand scheme of things, but that of all creatures.

Both these matters, then—first, the role of animal pain in theodicy, and, second, the question of animal redemption—can be viewed as variations on the main theme highlighted earlier. To the extent that an interpretation of the Christian ethic mimics the scope and content of secular humanism, to that extent we are likely to find both a theodicy that minimizes the importance of animal pain and a view of redemption that reserves life-after-death for humans only. To the extent that an interpretation of this ethic enlarges upon the borders drawn by a humanistic account of values in nature, however, to that extent the significance of animal pain for theodicy and the prospects of animal redemption in the after-life will be taken more seriously. The central question characterized above, the moral question, 'What do we owe the animals?' seems always to be hovering in the background.

That question increasingly has come to the fore in those contexts where the adequacy of secular humanism has been subjected to serious critical review. The intellectual leaders of the environmental as well as the animal rights movements, whatever their differences on some points, at least are agreed on the desirability of overthrowing the principles of secular humanism. We humans are not the measure of all things, these thinkers maintain, since there are values in the world apart from our needs and interests—values to be discovered, not created, by us. The impact of this major assault on secular humanism is perhaps nowhere more evident than in our institutions of higher learning. A decade ago it was all but impossible to find a college or university student discussing 'animal rights' in the classroom. Today, thanks to the creative work of many, tens of thousands of students discuss this idea every year, just in the United States, in classes in moral philosophy at our secular colleges and universities.

As for classes at our church-related colleges and universities, 'animal rights' now occupies the position that it occupied a decade earlier in their secular counterparts. One reason for this neglect may be the absence of an appropriate collection of readings, a collection that sets out the relevant issues against the backdrop of Christian thought and experience. The present collection seeks to remedy this. But another, no less important reason helps explain the absence of such a reader in the first place. In the internal dialectic we know as the history of Christian thought the past century has witnessed the gradual but certain ascent of Christian humanism, and so firm has the grip of this part of the Christian tradition become that discussion of the idea of animal rights has not even been on the agenda. And where no need is sensed, there nothing will be created to satisfy it.

Thus may the present anthology be viewed as itself a symptom of the growing sense that something is needed if contemporary Christians are to be in a position to respond with knowledge and insight to the mounting challenges being made against humanism, whether secular or religious. Other symptoms of this re-awakening are the increasing number of statements that are being made on behalf of animals by influential church leaders, as well as the steadily growing number of church services that are being performed in celebration of animals.

In light of these developments, we perhaps need not be as disheartened as Anna Kingsford was, by religion's lack of involvement in the cause of justice for the animals. A major force in the animal-protection movement of the nineteenth century, married to an Anglican priest and herself a convert to Catholicism, Anna Kingsford was moved to lament that 'the Church needs as much saving as the world.' How correct she is in her judgment, it would be rash to decide. But to the extent that she is correct, it is apposite to observe that one possible saving grace for all Christian churches, and all Christians, is to be found in seriously examining the merits of that 'great ethic' Hugo sensed, finding how, if possible, it can be given a distinctively Christian interpretation, and (assuming that it can) then struggling to give that ethic life through our deeds. For there are 'inconsiderate forms of domination' that need to be righted, and one need not any longer think oneself 'mad' for believing so.

Acknowledgments

The Scripture quotations in this publication are from the Revised Standard Version of the Bible, copyrighted 1946, 1952, © 1971, 1973 by the Division of Christian Education of the National Council of the Churches of Christ in the USA, and are used by permission.

We are grateful to the following for permission to reproduce copyright material:

Basil Blackwell Ltd for the extract from *The Concept of God* by Keith Ward.

Burns & Oates Ltd for the extract from *An Introduction to the Devout Life* by St Francis de Sales, trans. Michael Day.

Cambridge University Press for the extracts from *Philosophical Works of Descartes*, trans. E. S. Haldane and G. R. T. Ross, and from *Providence and Evil* by Peter Geach.

Centaur Press Ltd for the extract from Ruth Harrison's contribution to *Animals' Rights—A Symposium*, ed. David Paterson and R. D. Ryder.

T. & T. Clark Ltd for the extracts from *Church Dogmatics* by Karl Barth, trans. A. T. Mackay, T. H. L. Parker, H. Knight, H. A. Kennedy and J. Marks.

Anthony Clarke Books for the extract from *The Complete Works* of St John of the Cross, trans. A. E. Peers.

James Clarke & Co. for the extract from *The Mystical Theology of the Eastern Church* by Vladimir Lossky.

Collins Publishers for the extracts from John Austin Baker's contribution to *Man and Nature*, ed. Hugh Montefiore; from *Evil and the God of Love* by John Hick; from *Love Almighty and Ills Unlimited* by Austin Farrer; and from *The Problem of Pain* by C. S. Lewis.

Wm B. Eerdmans Publishing Co. for the extract from the essay by Paulos Mar Gregorios in *Tending the Garden: Essays on the Gospel and the Church*, ed. Wesley Granberg-Michaelson.

Epworth Press for the extract from *Tower Hill, 12.30* by Donald Soper.

Victor Gollancz Ltd for the extract from Edward Carpenter's contribution to *Against Hunting*, ed. Patrick Moore.

Grove Books Ltd for the extract from *The Human Use of Animals* by Richard Griffiths.

The publishers of *The Month* for the article 'The Pains of Animals' by C. E. M. Joad and C. S. Lewis.

The publishers of *New Blackfriars* for the article 'Animals in Heaven?' by Edward Quinn.

North River Press Inc for the extract from *The Right to Hunt* by James B. Whisker.

Oliver & Boyd for the extract from Calvin's *Commentaries*, ed. D. W. Torrance and T. F. Torrance, trans. Ross Mackenzie.

Oxford University Press for the extracts from *Descartes: Philosophical Letters*, trans. and ed. Anthony Kenny; from *Contra Gentes and De Incarnatione* by St Athanasius, trans. and ed. Robert W. Thomson; from *The Moral Status of Animals* by Stephen R. L. Clark; and from *Recollections and Essays* by Leo Tolstoy.

Penguin Books Ltd for the extract from *Concerning the City of God Against the Pagans* by St Augustine, trans. Henry Bettenson.

SCM Press for the extracts from *Systematic Theology* by Paul Tillich and for the sermon 'Animals' in *Windsor Sermons* by Alec R. Vidler.

Sheed & Ward Ltd for the extract from *Moral and Pastoral Theology* by Henry Davis.

Sphere/Abacus for the extract from *Small is Beautiful* by E. F. Schumacher.

Unwin Hyman Ltd for the extracts from *Civilization and Ethics* by Albert Schweitzer, trans. C. T. Campion, and for the quotations from St Irenaeus taken from *Basic Readings in Theology*, ed. A. D. Galloway.

Full publication details are given in a footnote to each reading.

Part One

◆

ATTITUDES
TO CREATION

Introduction to Part One

Our opening section begins by introducing some of the pivotal assumptions which frequently influence, directly or indirectly, Christian attitudes towards animals. Animals, we learn in the Bible, are created by God. They are made on the fifth and sixth days of creation and together with man they are the recipients of a common blessing. Animals, therefore, have some fundamental value to God—expressed by Genesis in the idea that God saw what he had made and 'behold it was very good.' According to Jesus even the sparrows sold in the market place, quite literally for two a penny, have value to their Creator. Animals are our fellow-creatures in creation. They share with man, according to Genesis 2, the fall of creation, and God's restorative covenant with Noah expressly includes all living things. The Psalmists repeatedly declare how all creatures, including the animals, praise their Creator. And yet it is also clear in the biblical material that humans have a special place in creation. They are made in God's image and are given dominion over the beasts of the field, as well as the fish of the sea and the birds of the air.

How we are to interpret that dominion over animals is the subject of our first two selections. Bishop John Austin Baker insists that dominion does not mean despotism. Dominion is 'poles apart from the kind of right to egoistical exploitation which it suggests to our ears.' To have divine power over animals, argues Baker, essentially means behaving as God's vice-regent, that is with responsibility and restraint. That this was the original intention of the Priestly writer is confirmed by the divine injunction to man—who has been given dominion—to be vegetarian. Baker, therefore, maintains that the Old Testament is free from exploitative attitudes. 'Although it recognises man's preying on nature as a fact, it characterises that fact as a mark of man's decline from the first perfect intention of God for him.'

St Thomas Aquinas, by contrast, insists that human mastery over animals belongs to man in his state of innocence. Unlike Baker, who sees carnivourousness as a mark of creation's fallenness, Aquinas argues that 'in the state of innocence man had mastership over the animals by commanding them.' Adam, after all, names the animals and thereby expresses sovereignty over them. But not only in commanding, or changing them, is man's mastery expressed but also 'in making use of them without hindrance.' This, Aquinas claims, is God's will in creation.

The purposes for which animals were created are among the issues raised by our next two selections. On the one hand, Calvin is clear that animals, like plants and vegetables, were created solely for the use of humans. Animals exist for human ends 'that none of the conveniences and necessities of life might be wanting to men.' 'Man was rich before he was born' because of the special generosity ordained by God in his creation. John Burnaby, on the other hand, protests against this anthropocentric view. The idea that the universe was made for man is not, he argues, an assumption required by the Christian faith. On the contrary, God's universal purposes extend to all creation; all life exists principally for the glory of God.

The three remaining authors address the question of the unity of creation. Metropolitan Gregorios, interpreting Colossians 1, lays great stress on the incarnation of God in Christ as the meeting of the 'spiritual' and the 'material' worlds. In Christ *all* things are reconciled. Christ's body 'is a *material* body—transformed, of course, but transformed *matter*. Thus he shares his being with the whole created order: animals and birds, snakes and worms, flowers and seeds.' St Bonaventure in an arguably similar vein emphasises how the unity between Christ and creation enabled the great saint, Francis, to call creatures 'brother or sister, because he knew they had the same source as himself.' The stories of St Francis caring for animals exemplify in a practical way this serious theological point, namely that the love of God in Christ embraces each and every creature. It could be that in the life of St Francis we see the living out of the ethical dimension of the Noachic covenant—summarised in the line that 'we are all in one boat together.'

Vladimir Lossky, too, opposes the view that man can be seen in isolation from creation. Interpreting the theology of St Maximus, he suggests that man is a microcosm of the whole creation and is therefore intimately bound up with all of its constituent parts. Indeed, man's own salvation is part and parcel of the universal work of redemption which confers on humans a unique ethical responsibility. 'In his way to union with God, man in no way leaves the creatures aside, but gathers together in his love the whole cosmos disordered by sin, that it may at last be transfigured by grace.'

We may summarise the main issues in this section as follows: (1) Does human dominion over animals mean mastery or service? (2) Are animals made for human use or the glory of God? and (3) If there is a unity between humans and animals should this be properly expressed in the form of a common moral obligation?

The Bible

On Creation, Covenant and Interdependence

Genesis 1:20–28 and 31a

And God said, "Let the waters bring forth swarms of living creatures, and let birds fly above the earth across the firmament of the heavens." So God created the great sea monsters and every living creature that moves, with which the waters swarm, according to their kinds, and every winged bird according to its kind. And God saw that it was good. And God blessed them, saying, "Be fruitful and multiply and fill the waters in the seas, and let birds multiply on the earth." And there was evening and there was morning, a fifth day.

And God said, "Let the earth bring forth living creatures according to their kinds: cattle and creeping things and beasts of the earth according to their kinds." And it was so.

And God made the beasts of the earth according to their kinds and the cattle according to their kinds, and everything that creeps upon the ground according to its kind. And God saw that it was good. Then God said, "Let us make man in our image, after our likeness; and let them have dominion over the fish of the sea, and over the birds of the air, and over the cattle, and over all the earth, and over every creeping thing that creeps upon the earth." So God created man in his own image, in the image of God he created him; male and female he created them. And God blessed them, and God said to them, "Be fruitful and multiply, and fill the earth and subdue it; and have dominion over the fish of the sea and over the birds of the air and over every living thing that moves upon the earth."

And God saw everything that he had made, and behold, it was very good.

Genesis 2:4b–7 and 15

In the day that the Lord made the earth and the heavens, when no plant of the field was yet in the earth and no herb of the field

6

had yet sprung up—for the Lord God had not caused it to rain upon the earth, and there was no man to till the ground; but a mist went up from the earth and watered the whole face of the ground—then the Lord God formed man of dust from the ground, and breathed into his nostrils the breath of life; and man became a living being.

The Lord God took the man and put him in the garden of Eden to till it and keep it.

Genesis 2:18–20

Then the Lord God said, "It is not good that the man should be alone; I will make him a helper fit for him." So out of the ground the Lord God formed every beast of the field and every bird of the air, and brought them to the man to see what he would call them; and whatever the man called every living creature, that was its name. The man gave names to all cattle, and to the birds of the air, and to every beast of the field; but for the man there was not found a helper fit for him.

Genesis 3:13–15

Then the Lord God said to the woman, "What is this that you have done?" The woman said, "The serpent beguiled me, and I ate." The Lord God said to the serpent.

> "Because you have done this,
>> cursed are you above all cattle,
>> and above all wild animals;
> upon your belly you shall go,
>> and dust you shall eat
>> all the days of your life.
> I will put enmity between you and the woman,
>> and between your seed and her seed;
> he shall bruise your head,
>> and you shall bruise his heel."

Genesis 6:5–8

The Lord saw that the wickedness of man was great in the earth, and that every imagination of the thoughts of his heart was only evil continually. And the Lord was sorry that he had made man on the earth, and it grieved him to his heart. So the Lord said, "I will blot out man whom I have created from the face of the ground, man and beast and creeping things and birds of the air, for I am sorry that I have made them." But Noah found favour in the eyes of the Lord.

Genesis 7:1–4

Then the Lord said to Noah, "Go into the ark, you and all your household, for I have seen that you are righteous before me in this generation. Take with you seven pairs of all clean animals, the male and his mate; and a pair of the animals that are not clean, the male and female, and seven pairs of the birds of the air also, male and female, to keep their kind alive upon the face of all the earth. For in seven days I will send rain upon the earth forty days and forty nights; and every living thing that I have made I will blot out from the face of the ground."

Genesis 9:8–11

Then God said to Noah and to his sons with him, "Behold, I establish my covenant with you and your descendants after you, and with every living creature that is with you, the birds, the cattle, and every beast of the earth with you, as many as came out of the ark. I establish my covenant with you, that never again shall all flesh be cut off by the waters of a flood, and never again shall there be a flood to destroy the earth."

Psalm 147:7–9

Sing to the Lord with thanksgiving;
    make melody to our God upon the lyre!
He covers the heavens with clouds,
    he prepares rain for the earth,
    he makes grass grow upon the hills.
He gives to the beasts their food,
    and to the young ravens which cry.

Psalm 148:7–10

Praise the Lord from the earth,
    you sea monsters and all deeps,

fire and hail, snow and frost,
stormy wind fulfilling his command!

Mountains and all hills,
fruit trees and all cedars!
Beasts and all cattle,
creeping things and flying birds!

Ezekiel 34:25–28

"I will make with them a covenant of peace and banish wild beasts
from the land, so that they may dwell securely in the wilderness
and sleep in the woods. And I will make them and the places round
about my hill a blessing; and I will send down the showers in their
season; they shall be showers of blessing. And the trees of the field
shall yield their fruit, and the earth shall yield its increase, and they
shall be secure in their land; and they shall know that I am the
LORD, when I break the bars of their yoke, and deliver them from
the hand of those who enslaved them. They shall no more be a
prey to the nations, nor shall the beasts of the land devour them;
they shall dwell securely, and none shall make them afraid."

Matthew 6:26

"Look at the birds of the air; they neither sow nor reap nor gather
into barns, and yet your heavenly Father feeds them. Are you not
of more value than they?"

Matthew 21:1b–5

Jesus sent two disciples, saying to them, "Go into the village opposite
you, and immediately you will find an ass tied, and a colt with her;
untie them and bring them to me. If any one say anything to you,
you shall say, 'The Lord has need of them,' and he will send them
immediately." This took place to fulfil what was spoken by the
prophet, saying.

"Tell the daughter of Zion,
Behold, your king is coming to you,
humble, and mounted on an ass,
and on a colt, the foal of an ass."

Mark 1:12

The Spirit immediately drove him out into the wilderness. And he was in the wilderness forty days, tempted by Satan; and he was with the wild beasts; and the angels ministered to him.

Luke 12:6–7

"Are not five sparrows sold for two pennies? And not one of them is forgotten before God. Why, even the hairs of your head are all numbered. Fear not; you are of more value than many sparrows."

John 1:1–3

In the beginning was the Word, and the Word was with God, and the Word was God. He was in the beginning with God; all things were made through him, and without him was not anything made that was made.

Hebrews 2:10

For it was fitting that he, for whom and by whom all things exist, in bringing many sons to glory, should make the pioneer of their salvation perfect through suffering.

JOHN AUSTIN BAKER

Old Testament Attitudes to Nature

The writers of the Old Testament did not have, as we do, an immense stock of general or semi-abstract terms. While this limited them in some directions—the development of Hebrew philosophy and metaphysics, for example, had to wait for the enrichment of the language in post-biblical times—it also saved them from certain woollinesses of thought to which we are peculiarly liable. Thus, the lack of a word corresponding to our term 'nature' deprived them of a collective noun

From "Biblical Attitudes to Nature", in Hugh Montefiore (ed.), *Man and Nature* (London: Collins, 1975), pp. 87–96.

useful enough if carefully handled; but it also meant that they were safe-guarded against lumping together things that have no obvious business together, and did not have (and so could not be taken in by) such phrases as 'communing with nature', or 'Nature, red in tooth and claw'. What they saw when they looked around them was not some undifferentiated global category, but concrete things—mountains, seas, rivers, crawling animals, oaktrees, birds, the sun and moon, and so on. Their nearest approach to an all-embracing word for their environment was 'the earth'. The title 'Friends of the Earth' they would have understood. 'Nature-lover' would have required some explanation.

One result of these terminological differences is that we sometimes fail to recognize our own questions, and indeed our own answers to those questions, when they appear in the Old Testament in what we regard as 'less sophisticated' language. (It may not in fact be less sophisticated, only less imprecise.) Several such common areas of concern will emerge in the course of this essay. One in particular, however, will form a good starting-point for our discussion.

How far is man involved in nature, and how far has he distanced himself from it? Between them the Old Testament writers are aware of the basic elements of this question. Man is part of the panorama of nature. Psalm 104, for example, places him firmly, with great artistry, in the context of all the other teeming life of the earth. Nothing is done to highlight him; he is just another figure in the landscape:

> Thou makest darkness, and it is night,
>   when all the beasts of the forests creep forth.
> The young lions roar for their prey,
>   seeking their food from God.
> When the sun rises, they get them away
>   and lie down in their dens.
> Man goes forth to his work
>   and to his labour until the evening.
> O Lord, how manifold are thy works!
>   In wisdom has thou made them all;
>   the earth is full of thy creatures (vv. 20–4).

By contrast, both the creation stories in Genesis, in their individual ways, stress the distinctness of man from the rest of creation, while in one of them his homogeneity with it is at least played down. In the older story (J), Genesis 2:4b–25, both man and the animals are formed out of the dust of the ground (vv. 7,19); but the birds and beasts are nevertheless not adequate companions and partners for man (v. 20). Only another human being, formed out of his own living substance, can be that (vv. 21–3). It is this unique kinship which, so the story claims, explains the all-surpassing force of the bond between man and woman (v. 24).

The superiority of man to the animals is further emphasized in his story by the incident of man's naming of all the living creatures. God brings the animals which he has created to man to see what will happen; and man expresses his innate superiority by giving them their names, names which from thenceforward are unalterably the ones that properly belong to them (vv. 19–20). This incident has two important implications. First, to give a name to some other being is to claim and exercise sovereignty over it. One obvious example is the authority of a parent over a newborn child; but the naming prerogative is also a mark of a political overlord (cf. 2 Kings 24:17). . . . Secondly, there is the strong conviction of the whole ancient world, which the biblical writers shared, that a true name expresses the nature and controls the destiny of its owner (cf., for example, Genesis 35:16–18, the two names of Rachel's last child). By giving the animals the truly appropriate name for each Adam proves that he has insight into their true nature, that he understands them. This at once puts him on a different plane from them; he is a creature nearer to God than they, and in fact sharing some at any rate of the insight that enabled God to create them in the first place. Man's natural role, therefore, is one of sovereignty over other creatures—not the absolute sovereignty that belongs to God alone, but at least a relative authority and superiority. That this is the correct reading of the story is confirmed by the form which man's own punishment for his disobedience takes in Genesis 3. Because he has rebelled against his proper overlord, God, his own subjects are to rebel against him; and the ground which once he tilled with ease (2:15) now yields less, and even that only to unremitting labour (3:17–19).

In the later creation narrative (Genesis 1:1–2:4a) man's supremacy is spelt out categorically. His kinship with God is given technical theological expression: he is 'in [God's] image' and 'after [his] likeness' (Genesis 1:26–7). The exact meaning of this phrase has been endlessly debated. There may be influence from the Egyptian formula according to which the Pharaoh is 'the image of Amun-Re', in which case there are viceregal overtones, made explicit in verse 28. But the Hebrew and Egyptian phrases are not truly parallel. Much more certain is the implication that man is the nearest visible pointer to what God looks like (cf. Ezekiel 1:26). The interesting question is how far is this sim-ilarity thought to go below the surface into the realm of understanding and moral character? To some degree it must do, since it is inherently improbable that any writer would make God give even a shadow of his own unique likeness to a creature that had nothing in common with him; and this common-sense conclusion is confirmed by the fact that God entrusts dominion over his new and wonderful earth and its inhabitants to man.

The major difference between this creation story and the older one, so far as our subject is concerned, is that in Genesis 1, while the superiority of man to the rest of the animal world, though expressed in more explicit imagery, is probably no more radical than it is in Genesis 2, the theme of a common physical origin for men and animals is suppressed altogether. The writer of Genesis 1 seems to have held a view, of which there are other instances in the ancient world, that the earth and the sea themselves 'brought forth' their various inhab-itants (vv. 20–1, 24–5), but he has combined this with safeguards against any divinization of earth and sea by insisting simultaneously that in fact God himself 'created' (v. 21) and 'made' (v. 25) the crea-tures which these primordial entities generated. The resultant picture, then, is that all animal life was 'produced' either by the earth or by the sea, as a result of God's creative edict and operation. There is here a very careful gradation upwards from the production of plant life (vv. 11–12), where God issues the creative fiat, 'Let the earth put forth vegetation, etc', but is not said to have 'made' or 'created' what is put forth. The writer seems to be saying that animal life, whether on land or in the sea, is more marvellous than mere plant life, and, although issuing from the womb of the earth and from the waters, required a special operation of God to bring it about. Now, in the case of man we take yet another step upwards. Here the divine edict and activity are everything: no intermediate creative source is named. Whereas in Genesis 2 both man and animals were fashioned by God from the soil, here man is presented as created by God directly, and the question whether he too came from the earth is at least passed over in silence . . .

Man in Genesis I, indeed, occupies much the same high place in the scheme of things as he does in Psalm 8:

> Yet thou hast made him little less than God,
>   and dost crown him with glory and honour.
> Thou hast given him dominion over the works of thy hands;
>   thou hast put all things under his feet,
> all sheep and oxen,
>   and also the beasts of the field,
> the birds of the air, and the fish of the sea,
>   whatever passes along the paths of the sea (vv. 5–8).

To our ears such words sound very like the most blatant human imperialism vis-à-vis the rest of nature, as does the divine commission to man in Genesis 1:28; and in modern times they may have fostered and been used to justify such an attitude. But what in their biblical context did they originally imply?

It is highly probable that one connection of this type of language is with the institution of kingship. Under the influence of Mesopotamian models even quite petty kings in the ancient Near East seem to have used cosmic iconography to express their status and authority. Solomon's lion throne, with six steps and a curved back (1 Kings 10:18–20), as we know from archaeological parallels, symbolized world dominion; and the embroidery on the collar of the later high priests, which was probably zodiacal and signified the whole cosmos, was almost certainly taken over from the royal robes of earlier times (cf. Wisdom of Solomon 18:24a). 'Kingship came down from heaven', the ancient Near East believed; and part of the mystique of kingship was that every king was God's vicegerent on earth. Now, one of a king's most important duties was to ensure fertility and prosperity by his obedience to the gods and by his observance of the yearly rituals. We can trace thinking of this kind in the Old Testament, not only in such an incident as the famine sent on Israel for the wickedness of Ahab (1 Kings 17:1) but, more positively, in a text like Psalm 72, where unimaginable abundance is to be a mark of the reign of the ideal ruler. The conditions pictured in this psalm certainly never obtained at any historical epoch—the world-wide dominion described in verse 8, for example, was never actually attained even by those Mesopotamian overlords from whose honorifics the phrase in question was borrowed— but the psalm is nonetheless not just a dream of an indefinite future. Verse 1 refers to an actual king; it is a prayer, perhaps used at his coronation, that the vision painted in the psalm may come true in *this* king's reign. Primarily, therefore, the 'man' and 'son of man' of Psalm 8 is also the king, whose sacred office endows him with the resources of divine power not just over his human subjects but over all other creatures within his domain; and it is only his sins which cause this power to be withheld. Inevitably, therefore, as hopes pinned on human rulers are falsified, the vision of a world of abundance and peace becomes part of a hope set on God alone. In his own good time he will bring this to pass, and all the anomalies of both man and nature will be ironed out, and harmony will reign. Perhaps the most famous Old Testament instance of this eschatological hope for nature is Isaiah 11. But, by a well-known feature of human mythical thinking, paradise in the end-time is thought of as the recreation of a primeval paradise at the dawn of creation, the lost 'golden age'. And that is how it comes about that in both the Old Testament creation stories we have the picture of man, the ideal king, God's perfect vicegerent, under whom nature is fertile and peaceful and all she was meant to be. A small but striking detail confirming this is the vegetarianism of the creation in Genesis 1: animals eat grass, man eats grains and fruits. It is no surprise, then, to find precisely this feature in Isaiah 11, the vision of paradise regained:

> The wolf shall dwell with the lamb,
>   and the leopard shall lie down with the kid,
> and the calf and the lion and the fatling together,
>   and a little child shall lead them.
> The cow and the bear shall feed;
>   their young shall lie down together;
>   and the lion shall eat straw like the ox . . .
> They shall not hurt or destroy
>   in all my holy mountain (vv. 6–7, 9a).

The 'dominion', therefore, which man is promised in Genesis 1 is poles apart from the kind of right to egotistical exploitation which it suggests to our ears. It is in essence a perfect obedience to the will of

God which is rewarded by a divinely ordained harmony and abundance in nature, which recognizes man as the greatest of all God's creatures and pays him homage. If this vision offers any goals or ideals for our present situation, they certainly are not the extermination of species or the ruthless exploitation for short-term gain of precious natural resources. On the contrary, they are much more akin to the aims of modern study of animal life and of environmental conservation. Their relevance to technological questions can only be very indirect, worked out by applying the underlying theological attitudes in situations unimaginable to the original writers.

The Old Testament expresses in a number of ways the idea that man declined drastically from the standards of the golden age. The story of Cain and Abel (Genesis 4) is but the first and best known instance. Another, of more direct interest in our present context, is the change in the divine laws of life after the Flood. Mankind had become so corrupt that a cataclysmic destruction was the only remedy; the family of righteous Noah, eight persons only, are the sole survivors. This new start for the human race is marked by a divine covenant which, being modelled ultimately on the treaties imposed unilaterally in some ancient Near Eastern empires by suzerains on their vassals, contains both promises by the overlord and obligations laid upon his subjects. The promise is that never again will God destroy all living things (Genesis 9:8–17). It is interesting and important that the covenant is made not just with man but also with all living creatures (five times repeated: vv. 10, 12, 15, 16, 17) and, indeed, with the earth itself (v. 13). The new laws of life (9:1–7) replace the ordinances established at the creation, and modify them in significant respects. No longer is man's food to be fruit and grain only: 'Every moving thing that lives shall be food for you; and as I gave you the green plants, I give you everything' (9:3). The Flood and the subsequent new start for the world are used as an opportunity to switch from the theoretic 'golden age' to the conditions actually obtaining; and one of the saddest features of this change is the degradation of relations between man and the animals from their first created beauty. The language of Genesis 9:1–2, when compared with the same writer's phrasing in 1:28f., betrays at once the poignancy of his feelings:

> The fear of you and the dread of you shall be upon every
> beast of the earth, and upon every bird of the air, upon

everything that creeps on the ground and all the fish of the
sea; into your hand they are delivered (v. 2).

The language is that normally used of a conqueror slaughtering a routed
army or sacking a fallen city. Man has become the enemy of all living
things.

The Old Testament, then, does nothing to justify the charge that
it represents an exploitative, humanly egotistical attitude to nature.
Although it recognizes man's preying on nature as a fact, it characterizes
that fact as a mark of man's decline from the first perfect intentions
of God for him.

ST THOMAS AQUINAS
Man as Master over Creation

QUESTION XCVI
Of the Mastership Belonging to Man
in the State of Innocence

FIRST ARTICLE
WHETHER ADAM IN THE STATE OF INNOCENCE HAD
MASTERSHIP OVER THE ANIMALS?

We proceed thus to the First Article:—

Objection 1. It would seem that in the state of innocence Adam had
no mastership over the animals. For Augustine says (*Gen. ad lit.* ix.
14), that the animals were brought to Adam, under the direction of
the angels, to receive their names from him. But the angels need not

From *Summa Theologica*, Part 1, QQ. LXXV–CII, ET by the Fathers of the English Dominican
Province (London and New York: Burns Oates & Washbourne and Benziger Brothers, 2nd and
revised ed. 1922), pp. 326–30.

have intervened thus, if man himself were master over the animals. Therefore in the state of innocence man had no mastership of the animals.

Obj. 2. Further, it is unfitting that the elements hostile to one another should be brought under the mastership of one. But many animals are hostile to one another, as the sheep and the wolf. Therefore all animals were not brought under the mastership of man.

Obj. 3. Further, Jerome[1] says: *God gave man mastership over the animals, although before sin he had no need of them: for God foresaw that after sin animals would become useful to man.* Therefore, at least before sin, it was unfitting for man to make use of his mastership.

Obj. 4. Further, it is proper to a master to command. But a command is not given rightly save to a rational being. Therefore man had no mastership over the irrational animals.

On the contrary, It is written (Gen. i. 26): *Let him have dominion over the fishes of the sea, and the birds of the air, and the beasts of the field* (Vulg., *and the whole earth*).

I answer that, As above stated (Q. XCV., A. 1) for his disobedience to God, man was punished by the disobedience of those creatures which should be subject to him. Therefore in the state of innocence, before man had disobeyed, nothing disobeyed him that was naturally subject to him. Now all animals are naturally subject to man. This can be proved in three ways. First, from the order observed by nature; for just as in the generation of things we perceive a certain order of procession of the prefect from the imperfect (thus matter is for the sake of form; and the imperfect form, for the sake of the perfect), so also is there order in the use of natural things; thus the imperfect are for the use of the perfect; as the plants make use of the earth for their nourishment, and animals make use of plants, and man makes use of both plants and animals. Therefore it is in keeping with the order of nature, that man should be master over animals. Hence the Philosopher says (*Politic.* i. 5) that the hunting of wild animals is just and natural, because man thereby exercises a natural right. Secondly, this is proved from the order of Divine Providence which always governs inferior things by the superior. Wherefore, as man, being made to the image of God, is above other animals, these are rightly subject to his government. Thirdly, this is proved from a property of man and of other

---

[1]The words quoted are not in S. Jerome's works. S. Thomas may have had in mind Bede, *Hexaem.*, as quoted in the *Glossa ordinaria* on Gen. i. 26.

animals. For we see in the latter a certain participated prudence of natural instinct, in regard to certain particular acts; whereas man possesses a universal prudence as regards all practical matters. Now whatever is participated is subject to what is essential and universal. Therefore the subjection of other animals to man is proved to be natural.

Reply Obj. 1. A higher power can do many things that an inferior power cannot do to those which are subject to them. Now an angel is naturally higher than man. Therefore certain things in regard to animals could be done by angels, which could not be done by man; for instance, the rapid gathering together of all animals.

Reply Obj. 2. In the opinion of some, those animals which now are fierce and kill others, would, in that state, have been tame, not only in regard to man, but also in regard to other animals. But this is quite unreasonable. For the nature of animals was not changed by man's sin, as if those whose nature now it is devour the flesh of others, would then have lived on herbs, as the lion and falcon. Nor does Bede's gloss on Gen. i. 30, say that trees and herbs were given as food to all animals and birds, but to some. Thus there would have been a natural antipathy between some animals. They would not, however, on this account have been excepted from the mastership of man: as neither at present are they for that reason excepted from the mastership of God, Whose Providence has ordained all this. Of this Providence man would have been the executor, as appears even now in regard to domestic animals, since fowls are given by men as food to the trained falcon.

Reply Obj. 3. In the state of innocence man would not have had bodily need of animals;—neither for clothing since then they were naked and not ashamed, there being no inordinate motions of concupiscence,—nor for food, since they fed on the trees of paradise,—nor to carry him about, his body being strong enough for that purpose. But man needed animals in order to have experimental knowledge of their natures. This is signified by the fact that God led the animals to man, that he might give them names expressive of their respective natures.

Reply Obj. 4. All animals by their natural instinct have a certain participation of prudence and reason: which accounts for the fact that cranes follow their leader, and bees obey their queen. So all animals would have obeyed man to their own accord, as in the present state some domestic animals obey him.

SECOND ARTICLE
WHETHER MAN HAD MASTERSHIP OVER ALL OTHER CREATURES?

We proceed thus to the Second Article:—

Objection 1. It would seem that in the state of innocence man would not have had mastership over all other creatures. For an angel naturally has a greater power than man. But, as Augustine says (*De Trin.* iii. 8), *corporeal matter would not have obeyed even the holy angels.* Much less therefore would it have obeyed man in the state of innocence.

Obj. 2. Further, the only powers of the soul existing in plants are nutritive, augmentative, and generative. Now these do not naturally obey reason; as we can see in the case of any one man. Therefore, since it is by his reason that man is competent to have mastership, it seems that in the state of innocence man had no dominion over plants.

Obj. 3. Further, whosoever is master of a thing, can change it. But man could not have changed the course of the heavenly bodies; for this belongs to God alone, as Dionysius says (*Ep. ad Polycarp,* vii.). Therefore man had no dominion over them.

On the contrary, It is written (Gen. i. 26): *That he may have dominion over . . . every creature.*

I answer that, Man in a certain sense contains all things; and so according as he is master of what is within himself, in the same way he can have mastership over other things. Now we may consider four things in man: his *reason* which makes him like to the angels; his *sensitive powers,* whereby he is like the animals; his *natural forces,* which liken him to the plants; and *the body* itself, wherein he is like to inanimate things. Now in man reason has the position of a master and not of a subject. Wherefore man had no mastership over the angels in the primitive state; so when we read *all creatures,* we must understand the creatures which are not made to God's image. Over the sensitive powers, as the irascible and concupiscible, which obey reason in some degree, the soul has mastership by commanding. So in the state of innocence man had mastership over the animals by commanding them. But of the natural powers and the body itself man is master not by commanding, but by using them. Thus also in the state of innocence man's mastership over plants and inanimate things consisted not in commanding or in changing them, but in making use of them without hindrance.

The answers to the objections appear from the above.

JOHN CALVIN
The Pre-eminence of Man

[Genesis 1:] 26 *Let us make man.* Although the tense here used is the future, all must acknowledge that this is the language of one apparently deliberating. Hitherto God has been introduced simply as *commanding;* now, when he approaches the most excellent of all his works, he enters into *consultation.* God certainly might here command by his bare word what he wished to be done: but he chose to give this tribute to the excellency of man, that he would, in a manner, enter into consultation concerning his creation. This is the highest honor with which he has dignified us; to a due regard for which, Moses, by this mode of speaking, would excite our minds. For God is not now first beginning to consider what form he will give to man, and with what endowments it would be fitting to adorn him, nor is he pausing as over a work of difficulty: but, just as we have before observed, that the creation of the world was distributed over six days, for our sake, to the end that our minds might the more easily be retained in the meditation of God's works: so now, for the purpose of commending to our attention the dignity of our nature, he, in taking counsel concerning the creation of man, testifies that he is about to undertake something great and wonderful. Truly there are many things in this corrupted nature which may induce contempt; but if you rightly weigh all circumstances, man is, among other creatures, a certain pre-eminent specimen of Divine wisdom, justice, and goodness, so that he is deservedly called by the ancients *microcosmos,* "a word in miniature." But since the Lord needs no other counsellor, there can be no doubt that he consulted with himself. . .

And let them have dominion. Here he commemorates that part of dignity with which he decreed to honour man, namely, that he should have authority over all living creatures. He appointed man, it is true, lord of the world; but he expressly subjects the animals to him, because they, having an inclination or instinct of their own, seem to be less under authority from without. The use of the plural number intimates

From *Commentaries on the First Book of Moses called Genesis,* Vol. I, ET by John King (Edinburgh: Calvin Translation Society, 1847), pp. 91–100. [The following two footnotes are in the original.—A.L.]

that this authority was not given to Adam only, but to all his posterity as well as to him. And hence we infer what was the end for which all things were created; namely, that none of the conveniences and necessaries of life might be wanting to men. In the very order of the creation the paternal solicitude of God for man is conspicuous, because he furnished the world with all things needful, and even with an immense profusion of wealth, before he formed man. Thus man was rich before he was born. But if God had such care for us before we existed, he will by no means leave us destitute of food and of other necessaries of life, now that we are placed in the world. Yet, that he often keeps his hand as if closed is to be imputed to our sins . . .

Subdue it. He confirms what he had before said respecting dominion. Man had already been created with this condition, that he should subject the earth to himself; but now, at length, he is put in possession of his right, when he hears what has been given to him by the Lord: and this Moses expresses still more fully in the next verse, when he introduces God as granting to him the herbs and the fruits. For it is of great importance that we touch nothing of God's bounty but what we know he has permitted us to do; since we cannot enjoy anything with a good conscience, except we receive it as from the hand of God. And therefore Paul teaches us that, in eating and drinking, we always sin, unless faith be present, (Rom. xiv. 23.) Thus we are instructed to seek from God alone whatever is necessary for us, and in the very use of his gifts, we are to exercise ourselves in meditating on his goodness and paternal care. For the words of God are to this effect: 'Behold, I have prepared food for thee before thou wast formed; acknowledge me, therefore, as thy Father, who have so diligently provided for thee when thou wast not yet created. Moreover, my solicitude for thee has proceeded still further; it was thy business to nurture the things provided for thee, but I have taken even this charge also upon myself. Wherefore, although thou art, in a sense, constituted the father of the earthly family, it is not for thee to be over-anxious about the sustenance of animals.'[1]

Some infer, from this passage, that men were content with herbs and fruits until the deluge, and that it was even unlawful for them to eat flesh. And this seems the more probable, because God confines,

---

[1]See verses 29, 30, in which God promises the herbs and fruits of the earth, and every green herb, to the beasts of the earth for food. The reader will perceive that the subsequent observations of Calvin refer more especially to these verses.—*Ed.*

in some way, the food of mankind within certain limits. Then, after the deluge, he expressly grants them the use of flesh. These reasons, however, are not sufficiently strong: for it may be adduced on the opposite side, that the first men offered sacrifices from their flocks.[2] This, moreover, is the law of sacrificing rightly, not to offer unto God anything except what he has granted to our use. Lastly, men were clothed in skins; therefore it was lawful for them to kill animals. For these reasons, I think it will be better for us to assert nothing concerning this matter. Let it suffice for us, that herbs and the fruits of trees were given them as their common food; yet it is not to be doubted that this was abundantly sufficient for their highest gratification. For they judge prudently who maintain that the earth was so marred by the deluge, that we retain scarcely a moderate portion of the original benediction. Even immediately after the fall of man, it had already begun to bring forth degenerate and noxious fruits, but at the deluge, the change became still greater. Yet, however this may be, God certainly did not intend that man should be slenderly and sparingly sustained; but rather, by these words, he promises a liberal abundance, which should leave nothing wanting to a sweet and pleasant life. For Moses relates how beneficient the Lord had been to them, in bestowing on them all things which they could desire, that their ingratitude might have the less excuse.

JOHN BURNABY

The Purpose of Creation*

The difficulties raised for our belief in a good Creator by the evils of the world are unnecessarily exaggerated by certain assumptions which we sometimes make without considering whether they are required by

[2]It does not appear that there is much force in Calvin's objections to the opinion, that flesh was not allowed for human food till after the deluge. For if the sacrifices offered were *holocausts*, then the skin only would be left for the use of man. See notes on the offering of Cain and Abel in the fourth chapter; and, especially, Dr Magee's work on the Atonement, Dissertation LII., *On the date of the permission of animal food to man.*—Ed.

*From *The Belief of Christendom: A Commentary on the Nicene Creed* (London: SPCK, 1963), pp. 40–42.

our Christian faith. In the first chapter of Genesis it is the making of this earth and the provision for life upon it which leads up to and is crowned by the creation of man. With our immensely wider horizons, we easily read the story as though the whole structure of the universe had no other purpose but the production of the human species and that all things in it had been made for the use of man. And we may slip from there into the further assumption that the "use" of man can only mean his happiness or even his material comfort.

Now the human species does appear to be the species most highly organized and adapted for life on this planet—as indeed the Biblical story of creation implies. Man has "all things in subjection under his feet . . . sheep and oxen and the beasts of the field". Yet the Psalmist can still exclaim: "What is man, that thou art mindful of him?" And the Book of Job enforces the counsel of humility from the sheer mystery of creation, and the limits to all human powers of understanding or controlling it.[1]

It is also true that all increase in our knowledge of natural law emphasizes the fact that mankind is the product not only of this earth but of the whole stellar universe, which is the setting, the cosmic order that has made possible the evolution of humanity on this particular planet. We are not to be stampeded by the *vastness* of creation into belittling ourselves; for quantity has nothing to do with quality, extension in space or time has nothing to do with significance or value. We do not know that we are the only beings in the universe capable of becoming children of God: but there would be nothing irrational in the supposition that we *are* the only such beings—unless it is irrational to suppose that a man is more "important" than a mountain. Nevertheless, these considerations do not justify us in affirming that the universe was made for man.

God, says the Creed, is the Maker of heaven and earth; and the Nicene Creed adds: "and of all things visible and invisible". "Heaven and earth" in the language of the creed-makers would naturally be taken to describe the material world known to us through our senses. The added clause makes it clear that the range of God's creation is not so limited: it widens out to embrace things beyond the reach of our powers of perception. For the creedmakers, the "things invisible" will certainly have included the "heavenly powers"—the angels who

[1]Ps. 8; Job 38–41.

are God's "ministering spirits". If there are angels, it would be gratuitous to suppose that their ministry is limited to us men. But whatever "powers" the universe contains—physical energies or spiritual agents unknown to us—all is of God.

We cannot then assume that even if the things that are "in subjection under our feet" extend far more widely than the author of Job supposed, it follows that God's universal purpose reaches no further than ourselves. The purpose of creation as a whole must be beyond our comprehension. But we can believe that God, in revealing himself to us in Christ, has therewith shown us his purpose *"for us men"*— what *man* is meant to be. And this should make it impossible for us to think that God has created all things with no other purpose than the satisfaction of men's natural desires and needs. We need not abandon the ancient insight, whereby the purpose of man's being, that in which he is to find his fulfilment, is embraced in the purpose of all creation—the *glory* of God. The glory of God in the Bible and Christian tradition has always been linked with the idea of light. The light of the sun enables those who have eyes to see the world lit up with splendour. God is glorified on earth when the eyes of men are enlightened, when they see his goodness in his works and come to worship him. But it would be presumptuous to imagine that the glory of God *depends* on the existence of the human eye.

PAULOS MAR GREGORIOS
Christology and Creation

He, Christ, the Beloved Son, is the manifest presence (icon) of the unmanifest God. He is the Elder Brother of all things created, for it was by him and in him that all things were created, whether here on earth in the sensible world or in the world beyond the horizon of your senses which we call heaven, even institutions like royal thrones, seats of lords

From "New Testament Foundations for Understanding the Creation", in Wesley Granberg-Michaelson (ed.), *Tending the Garden: Essays on the Gospel and the Church* (Grand Rapids, Michigan: William B. Eerdmans, 1987), pp. 87-9.

and rulers—all forms of authority. All things were created through him, by him, in him. But he himself is before all things; in him they consist and subsist; he is the head of the body, the Church. He is the New Beginning, the Firstborn from the dead; thus he becomes in all respects preeminent. For it was (God's) good pleasure that in Christ all fullness should dwell; it is through him and in him that all things are to be reconciled and reharmonized. For he has removed the contradiction and made peace by his own blood. So all things in the visible earth and in the invisible heaven should dwell together in him.

That includes you, who were once alienated, enemies in your own minds to God's purposes, immersed in evil actions; but now you are bodily reconciled in his fleshly body which has tasted death. Christ intends to present you—holy, spotless, and blameless—in God's presence, if you remain firm in the faith, rooted and grounded in him, unswerving from the hope of the good news you have heard, the good news declared not only to men and women on earth, but to all created beings under heaven. It is this gospel that I, Paul, have also been called to serve.

(Col. 1:15–23)

Principle: Christ himself should be seen in his three principal relationships: (1) to members incorporated into his body, (2) to the human race, and (3) to the other than human orders of created existence in a many-planed universe. Each of these is related to the other.

A Christology based on this principle will not conceive of a Christ as somehow other than the created order. Today much of Christology sees Christ as being separate from the world, from culture, and so forth; we try to affirm the Lordship of Christ *over* world and culture by conceiving even the incarnate Christ as somehow totally distinct from the created order. We then think of him as Lord of the world, Lord of the church, and so on. In the more individualistic versions of Christology-soteriology, some make him "sole mediator" between the person and God. This perception involves three realities: God, Christ, and the individual. God is there, the individual is here, and Christ stands in between. And the world and the church are fourth and fifth realities.

This kind of disjunctive thinking has to give way to an integral and participative way of understanding Christ. Jesus Christ in not an abstract or "purely spiritual" entity. He is incarnate. He took a material body, becoming part of the created order while remaining unchanged as one of the three persons in the Trinity who is Creator. He is one of us. He is fully consubstantial with us.

As Christians we are united with him in an especially intimate way. By baptism and by faith, he has incorporated us as members of his body. By participation in his body and blood, we grow to be integral parts of him. Once he had a human body like ours. In fact, he still does—though it has already been transformed and resurrected and is therefore no longer subject to the ordinary laws of our physics, which govern only mortal bodies and material objects. But he has chosen to have a larger body, partly in heaven (i.e., beyond the horizon of our senses) and partly here on earth. We belong to that body as a whole, but particularly to the earthly part of it. Christ is always with us, the members of his body, particularly as he continues to fulfill his ministry as High Priest of creation and as Prophet and Servant to the world.

Christ incarnate is a human being, consubstantial with all other human beings. He did not become simply an individual human person or a Christian. He became *humankind*—male and female. He assumed the whole of human nature, and now there is no humanity other than the one which Christ took on—our humanity, in which all human beings participate, whether or not they believe in Christ, whether or not they recognize the nature of their humanity. This aspect of the Redeemer's relationship to the whole of humanity, independent of human faith, is seldom fully recognized by Christians and its implications worked out. No human beings are alien to Christ, whether they be Hindu, Muslim, Communist, or Buddhist. They share in Christ's humanity in ways that we have to spell out elsewhere. They are not members of the body of Christ, but they are not unrelated to Christ.

Christ the Incarnate One assumed flesh—organic, human flesh; he was nurtured by air and water, vegetables and meat, like the rest of us. He took matter into himself, so matter is not alien to him now. His body is a *material* body—transformed, of course, but transformed *matter*. Thus he shares his being with the whole created order: animals and birds, snakes and worms, flowers and seeds. All parts of creation are now reconciled to Christ. And the created order is to be set free and to share in the glorious freedom of the children of God. Sun and moon, planets and stars, pulsars and black holes—as well as the planet earth—are to participate in that final consummation of the redemption.

The risen Christ is thus active, by the Spirit, in all three realms: in the church, in the whole of humanity, and in the cosmos. Each of these relationships is fundamentally different, but all are real and meaningful to Christ the Incarnate One.

Our theology's weakness has been its failure to recognize the wider scope of the redemption beyond the "individual soul" or the person. Liberalism still spiritualizes the incarnate Christ by confining his actions to so-called history, as if that were a realm in which "nature" and the material elements of creation were not present. We must move beyond personal salvation to declare and teach the three basic dimensions of the redemption.

ST BONAVENTURE
The Life of St Francis

When he considered the primordial source of all things, he was filled with even more piety, calling creatures, no matter how small, by the name of brother or sister, because he knew they had the same source as himself.[1] However, he embraced more affectionately and sweetly those creatures which present a natural reflection of Christ's merciful gentleness and represent him in Scriptural symbolism. He often paid to ransom lambs that were being led to their death, remembering that most gentle Lamb who willed to be *led to slaughter* (Isa. 53:7) to pay the ransom of sinners.

One time when God's servant was lodging at the monastery of San Verecondo in the diocese of Gubbio, a sheep gave birth to a little lamb during the night. There was a ferocious sow there, which did not spare the life of the innocent lamb, but killed it with her ravenous

From *Bonaventure: The Soul's Journey into God, The Tree of Life and The Life of St. Francis*, ET and introduction by Ewert Cousins, preface by Ignatius Brady, The Classics of Western Spirituality (Mahwah, N.J., and London: SPCK and Paulist Press, 1978), pp. 254–61.
[1]This is an application of Bonaventure's exemplarism, whereby creatures reflect God, a theme developed throughout *The Soul's Journey into God.*

bite. When he heard of this, the devoted father was moved by wonderful compassion and, remembering the Lamb without stain, grieved
in the presence of all over the death of the little lamb, saying: "Alas,
brother lamb, innocent animal, you represent Christ to men. A curse
on that impious beast that killed you; may no man or beast ever eat
of her." Remarkably, the evil sow immediately became ill and after
paying for her deed with three days of bodily punishment she finally
suffered avenging death. She was thrown into the monastery ditch
and lay there for a long time dried up like a board, and did not serve
as food for any hungry animal.

> Let the impiety of men, therefore,
> be warned
> how great a punishment will be inflicted on it
> at the end of time,
> if the cruelty of an animal
> was punished
> with so horrible a death.
> Let also the devotion of the faithful consider
> that the marvelous power and abundant sweetness
> of the piety of God's servant
> was so great
> that it was acknowledged in their own way
> even by animals.[2]

When Francis was traveling near the city of Siena, he came upon
a large flock of sheep in a pasture. When he greeted them kindly, as
he was accustomed to do, they all stopped grazing and ran to him,
lifting their heads and fixing their eyes on him. They gave him such
a welcome that the shepherds and the friars were amazed to see the
lambs and even the rams frisking about him in such an extraordinary
way.

Another time at St. Mary of the Portiuncula the man of God was
offered a sheep, which he gratefully accepted in his love of that innocence and simplicity which the sheep by its nature reflects. The
pious man admonished the little sheep to praise God attentively and

[2]Major sources: I C 80–81, 77, 79; II C 111. Cf, I C 77, 80–81; II C 165, and IX, 1, pp.
262–263.

to avoid giving any offense to the friars. The sheep carefully observed his instructions, as if it recognized the piety of the man of God. For when it heard the friars chanting in choir, it would enter the church, genuflect without instructions from anyone, and bleat before the altar of the Virgin, the mother of the Lamb, as if it wished to greet her. Besides, when the most sacred body of Christ was elevated at mass, it would bow down on bended knees as if this reverent animal were reproaching those who were not devout and inviting the devout to reverence the sacrament.

Once in Rome he had with him a little lamb out of reverence for the most gentle Lamb of God. At his departure he left it in the care of the noble matron, the Lady Jacoba of Settesoli.[3] Now the lamb went with the lady to church, standing reverently by her side as her inseparable companion, as if it had been trained in spiritual matters by the saint. If the lady was late in rising in the morning, the lamb rose and nudged her with its horns and woke her with its bleating, urging her with its nods and gestures to hurry to the church. On account of this, the lamb, which was Francis's disciple and had now become a master of devotion, was held by the lady as an object of wonder and love.[4]

Another time at Greccio a live hare was offered to the man of God, which he placed on the ground and let it free to go where it wished. But when the kind father called, it ran and jumped into his arms. He fondled it with warm affection and seemed to pity it like a mother. After warning it gently not to let itself be caught again, he let it go free. But as often as he placed it on the ground to run away, it always came back to the father's arms, as if in some secret way it perceived the kind feeling he had for it. Finally, at the father's command, the friars carried it away to a safer place far from the haunts of men.

In the same way on an island in the lake of Perugia[5] a rabbit was caught and offered to the man of God. Although it fled from everyone else, it entrusted itself to his hands and his heart as if to the security of its home. When he was hurrying across the Lake of Rieti to the

---

[3] A noble Roman lady, widow of Graziano Frangipani, Lord of the Septizonium; she was a close friend of Francis, (who called her "Brother Jacoba"), and was summoned to his deathbed. Cf. III C 37–38–39.

[4] Major source: III C 31. The two incidents of a lamb are not found in Celano or Julian.

[5] Lago Trasimeno.

hermitage of Greccio, out of devotion a fisherman offered him a waterfowl. He took it gladly and opened his hands to let it go, but it did not want to. He prayed for a long time with his eyes turned to heaven. After more than an hour, he came back to himself as if from another realm and gently told the bird again to go away and praise God. Having received his permission with a blessing, the bird expressed its joy in the movements of its body, and flew away. On the same lake in a similar way he was offered a large live fish which he addressed as brother in his usual way and put it back into the water by the boat. The fish played about in the water in front of the man of God; and as if it were attracted by his love, it would not go away from the ship until it received from him his permission with a blessing.[6]

Another time when he was walking with a friar through the marshes of Venice, he came upon a large flock of birds singing among the reeds. When he saw them, he said to his companion: "Our sisters the birds are praising their Creator; so we should go in among them and chant the Lord's praises and the canonical hours." When they had entered among them, the birds did not move from the place; and on account of the noise the birds were making, they could not hear each other saying the hours. The saint turned to the birds and said: "Sister birds, stop singing until we have done our duty of praising God!" At once they were silent and remained in silence as long as it took the friars to say the hours at length and to finish their praises. Then the holy man of God gave them permission to sing again. When the man of God gave them permission, they immediately resumed singing in their usual way.[7]

A cricket used to perch on a figtree beside the cell of the man of God at St. Mary of the Portiuncula and sing, arousing with its songs the Lord's servant to sing more frequently the divine praises, for he had learned to marvel at the Creator's magnificence even in insignificant creatures. He called it one day, and it flew upon his hand as if it had been taught by God. He said to it: "Sing, my sister cricket, praise the Lord Creator with your joyful song!" It obeyed without delay and began to sing; nor did it stop until at his command it flew back to its usual place. There it remained for eight days, coming each day, singing and returning, all at his command. Finally the man of God

[6]Major sources: III C 29; I C 60; III C 30. 23–24; minor source: Jul. 40.
[7]This incident is not found in Celano or Julian.

said to his companions: "Let us give our sister cricket permission to go away now, for she has cheered us enough with her singing and has aroused us to praise God over the space of eight days." With his permission, it departed and never appeared there again, as if it did not dare to disobey his command in the slightest way.[8]

When he was ill at Siena, a nobleman sent him a live pheasant he had recently caught. The moment it saw and heard the holy man, it was drawn to him with such affection that it would in no way allow itself to be separated from him. Many times it was placed outside the friar's place in the vineyard so that it could go away if it wanted. But every time it ran right back to the father as if it had always been reared by him. Then it was given to a man who used to visit God's servant out of devotion but it absolutely refused to eat, as if it were upset at being out of the sight of the devoted father. It was finally brought back to God's servant, and as soon as it saw him, showed signs of joy and ate heartily.[9]

When he went to the hermitage of La Verna to observe a forty-day fast in honor of the Archangel Michael, [10] birds of different kinds flew around his cell, with melodious singing and joyful movements, as if rejoicing at his arrival, and seemed to be inviting and enticing the devoted father to stay. When he saw this, he said to his companion: "I see, brother, that it is God's will that we stay here for some time, for our sisters the birds seem so delighted at our presence."[11] When he extended his stay there, a falcon that had built its nest there became deeply attached to him as a friend. For at the hour of the night when the holy man used to rise for the divine office, the falcon always came to wake him by making noise and singing. This pleased God's servant very much because the falcon was so solicitous toward him that it shook out of him all sluggish laziness. But when Christ's servant was more than usually weighed down with illness, the falcon had pity and did not impose such early vigils on him. As if instructed by God, about dawn it would ring the bell of its voice with a light touch.[12]

---

[8]Major source: III C 27; minor source III C 20.
[9]Major source: III C 26.
[10]Cf. IX, 3 and XIII, 1, pp. 264–265, 303–304.
[11]This incident is not found in Celano or Julian.
[12]Major source: III C 25.

There certainly seems to have been
a divine prophecy
both in the joy of the different kinds of birds
and in the song of the falcon—
a prophecy
of the time when
this praiser and worshiper of God
would be lifted up
on the wings of contemplation
and there would be exalted
with a Seraphic vision.[13]

Once when he was staying in the hermitage at Greccio, the local inhabitants were being troubled by many evils. For a pack of ravenous wolves were devouring not only animals but even men, and every year hail storms were devastating the fields and vineyards. When the herald of the holy Gospel preached to these people who were thus afflicted, he said to them: "For the honor and praise of Almighty God I promise you that all this pestilence will depart and the Lord will look kindly upon you and give you an increase of temporal goods if you believe me and show mercy to yourselves by making a good confession and *bring forth fruits worthy of repentance* (Matt. 3:8). Again I announce to you that if you are ungrateful for his gifts and *return to your vomit* (Prov. 26:11), the plague will be renewed, punishment will be doubled and even greater *wrath will rage* against you" (Jos. 22:18). The people did penance at his exhortation, and from that hour, the damage ceased, the dangers passed and neither the wolves nor the hail caused any further trouble. Furthermore, what is even greater, if hail came over the fields of their neighbors and approached their borders, it either stopped there or was diverted to another area.[14]

The hail kept the pact
of God's servant
and so too did the wolves;
nor did they try to rage anymore

[13]Cf. XIII, 1–3, pp. 303–306.
[14]Major source: II C 35–36.

contrary to the law of piety
against men who had been converted to piety,
as long as, according to their agreement,
the people did not act impiously
against God's most pious laws.
Therefore, we should respond piously
to the piety
of this blessed man,
which had such remarkable
sweetness and power
that it subdued ferocious beasts,
tamed the wild,
trained the tame
and bent to his obedience
the brute beasts that had rebelled
against fallen mankind.
Truly this is the virtue
that unites all creatures in brotherhood
and is helpful *for all things*
since it has the promise of the present life,
and of the life to come.[15]

VLADIMIR LOSSKY

Cosmic Awareness*

It was the divinely appointed function of the first man, according
to St. Maximus, to unite in himself the whole of created being; and
at the same time to reach his perfect union with God and thus grant
the state of deification to the whole creation. It was first necessary
that he should suppress in his own nature the division into two sexes,
in his following of the impassible life according to the divine archetype.

---

[15] 1 Tim. 4:8.
*From *The Mystical Theology of the Eastern Church*, ET by the Fellowship of St Alban and St
Serguis (Cambridge and London: James Clarke and Co., 3rd ed., 1973), pp. 109–111.

He would then be in a position to reunite paradise with the rest of the earth, for, constantly bearing paradise within himself, being in ceaseless communion with God, he would be able to transform the whole earth into paradise. After this, he must overcome spatial conditions not only in his spirit but also in the body, by reuniting the heavens and the earth, the totality of the sensible universe. Having surpassed the limits of the sensible, it would then be for him to penetrate into the intelligible universe by knowledge equal to that of the angelic spirits, in order to unite in himself the intelligible and the sensible worlds. Finally, there remaining nothing outside himself but God alone, man had only to give himself to Him in a complete abandonment of love, and thus return to Him the whole created universe gathered together in his own being. God Himself would then in His turn have given Himself to man, who would then, in virtue of this gift, that is to say by grace, possess all that God possesses by nature. The deification of man and of the whole created universe would thus be accomplished. Since this task which was given to man was not fulfilled by Adam, it is in the work of Christ, the second Adam, that we can see what it was meant to be.

Such is the teaching of St. Maximus on the divisions of created being, which is borrowed, in part, by John Scotus Eriugena in his *De divisione naturae*. These divisions of St. Maximus express the limited character of the creation which is indeed the very condition of its existence; at the same time they are problems to be resolved, obstacles to be surmounted on the way towards union with God. Man is not a being isolated from the rest of creation; by his very nature he is bound up with the whole of the universe, and St. Paul bears witness that the whole creation awaits the future glory which will be revealed in the sons of God (Rom. viii, 18–22). This cosmic awareness has never been absent from Eastern spirituality, and is given expression in theology as well as in liturgical poetry, in iconography and, perhaps above all, in the ascetical writings of the masters of the spiritual life of the Eastern Church. 'What is a charitable heart?'—asks St. Isaac the Syrian—'It is a heart which is burning with charity for the whole of creation, for men, for the birds, for the beasts, for the demons—for all creatures. He who has such a heart cannot see or call to mind a creature without his eyes becoming filled with tears by reason of the immense compassion which seizes his heart; a heart which is softened and can no longer bear to see or learn from others of any suffering, even the smallest pain, being inflicted upon a creature. This is why such a man never ceases to pray also for the animals, for the enemies of Truth, and for those who do him evil, that they may be preserved and purified. He will pray even for the reptiles, moved by the infinite pity which reigns in the hearts of those who are becoming united to God.' In his way to union with God, man in no way leaves creatures aside, but gathers together in his love the whole cosmos disordered by sin, that it may at last be transfigured by grace.

Part Two

◆

THE
PROBLEM OF
ANIMAL PAIN

Introduction to Part Two

The question of the interdependence and unity of creation, explored by some of the contributors to the last section, is graphically illustrated by our biblical selections which open this second section. For so close indeed are humans and animals thought to be within creation that a significant number of biblical passages speak of their condition in similar or identical terms. Thus, according to the Prophets, animals, as well as humans, suffer chastisement from the Lord. Both animals as well as humans are dependent upon the providence of the Lord, according to the Psalmist. In Joel, animals and humans both suffer common deprivation and common restoration. Indeed, if Jonah is right, the Lord takes pity on the city of Nineveh because of its many thousands of inhabitants, and also because of 'much cattle.'

In the light of this biblically based view of the fundamental closeness between humans and animals, there is, of course, no suggestion in the Old and New Testaments that animals do not suffer pain. Indeed the idea that there is a misery common to both is well documented by the prophetic writers, such as Isaiah. And yet the idea that animals can suffer pain like humans has not been a unanimous view throughout Christian history.

René Descartes is an example of this contrary view. In our first selection, he inveighs against the common notion that animals 'think' and are possessed of 'minds' or 'reason.' Because the rational soul is not to be found in non-human creatures, it follows, according to Descartes, that they cannot have the necessary self-consciousness to experience pain. Animals, in other words, are machines like clocks. In this way, Descartes is free from having to confront the problem of 'natural' evil especially apparent in pain and suffering in animals. His answer is straightforward: since animals cannot experience pain, there is no case for God to answer. Peter Geach's answer, represented in our second selection, is more subtle. He does not deny that animals feel pain or suffering, he simply denies that God is in any way whatever concerned about such pain or suffering in animals. 'The Creator's mind, as manifested in the living world, seems to be characterised by mere indifference to the pain that the elaborate interlocking teleologies of life involve.' Again, God does not 'share with his creatures . . . the virtue of sympathy with physical suffering.'

In contrast, C. E. M. Joad and C. S. Lewis both agree that animal pain is a serious matter and one that requires theological explanation. But finding a sufficiently comprehensive and satisfying explanation, however, is not an easy task as their long and thought-provoking discussion reveals. For Joad, animal pain actually constitutes 'an insuperable objection' to Christian faith. 'Either God could abolish [it] but did not, in which case, since he deliberately tolerated the presence in the universe of a state of affairs which was bad, I did not see how He could be good; or He wanted to abolish [it] but could not, in which case I did not see how He could be all-powerful.' Like Joad, Lewis accepts that animal pain is indeed problematic for faith but suggests, speculatively, both that God alone was not responsible for all the evil in the world let loose through the fall of man or the agency of Satan, and also, that God may yet redeem suffering animal creation in a way that few Christian writers have as yet sufficiently understood.

John Hick, in contrast, does not believe that 'an eschatological new heaven and earth could relieve the problem of earthly animal pain.' He accepts that animal pain is theologically 'baffling,' but opts for a refashioned Augustinian position that suffering in creation is there to make possible its 'human apex.' In other words, the world of non-human suffering is somehow necessary for human 'soul-making' and therefore essential to the fullness of the created world. Austin Farrer concurs with Hick's view that pain is inevitable in creation. 'If we say that God . . . should have spared his creatures all suffering, we are surely talking nonsense,' argues Farrer. What then is the point of suffering? Farrer's answer appears to be that suffering is essential if there is to be compassion. 'It is only because God allows pain that there is any object for his compassion, or any sense in speaking of it.'

Our concluding piece by A. Richard Kingston points us to the theological and moral unsatisfactoriness of almost all the preceding arguments. He sees a fundamental 'callousness' to suffering exhibited, on the one hand by Descartes and others, who deny the reality of animal pain, and by Hick and others on the other hand, who suggest that God is really unconcerned about the status and suffering of non-human creatures. Kingston insists that the record of Christian theologians in this area lacks both a sufficient conception of God's moral rule as well as ordinary human compassion. 'Our search clearly must continue for a theodicy which really does justice both to the Creator and to all his creatures, which points to a God of love and pin-points our duty to love.'

We may summarise the issues raised in this section as follows: (1) Can animals experience pain and suffering? (2) Is God concerned about suffering in animals? (3) Are animals, like humans, to be redeemed? (4) Is animal suffering the result of the 'fall' of creation or the agency of Satan? (5) Is animal pain essential in order for there to be a human species at all, or a human species which can exhibit compassion? and (6) Are (4) and (5) morally or theologically satisfactory 'explanations' of suffering in the non-human world?

The Bible
On the Pains and Status of Animals

Deuteronomy 13:12–15

"If you hear in one of your cities, which the Lord your God gives you to dwell there, that certain base fellows have gone out among you and have drawn away the inhabitants of the city, saying, 'let us go and serve other gods,' which you have not known, then you shall inquire and make search and ask diligently; and behold, if it be true and certain that such an abominable thing has been done among you, you shall surely put the inhabitants of that city to the sword, destroying it utterly, all who are in it and its cattle, with the edge of the sword."

1 Samuel 15:2–3

Thus says the Lord of hosts, "I will punish what Amalek did to Israel in opposing them on the way, when they came up out of Egypt. Now go and smite Amalek, and utterly destroy all that they have; do not spare them, but kill both man and woman, infant and suckling, ox and sheep, camel and ass."

Job 41:1–10 and 33–34

"Can you draw out Leviathan with a fishhook
    or press down his tongue with a cord?
Can you put a rope in his nose,
    or pierce his jaw with a hook?
Will he make many supplications to you?
    Will he speak to you soft words?
Will he make a covenant with you
    to take him for your servant for ever?

Will you play with him as with a bird,
    or will you put him on a leash for your maidens?
Will traders bargain over him?
    Will they divide him up among the merchants?
Can you fill his skin with harpoons,
    or his head with fishing spears?
Lay hands on him;
    think of the battle; you will not do it again!
Behold, the hope of a man is disappointed;
    he is laid low even at the sight of him.
No one is so fierce that he dares to stir him up.
    Who then is he that can stand before me?
Who has given to me, that I should repay him?
    Whatever is under the whole heaven is mine.

Upon earth there is not his like,
    a creature without fear,
He beholds everything that is high;
    he is king over all the sons of pride."

Psalm 104:27–31

These all look to thee,
    to give them their food in due season.
When thou givest to them, they gather it up;
    when thou openest thy hand,
    they are filled with good things.
When thou hidest thy face, they are dismayed;
    when thou takest away their breath,
    they die and return to their dust.
When thou sendest forth thy Spirit, they are created;
    and thou renewest the face of the ground.

Jeremiah 7:20

Therefore thus says the Lord God: "Behold, my anger and my wrath will be poured out on this place, upon man and beast, upon the trees of the field and the fruit of the ground; it will burn and not be quenched."

Joel 1:15–16, 18 and 2:21–22

> Alas for the day!
> For that day of the Lord is near,
>   and as destruction from the Almighty it comes.
> Is it not the food cut off before our eyes,
>   joy and gladness from the house of our God?
>
> How the beasts groan!
>   The herds of cattle are perplexed
> because there is no pasture for them;
>   Even that flocks of sheep are dismayed.
>
> "Fear not, O Lord;
>   be glad and rejoice,
>   for the Lord has done great things!
> Fear not you beasts of the field,
>   for the pastures of the wilderness are green;
> the tree bears its fruit,
>   the fig tree and vine give their full yield."

Jonah 3:6–9

The tidings reached the king of Nineveh, and he arose from his throne, removed his robe, and covered himself with sackcloth and sat in ashes. And he made proclamation and published through Nin'eveh, "By the decree of the king and his nobles: Let neither man nor beast, herd nor flock, taste anything; let them not feed, or drink water, but let man and beast be covered with sackcloth and let them cry mightily to God; yea, let every one turn from his evil way and from the violence which is in his hands. Who knows, God may yet repent and turn from his fierce anger, so that we perish not?"

Jonah 4:9–11

But God said to Jonah, "Do you do well to be angry for the plant?" And he said, "I do well to be angry, angry enough to die." And the Lord said, "You pity the plant, for which you did not labour, nor did you make it grow, which came into being in a night, and perished in a night. And should not I pity Nineveh, that great city, in which there are more than a hundred and twenty thousand persons who do not know their right hand from their left, and also much cattle?"

Luke 12:24 and 27

"Consider the ravens: they neither sow nor reap, they have neither storehouse nor barn, and yet God feeds them. Of how much more value are you than the birds!

Consider the lilies, how they grow; they neither toil nor spin; yet I tell you, even Solomon in all his glory was not arrayed like one of these."

RENÉ DESCARTES
Animals Are Machines

I

I had explained all these matters in some detail in the Treatise which I formerly intended to publish. And afterwards I had shown there, what must be the fabric of the nerves and muscles of the human body in order that the animal spirits therein contained should have the power to move the members, just as the heads of animals, a little while after decapitation, are still observed to move and bite the earth, notwithstanding that they are no longer animate; what changes are necessary in the brain to cause wakefulness, sleep and dreams; how light, sounds, smells, tastes, heat and all other qualities pertaining to external objects are able to imprint on it various ideas by the intervention of the senses; how hunger, thirst and other internal affections can also convey their impressions upon it; what should be regarded as the "common sense" by which these ideas are received, and what is

Selection I is from Descartes, *Discourse on Method in Philosophical Works of Descartes*, trans. E. S. Haldane and G. R. T. Ross (London: Cambridge University Press), vol. I, pp. 115–18. Selections II and III are from two letters by Descartes, to the Marquess of Newcastle (November 23, 1646) and to Henry More (February 5, 1649), in *Descartes: Philosophical Letters*, trans. and ed. Anthony Kenny (Oxford: The Clarendon Press, 1970).

meant by the memory which retains them, by the fancy which can change them in diverse ways and out of them constitute new ideas, and which, by the same means, distributing the animal spirits through the muscles, can cause the members of such a body to move in as many diverse ways, and in a manner as suitable to the objects which present themselves to its senses and to its internal passions, as can happen in our own case apart from the direction of our free will. And this will not seem strange to those, who, knowing how many different *automata* or moving machines can be made by the industry of man, without employing in so doing more than a very few parts in comparison with the great multitude of bones, muscles, nerves, arteries, veins, or other parts that are found in the body of each animal. From this aspect the body is regarded as a machine which, having been made by the hands of God, is incomparably better arranged, and possesses in itself movements which are much more admirable, than any of those which can be invented by man. Here I specially stopped to show that if there had been such machines, possessing the organs and outward form of a monkey or some other animal without reason, we should not have had any means of ascertaining that they were not of the same nature as those animals. On the other hand, if there were machines which bore a resemblance to our body and imitated our actions as far as it was morally possible to do so, we should always have two very certain tests by which to recognise that, for all that, they were not real men. The first is, that they could never use speech or other signs as we do when placing our thoughts on record for the benefit of others. For we can easily understand a machine's being constituted so that it can utter words, and even emit some responses to action on it of a corporeal kind, which brings about a change in its organs; for instance, if it is touched in a particular part it may ask what we wish to say to it; if in another part it may exclaim that it is being hurt, and so on. But it never happens that it arranges its speech in various ways, in order to reply appropriately to everything that may be said in its presence, as even the lowest type of man can do. And the second difference is, that although machines can perform certain things as well as or perhaps better than any of us can do, they infallibly fall short in others, by the which means we may discover that they did not act from knowledge, but only from the disposition of their organs. For while reason is a universal instrument which can serve for all contingencies, these organs have need of some special adaptation for every particular action.

From this it follows that it is morally impossible that there should be sufficient diversity in any machine to allow it to act in all the events of life in the same way as our reason causes us to act.

By these two methods we may also recognise the difference that exists between men and brutes. For it is a very remarkable fact that there are none so depraved and stupid, without even excepting idiots, that they cannot arrange different words together, forming of them a statement by which they make known their thoughts; while, on the other hand, there is no other animal, however perfect and fortunately circumstanced it may be, which can do the same. It is not the want of organs that brings this to pass, for it is evident that magpies and parrots are able to utter words just like ourselves, and yet they cannot speak as we do, that is, so as to give evidence that they think of what they say. On the other hand, men who, being born deaf and dumb, are in the same degree, or even more than the brutes, destitute of the organs which serve the others for talking, are in the habit of themselves inventing certain signs by which they make themselves understood by those who, being usually in their company, have leisure to learn their language. And this does not merely show that the brutes have less reason than men, but that they have none at all, since it is clear that very little is required in order to be able to talk. And when we notice the inequality that exists between animals of the same species, as well as between men, and observe that some are more capable of receiving instruction than others, it is not credible that a monkey or a parrot, selected as the most perfect of its species, should not in these matters equal the stupidest child to be found, or at least a child whose mind is clouded, unless in the case of the brute the soul were of an entirely different nature from ours. And we ought not to confound speech with natural movements which betray passions and may be imitated by machines as well as be manifested by animals; nor must we think, as did some of the ancients, that brutes talk, although we do not understand their language. For if this were true, since they have many organs which are allied to our own, they could communicate their thoughts to us just as easily as to those of their own race. It is also a very remarkable fact that although there are many animals which exhibit more dexterity than we do in some of their actions, we at the same time observe that they do not manifest any dexterity at all in many others. Hence the fact that they do better than we do, does not prove that they are endowed with mind, for in this case they would have more reason than any of us, and would surpass us in all other things. It rather shows that they have no reason at all, and that it is nature which acts in them according to the disposition of their organs, just as a clock, which is only composed of wheels and weights is able to tell the hours and measure the time more correctly than we can do with all our wisdom.

I had described after this the rational soul and shown that it could not be in any way derived from the power of matter, like the other things of which I had spoken, but that it must be expressly created. I showed, too, that it is not sufficient that it should be lodged in the human body like a pilot in his ship, unless perhaps for the moving of its members, but that it is necessary that it should also be joined and united more closely to the body in order to have sensations and appetites similar to our own, and thus to form a true man. In conclusion, I have here enlarged a little on the subject of the soul, because it is one of the greatest importance. For next to the error of those who deny God, which I think I have already sufficiently refuted, there is none which is more effectual in leading feeble spirits from the straight path of virtue, than to imagine that the soul of the brute is of the same nature as our own, and that in consequence, after this life we have nothing to fear or to hope for, any more than the flies and ants. As a matter of fact, when one comes to know how greatly they differ, we understand much better the reasons which go to prove that our soul is in its nature entirely independent of body, and in consequence that it is not liable to die with it. And then, inasmuch as we observe no other causes capable of destroying it, we are naturally inclined to judge that it is immortal.

II

I cannot share the opinion of Montaigne and others who attribute understanding or thought to animals. I am not worried that people say that men have an absolute empire over all the other animals; because I agree that some of them are stronger than us, and believe that there may also be some who have an instinctive cunning capable of deceiving the shrewdest human beings. But I observe that they only imitate or surpass us in those of our actions which are not guided by our thoughts. It often happens that we walk or eat without thinking at all about what we are doing; and similarly, without using our reason, we reject things which are harmful for us, and parry the blows aimed at us. Indeed, even if we expressly willed not to put our hands in front of our head when we fall, we could not prevent ourselves. I think also that if we had no thought we would eat, as the animals do, without having to learn to; and it is said that those who walk in their sleep sometimes swim across streams in which they would drown if they were awake. As for the movements of our passions, even though in us they are accompanied with thought because we have the faculty of thinking, it is none the less very clear that they do not depend on thought, because they often occur in spite of us. Consequently they can also occur in animals, even more violently than they do in human beings, without our being able to conclude from that that they have thoughts.

In fact, none of our external actions can show anyone who examines them that our body is not just a self-moving machine but contains a soul with thoughts, with the exception of words, or other signs that are relevant to particular topics without expressing any passion. I say words or other signs, because deaf-mutes use signs as we use spoken words; and I say that these signs must be relevant, to exclude the speech of parrots, without excluding the speech of madmen, which is relevant to particular topics even though it does not follow reason. I add also that these words or signs must not express any passion, to rule out not only cries of joy or sadness and the like, but also whatever can be taught by training to animals. If you teach a magpie to say good-day to its mistress, when it sees her approach, this can only be by making the utterance of this word the expression of one of its passions. For instance it will be an expression of the hope of eating, if it has always been given a titbit when it says it. Similarly, all the things which dogs, horses, and monkeys are taught to perform are only expressions of their fear, their hope, or their joy; and consequently they can be performed without any thought. Now it seems to me very striking that the use of words, so defined, is something peculiar to human beings. Montaigne and Charron may have said that there is more difference between one human being and another than between a human being and an animal; but there has never been known an animal so perfect as to use a sign to make other animals understand something which expressed no passion; and there is no human being so imperfect as not to do so, since even deaf-mutes invent special signs to express their thoughts. This seems to me a very strong argument to prove that the reason why animals do not speak as we do is not that they lack the organs but that they have no thoughts. It cannot be said that they speak to each other and that we cannot understand them; because since dogs and some other animals express their passions to us, they would express their thoughts also if they had any.

I know that animals do many things better than we do, but this does not surprise me. It can even be used to prove they act naturally and mechanically, like a clock which tells the time better than our judgement does. Doubtless when the swallows come in spring, they operate like clocks. The actions of honeybees are of the same nature, and the discipline of cranes in flight, and of apes in fighting, if it is true that they keep discipline. Their instinct to bury their dead is no stranger than that of dogs and cats who scratch the earth for the purpose of burying their excrement; they hardly ever actually bury it, which shows that they act only by instinct and without thinking. The most that one can say is that though the animals do not perform any action which shows us that they think, still, since the organs of their body are not very different from ours, it may be conjectured that there is attached to those organs some thoughts such as we experience in ourselves, but of a very much less perfect kind. To which I have nothing to reply except that if they thought as we do, they would have an immortal soul like us. This is unlikely, because there is no reason to believe it of some animals without believing it of all, and many of them such as oysters and sponges are too imperfect for this to be credible. But I am afraid of boring you with this discussion, and my only desire is to show you that I am, etc.

III

But there is no prejudice to which we are all more accustomed from our earliest years than the belief that dumb animals think. Our only reason for this belief is the fact that we see that many of the organs of animals are not very different from ours in shape and movement. Since we believe that there is a single principle within us which causes these motions—namely the soul, which both moves the body and thinks—we do not doubt that some such soul is to be found in animals also. I came to realize, however, that there are two different principles causing our motions: one is purely mechanical and corporeal and depends solely on the force of the spirits and the construction of our organs, and can be called the corporeal soul; the other is the incorporeal mind, the soul which I have defined as a thinking substance. Thereupon I investigated more carefully whether the motions of animals originated from both these principles or from one only. I soon saw clearly that they could all originate from the corporeal and mechanical principle, and I thenceforward regarded it as certain and established that we cannot at all prove the presence of a thinking soul in animals. I am not disturbed by the astuteness and cunning of dogs and foxes, or all the things which animals do for the sake of food, sex, and fear; I claim that I can easily explain the origin of all of them from the constitution of their organs.

But though I regard it as established that we cannot prove there is any thought in animals, I do not think it is thereby proved that there is not, since the human mind does not reach into their hearts. But when I investigate what is most probable in this matter, I see no argument for animals having thoughts except the fact that since they have eyes, ears, tongues, and other sense-organs like ours, it seems likely that they have sensation like us; and since thought is included in our mode of sensation, similar thought seems to be attributable to them. This argument, which is very obvious, has taken possession of the minds of all men from their earliest age. But there are other arguments, stronger and more numerous, but not so obvious to everyone, which strongly urge the opposite. One is that it is more probable that worms and flies and caterpillars move mechanically than that they all have immortal souls.

It is certain that in the bodies of animals, as in ours, there are bones, nerves, muscles, animal spirits, and other organs so disposed that they can by themselves, without any thought, give rise to all animals the motions we observe. This is very clear in convulsive movements when the machine of the body moves despite the soul, and sometimes more violently and in a more varied manner than when it is moved by the will.

Second, it seems reasonable, since art copies nature, and men can make various automata which move without thought, that nature should produce its own automata, much more splendid than artificial ones. These natural automata are the animals. This is especially likely since we have no reason to believe that thought always accompanies the disposition of organs which we find in animals. It is much more wonderful that a mind should be found in every human body than that one should be lacking in every animal.

But in my opinion the main reason which suggests that the beasts lack thought is the following. Within a single species some of them are more perfect than others, as men are too. This can be seen in horses and dogs, some of whom learn what they are taught much better than others. Yet, although all animals easily communicate to us, by voice or bodily movement, their natural impulses of anger, fear, hunger and so on, it has never yet been observed that any brute animal reached the stage of using real speech, that is to say, of indicating by word or sign something pertaining to pure thought and not to natural impulse. Such speech is the only certain sign of thought hidden in a body. All men use it, however stupid and insane they may be, and though they may lack tongue and organs of voice; but no animals do. Consequently it can be taken as a real specific difference between men and dumb animals.

For brevity's sake I here omit the other reasons for denying thought to animals. Please note that I am speaking of thought, and not of life or sensation. I do not deny life to animals, since I regard it as consisting simply in the heat of the heart; and I do not deny sensation, in so far as it depends on a bodily organ. Thus my opinion is not so much cruel to animals as indulgent to men—at least to those who are not given to the superstitions of Pythagoras—since it absolves them from the suspicion of crime when they eat or kill animals.

Perhaps I have written at too great length for the sharpness of your intelligence; but I wished to show you that very few people have yet sent me objections which were as agreeable as yours. Your kindness and candour has made you a friend of that most respectful admirer of all who seek true wisdom, etc.

PETER GEACH
Divine Indifference

[T]he ostensibly teleological structures and processes by which animals and plants live include complex reproductive processes which give a strong impression of teleology. Now in order that there should

From *Providence and Evil* (Cambridge: Cambridge University Press, 1977), pp. 76—80.

be an origin of *species* by evolution at all, rather than the production of an Empedoclean chaos of monsters, it is necessary that these offspring should have, in each successive generation, a considerable, though not complete, resemblance to their parents, including a resemblance in manner of reproduction. Otherwise a method of reproduction evolved by chance variation would serve for the survival only of *that* generation, not of subsequent ones. The reproductive mechanisms certainly cannot be explained just by saying that creatures which failed to develop them failed to reproduce their kind and perished: without these mechanisms there would be no raw material for any cause of evolution to work upon. So in this case there can be no story of natural selection to replace the ostensible teleological account; why then need we think some such story must account for other ostensibly teleological structures and activities of living things?

In arguing to this conclusion, I have not been trying to ease the task of theodicy: quite the contrary. For among the most striking cases of ostensible teleology are the ways that predators are adapted to catch their prey and the way that parasitic animals like the liver-fluke live and reproduce their kind. By what I am arguing, this telelogy should be accepted as genuine. The spectacle of the living world, to an un-captive mind, is a manifestation of great power and of great wisdom, for which no detail is too small; but there is no evidence or hint that the whole show is organized to minimize pain; nor, for that matter, is there any evidence that pain as such is elaborately contrived, as by Lewis's Devil. The Creator's mind, as manifested in the living world, seems to be characterized by mere indifference to the pain that the elaborate interlocking teleologies of life involve . . .

At this point I make a change of subject. Ought we to expect God the Creator of the world to have virtues like those of men? And ought we to admire and love him above all things even if he has not the character that would be deemed morally good in man? I shall argue that many human virtues cannot possibly be ascribed to God, and that all the same there can be nothing more worthy of love and admiration than God is.

There are certain human virtues that must be ascribed to God in a way befitting his kind of life: God is provident and wise and truthful and faithful to his promises. One cannot think of an illogical world, not therefore of a world made by an improvident or foolish God; and only a revelation according to which God is truthful and faithful to his promises can begin to be credible. But there are many virtues that it would be obviously absurd to ascribe to God: chastity, courage, honesty, gratitude. Even justice raises severe problems. Commutative justice is out of the question: what can God be given so that he owes something in return? Distributive justice seems very difficult too: since all that a creature has and is is God's gift, how can the question be raised whether God treats equals unequally or not, or whether the differences he has regard to are relevant or irrelevant ones? We may, I believe, ascribe to God retributive justice: reward and punishment; but his rewards and punishments are not arbitrarily annexed by positive law to human deeds.

These considerations are pretty straightforward, but are liable then to provoke the reaction that if God is not like a virtuous man then we ought not to admire and love him, or at least not as much as we admire and love virtuous men. But the reaction is perverse. What is being asked is that God should be admired and loved for his great glory, for being God, for being utterly unlike man in nature . . .

God is to be loved and admired above all things because he is all truth and all beauty: the truth and beauty that in the universe is scattered in separate pages, to use Dante's figure, is in God bound up orderly into one volume. And we love truth and beauty by our nature, in so far as our vices and follies do not prevent us. So it is only vice and folly that stop us from loving God above all things. The protest that we ought not so to love and admire him if he does not share the moral perfections proper to his creatures is a mere impertinence.

One virtue, if I am right, that God cannot share with his creatures is the virtue of sympathy with physical suffering. It is virtuous that a man should in measure sympathize with the sufferings of the lower animals: only in measure, for someone who tried to sympathize with a shark or octopus or herring would be erring by excess as Dr Moreau erred by defect; their life is too alien to ours for sympathy to be anything but folly or affectation. I once heard of a moral philosopher who worried, as he attacked his lamb chop, whether we ought not to avoid unnecessary suffering to animals by turning vegetarian; but then he reflected on all the slugs and bugs that would have to be killed in order to feed the human population; then if we reckon how many slugs and bugs add up, in the way of pain, to one lamb—and so he attacked his lamb chop with renewed zest. And I have never heard the conservationists protest against our genocidal war with the rat, a war prosecuted quite ruthlessly and with means that may cause extreme pain. Let us clear our minds of cant. Sympathy with the pains of animals whose nature we share is, I repeat, a virtue in men, so long as the Aristotelian mean is observed. But it is not a virtue that can reasonably be ascribed to the Divine Nature. God is not an animal as men are, and if he does not change his designs to avoid pain and suffering to animals he is not violating any natural sympathies as Dr Moreau did. Only anthropomorphic imagination allows us to accuse God of cruelty in this regard.

C. E. M. JOAD and C. S. LEWIS
The Pains of Animals

C. E. M. JOAD: For many years the problem of pain and evil seemed to me to offer an insuperable objection to Christianity. Either God could abolish them but did not, in which case, since He deliberately tolerated the presence in the universe of a state of affairs which was bad, I did not see how He could be good; or He wanted to abolish them but could not, in which case I did not see how He could be all-powerful. The dilemma is as old as Saint Augustine, and nobody pretends that there is an easy way of escape.

Moreover, all the attempts to explain pain away, or to mitigate its stark ferocity, or to present it as other than a very great evil, perhaps the greatest of evils, are palpable failures. They are testimonies to the kindness of men's hearts or perhaps to the queasiness of their consciences, rather than to the sharpness of their wits.

And yet, granting pain to be an evil, perhaps the greatest of evils, I have come to accept the Christian view of pain as not incompatible with the Christian concept of the Creator and of the world that He has made. That view I take to be briefly as follows: It was of no interest to God to create a species consisting of virtuous automata, for the "virtue" of automata who can do no other than they do, is a courtesy title only; it is analogous to the "virtue" of the stone that rolls downhill

From *The Month*, vol. 3, no. 2 (February 1950), pp. 95–102

or of the water that freezes at 32°. To what end, it may be asked, should God create such creatures? That he might be praised by them? But automatic praise is a mere succession of noises. That he might love them? But they are essentially unlovable; you cannot love puppets. And so God gave man freewill that he might increase in virtue by his own efforts and become, as a free moral being, a worthy object of God's love. Freedom entails freedom to go wrong: man did, in fact, go wrong, misusing God's gift and doing evil. Pain is a by-product of evil; and so pain came into the world as a result of man's misuse of God's gift of freewill.

So much I can understand; so much, indeed, I accept. It is plausible; it is rational; it hangs together.

But now I come to a difficulty, to which I see no solution; indeed, it is in the hope of learning of one that this article is written. This is the difficulty of animal pain, and, more particularly, of the pain of the animal world, before man appeared upon the cosmic scene. What account do theologians give of it? The most elaborate and careful account known to me is that of C. S. Lewis.

He begins by making a distinction between sentience and consciousness. When we have the sensations *a*, *b* and *c*, the fact that we have them and the fact that we know that we have them imply that there is something which stands sufficiently outside them to notice that they occur and that they succeed one another. This is consciousness, the consciousness to which the sensations happen. In other words, the experience of succession, the succession of sensations, demands a self or soul which is other than the sensations which it experiences. (Mr. Lewis invokes the helpful metaphor of the bed of a river along which the stream of sensations flows.) Consciousness, therefore, implies a continuing *ego* which recognizes the succession of sensations; sentience is their mere succession. Now animals have sentience but not consciousness. Mr. Lewis illustrates as follows:

> This would mean that if you give such a creature two blows with a whip, there are, indeed, two pains; but there is no co-ordinating self which can recognise that "I have had two pains." Even in the single pain there is no self to say "I am in pain"—for if it could distinguish itself from the sensation— the bed from the stream—sufficiently to say "I am in pain," it would also be able to connect the two sensations as *its* experience.

(*a*) I take Mr. Lewis's point or, rather, I take it without perceiving its relevance. The question is how to account for the occurence of pain (i) in a universe which is the creation of an all-good God; (ii) in creatures who are not morally sinful. To be told that the creatures are not really creatures, since they are not conscious in the sense of consciousness defined, does not really help matters. If it be true, as Mr. Lewis says, that the right way to put the matter is not "This animal is feeling pain" but "Pain is taking place in this animal," pain is nevertheless taking place. Pain is felt even if there is no continuing *ego* to feel it and to relate it to past and to future pains. Now it is the fact that pain is felt, no matter who or what feels it, or whether any continuing consciousness feels it, in a universe planned by a good God that demands explanation.

(*b*) Secondly, the theory of sentience as mere succession of sensations presupposes that there is no continuing consciousness. No continuing consciousness presupposes no memory. Now it seems to me to be non-sense to say that animals do not remember. The dog who cringes at the sight of the whip by which he has been constantly beaten *behaves* as if he remembers, and behaviour is all that we have to go by. In general, we all act upon the assumption that the horse, the cat and the dog with which we are acquainted, remember very well, remember sometimes better than we do. Now I do not see how it is possible to explain the fact of memory without a continuing consciousness.

Mr. Lewis recognizes this and concedes that the higher animals— apes, elephants, dogs, cats, and so on—have a self which connects experiences, have, in fact, what he calls a soul. But this assumption presents us with a new set of difficulties.

(*a*) If animals have souls, what is to be done about their immortality? The question, it will be remembered, is elaborately debated in Heaven at the beginning of Anatole France's *Penguin Island* after the short sighted St. Mael has baptized the penguins, but no satisfactory solution is offered.

(*b*) Mr. Lewis suggests that the higher domestic animals achieve immortality as members of a corporate society of which the head is man. It is, apparently, "The-goodman-and-the-goodwife-ruling-their-children-and-their-beasts-in-the-good-homestead" who survive. "If you ask," he writes, "concerning an animal thus raised as a member of the whole Body of the homestead, where its personal identity resides, I answer, 'Where its identity always did reside even in the earthly life—in its relation to the Body and, specially, to the master who is the head of that Body.' In other words, the man will know his dog: the dog will know its master and, in knowing him, will *be* itself."

Whether this is good theology, I do not know, but to our present enquiry it raises two difficulties.

(i) It does not cover the case of the higher animals who do not know man, for example apes and elephants, but who are yet considered by Mr. Lewis to have souls.

(ii) If one animal may attain good immortal selfhood in and through a good man, he may attain bad immortal selfhood in and through a bad man. One thinks of the over-nourished lapdogs of idle over-nourished women. It is a little hard that when, through no fault of their own, animals fall to selfish, self-indulgent or cruel masters, they should through eternity form part of selfish, self-indulgent or cruel super-personal wholes and perhaps be punished for their participation in them.

(c) If the animals have souls and, presumably, freedom, the same sort of explanation must be adopted for pain in animals as is offered for pain in men. Pain, in other words, is one of the evils consequent upon sin. The higher animals, then, are corrupt. The question arises, who corrupted them? There seem to be two possible answers: (1) The Devil; (2) Man.

(I) Mr. Lewis considers this answer. The animals, he says, may originally all have been herbivorous. They became carnivorous, that is to say, they began to prey upon, to tear, and to eat one another because "some mighty created power had already been at work for ill on the material universe, or the solar system, or, at least, the planet Earth, before ever man came on the scene. If there is such a power, it may well have corrupted the animal creation before man appeared."

I have three comments to make:

(i) I find the supposition of Satan tempting monkeys frankly incredible. This, I am well aware, is not a logical objection. It is one's imagination—or is it perhaps one's common sense?—that revolts against it.

(ii) Although most animals fall victims to the redness of Nature's "tooth and claw," many do not. The sheep falls down the ravine, breaks its leg and starves; hundreds of thousands of migrating birds die every year of hunger; creatures are struck and not killed by lightning, and their seared bodies take long to die. Are these pains due to corruption?

(iii) The case of animals without souls cannot, on Mr. Lewis's own showing, be brought under the "moral corruption" explanation. Yet consider just one instance of nature's arrangements. The wasps, ichneumonidae, sting their caterpillar prey in such a way as to paralyse its nerve centres. They then lay their eggs on the helpless caterpillar. When the grubs hatch from the eggs, they immediately proceed to feed upon the living but helpless flesh of their incubators, the paralysed but still sentient caterpillars.

It is hard to suppose that the caterpillar feels no pain when slowly consumed; harder still to ascribe the pain to moral corruption; hardest of all to conceive how such an arrangement could have been planned by an all-good and all-wise Creator.

(2) The hypothesis that the animals were corrupted by man does not account for animal pain during the hundreds of millions of years (probably about nine hundred million) when the earth contained living creatures, but did not contain man.

In sum, either animals have souls or they have no souls. If they have none, pain is felt for which there can be no moral responsibility, and for which no misuse of God's gift of moral freedom can be invoked as an excuse. If they have souls, we can give no plausible account (a) of their immortality—how draw the line between animals with souls and men with souls?—or (b) of their moral corruption, which would enable Christian apologists to place them in respect of their pain under the same heading of explanation as that which is proposed and which I am prepared to accept for man?

It may well be that there is an answer to this problem. I would be grateful to anyone who would tell me what it is.

C. S. Lewis: Though there is always some pleasure, as well as danger, in encountering so sincere and economical a disputant as Dr. Joad, I do so (at the Editor's request) with no little reluctance. Dr. Joad writes not merely as a controversialist who demands, but as an enquirer who really desires, an answer. I come into the matter at all only because my answers have already failed to satisfy him. And it is embarrassing to me, and possibly depressing to him, that he should, in a manner, be sent back to the same shop which has once failed to supply the goods. If it were wholly a question of defending the original goods I think I would let it alone. But it is not exactly that. I think he has perhaps slightly misunderstood what I was offering for sale.

Dr. Joad is concerned with the ninth chapter of my *Problem of Pain*. And the first point I want to make is that no one would gather from his article how confessedly speculative that chapter was. This was acknowledged in my preface and repeatedly emphasized in the chapter itself. This, of course, can bring no ease to Dr. Joad's difficulties; unsatisfactory answers do not become satisfactory by being tentative. I mention the character of the chapter to underline the fact that it stands on a rather different level from those which preceded it. And that difference suggests the place which my "guess-work" about Beasts (so I called it at the time and call it still) had in my own thought, and which I would like this whole question to have in Dr. Joad's thought too.

The first eight chapters of my book attempted to meet the *prima facie* case against Theism based on Human Pain. They were the fruit of a slow change of mind not at all unlike that which Dr. Joad himself has undergone and to which, when it had been completed, he at once bore honourable and (I expect) costly witness. The process of his thought differed at many points (very likely for the better) from the process of mine. But we came out, more or less, at the same place. The position of which he says in his article "So much I understand; so much, indeed, I accept" is very close to that which I reached in the first eight chapters of my *Problem*.

So far, so good. Having "got over" the problem of human pain, Dr. Joad and I both find ourselves faced with the problem of animal pain. We do not at once part company even then. We both (if I read him correctly) turn with distaste from "the easy speeches that comfort cruel men," from the theologians who do not seem to see that there is a real problem, who are content to say that animals are, after all, only animals. To us, pain without guilt or moral fruit, however low and contemptible the sufferer may be, is a very serious matter.

I now ask Dr. Joad to observe rather closely what I do at this point, for I doubt if it is exactly what he thinks. I do not advance a doctrine of animal sentience as proved and thence conclude "Therefore beasts are not sacrificed without recompense, and therefore God is just." If he will look carefully at my ninth chapter he will see that it can be divided into two very unequal parts; Part One consisting of the first paragraph, and Part Two of all the rest. They might be summarized as follows:

"*Part One.* The data which God has given us enable us in some degree to understand Human Pain. We lack such data about beasts.

We know neither what they are nor why they are. All that we can say for certain is that if God is good (and I think we have grounds for saying that He is) then the appearance of divine cruelty in the animal world must be a false appearance. What the reality behind the false appearance may be we can only guess.

Part Two. And here are some of my own guesses."

Now it matters far more whether Dr. Joad agrees with Part One than whether he approves any of the speculations in Part Two. But I will first deal, so far as I can, with his critique of the speculations.

(1) Conceding (positionis causa) my distinction between sentience and consciousness, Dr. Joad thinks it irrelevant. "Pain is felt," he writes, "even if there is no continuing ego to feel it and to relate it to past and future pain," and "it is the fact that pain is felt, no matter who or what feels it . . . that demands explanation." I agree that in one sense it does not (for the present purpose) matter "who or what" feels it. That is, it does not matter how humble, or helpless, or small, or how removed from our spontaneous sympathies, the sufferer is. But it surely does matter how far the sufferer is capable of what we can recognize as misery, how far the genuinely pitiable is consistent with its mode of existence. It will hardly be denied that the more coherently conscious the subject is, the more pity and indignation its pains deserve. And this seems to me to imply that the less coherently conscious, the less they deserve. I still think it possible for there to be a pain so instantaneous (through the absence of all perception of succession) that its "unvalue," if I may coin the word, is indistinguishable from zero. A correspondent has instanced shooting pains in our own experience on those occasions when they are unaccompanied by fear. They may be intense: but they are gone as we recognize their intensity. In my own case I do not find anything in them which demands pity; they are, rather, comical. One tends to laugh. A series of such pains is, no doubt, terrible; but then the contention is that the series could not exist for sentience without consciousness.

(2) I do not think that behaviour "as if from memory" proves memory in the conscious sense. A non-human observer might suppose that if we blink our eyes at the approach of an object we are "remembering" pains received on previous occasions. But no memories, in the full sense, are involved. (It is, of course, true that the behaviour of the organism is modified by past experiences, and we may thus by metonymy say that the nerves remember what the mind forgets: but that is not what Dr. Joad and I are talking of.) If we are to suppose memory

in all cases where behaviour adapts itself to a probable recurrence of past events, shall we not have to assume in some insects an inherited memory of their parents' complex breeding habits? And are we prepared to believe this?

(3) Of course my suggested theory of the tame animals' resurrection "in" its human (and therefore, indirectly, divine) context, does not cover wild animals nor ill-treated tame ones. I had made the point myself, and added "it is intended only as an illustration . . . of the general principles to be observed in framing a theory of animal resurrection." I went on to make an alternative suggestion, observing, I hope, the same principles. My chief purpose at this stage was at once to liberate imagination and to confirm a due agnosticism about the meaning and destiny of brutes. I had begun by saying that if our previous assertion of divine goodness was sound, we might be sure that *in some way or other* "all would be well, and all manner of thing would be well." I wanted to reinforce this by indicating how little we knew and, therefore, how many things one might keep in mind as possibilities.

(4) If Dr. Joad thinks I picture Satan "tempting monkeys" I am myself to blame for using the word "encouraged." I apologize for the ambiguity. In fact, I had not supposed that "temptation" (i.e. solicitation of the will) was the only mode in which the devil could corrupt or impair even human beings; when Our Lord spoke of the deformed woman as one "bound by Satan," I presume He did not mean that she had been tempted into deformity. Moral corruption is not the only kind of corruption. But the word *corruption* was perhaps ill-chosen and invited misunderstanding. *Distortion* would have been safer.

JOHN HICK
Explaining Animal Pain

To some, the pain suffered in the animal kingdom beneath the human level has constituted the most baffling aspect of the problem of evil. For the considerations that may lighten the problem as it affects

From *Evil and the God of Love*, Fontana Library of Theology and Philosophy (London: Collins, 4th ed., 1975), pp. 345–53.

mankind—the positive value of moral freedom despite its risks; and the necessity that a world which is to be the scene of soul-making should contain real challenges, hardships, defeats, and mysteries—do not apply in the case of the lower animals. These are not moral personalities who might profit from the hazards of freedom or from the challenges of a rough environment. Why, then, we have to ask, does an all-powerful and infinitely loving Creator permit the pain and carnage of animal life? . . .

There are . . . two important respects in which the animal's situation, as a being liable to pain, differs from man's. Whereas most human beings die through the eventual wearing out of their bodily fabric and its functions, most animals are violently killed and devoured by other species which, in the economy of nature, live by preying upon them. The animal kingdom forms a vast self-sustaining organism in which every part becomes, directly or indirectly, food for another part. And if we project ourselves imaginatively into this process, and see each creature as a self-conscious individual, its situation must seem agonizing indeed. But to do this is to miss the animal's proper good whilst feeling evils of which it is not conscious. Each individual—or at least each healthy individual—has its own fulfilment in the natural activity of its species, uncomplicated by knowledge of the future or a sense of the passage of time; and its momentary appreciations of its own physical impressions and activities are totally unaffected by the fact that after this thin thread of consciousness has snapped some other creature will devour the carcase. Death is not a problem to the animals, as it is to us; and herein lies the second major difference between the quality of human and animal experience. They do not wonder, 'in that sleep of death what dreams may come, When we have shuffled off this mortal coil', or dread 'To lie in cold obstruction and to rot, This sensible warm motion to become, A kneaded clot'. We may indeed say of them that 'Death is not an injury, but rather life a privilege'.

Not only is the animal's experience not shadowed by any anticipation of death or by any sense of its awesome finality; it is likewise simplified, in comparison with human consciousness, by a happy blindness to the dangers and pains that may lie between the present moment of this inevitable termination; and again by a similar oblivion to the past. Although possibly not total at every level of animal life, these restrictions must render all but the occasional animal genius immune to the distinctively human forms of suffering, which depend upon our capacity imaginatively to anticipate the future. The animal's goods and evils are exclusively those of the present moment, and in general it lives from instant to instant either in healthy and presumably pleasurable activity, or in a pleasant state of torpor. The picture, then, of animal life as a dark ocean of agonizing fear and pain is quite gratuitous, and arises from the mistake of projecting our distinctively human quality of experience into creatures of a much lower and simpler order.

The more fruitful question for theodicy is not why animals are liable to pain as well as pleasure—for this follows from their nature as living creatures—but rather why these lower forms of life should exist at all. Christian theology enables us to understand, within its own presuppositions, why the human creature exists: he is a rational and moral being who may freely respond to his Maker's love and so become a 'child of God' and 'heir of eternal life'. But this explanation cannot cover the lower animals, lacking as they do a rational and moral nature. Their existence remains as a problem.

. . . [T]he Augustinian theodicy resolves this problem by means of the principle of plenitude. The infinite divine nature expresses itself *ab extra* in the creation of every grade of dependent being, from the highest to the lowest, and accordingly the created world includes not only man but also monkeys and dogs and snakes and snails and germs. Each level of life makes its own valid contribution to the harmonious perfection of the whole; and the preying of life upon life is a proper feature of the lower ranges of the animal creation, where individuals are but fleeting ripples in a flowing stream of animate life. Thus the sub-human animals exist because they represent possible forms of being, and therefore of goodness, and because their existence is accordingly necessary to the fullness of the created world.

Modern theologians have been more troubled than were the ancients by the evil of animal pain and the spectacle of 'nature, red in tooth and claw'; and as a comparatively recent development within the broadly Augustinian tradition the suggestion has been made that either the fall of man or the prior fall of the angels has affected the natural order and perverted the realms of animal life, causing the various species to attack and devour one another . . .

Suppose, however, we find these theories unsatisfying: is there any alternative way of relating sub-human life, in the varied forms that it actually takes, to the creative activity of God? If we conduct our thinking upon the basis of what are, for the Christian theologian, assured data, we shall start from God's purpose for man revealed in the person and life of Jesus, the Christ, and try to work outwards from this centre towards an understanding of animal life. As a possible way of doing this, the concept of epistemic distance . . . suggests that man's embeddedness within a larger stream of organic life may be one of the conditions of his cognitive freedom in relation to the infinite Creator. Seeing himself as related to the animals and as, like them, the creature of a day, made out of the dust of the earth, man is set in a situation in which the awareness of God is not forced upon him but in which the possibility remains open to him of making his own free response to his unseen Maker. Protestant theology has generally affirmed that the animals exist for the sake of man, but has interpreted this in terms of man's rule over the lower creation. Possibly, however, another and more fundamental way in which, within the divine purpose, sentient nature supports and serves its human apex is by helping to constitute an independent natural order to which man is organically related and within which he exists at an epistemic distance from which he may freely come to the God who has thus bestowed upon him the autonomous status of a person.

One further question must be raised: What is the meaning of the eschatological hope, expressed by St. Paul, that 'the creation itself will be set free from its bondage to decay and obtain the glorious liberty of the children of God'? In particular, can this contribute to a Christian theodicy in respect of animal pain? . . . [I]t does not seem that an eschatological new heaven and new earth, with a new animal creation, could relieve the problem of earthly animal pain. For, unless we postulate a heaven for the millions of millions of individual animals that have perished since sentient life first appeared, no future state of the universe will be relevant to the pains that these creatures have undergone. And, indeed, it is extremely doubtful whether even a zoological paradise, filled with pleasure and devoid of pain, could have any compensatory value in relation to the momentary pangs of creatures who cannot carry their past experience with them in conscious memory.

We come back, then, to our previous suggestion. The justification of animal pain is identical with the justification of animal existence. And from the point of view of the divine purpose of soul-making, animal life is linked with human life as the latter's natural origin and setting, an origin and setting that contribute to the 'epistemic distance' by which man is enabled to exist as a free and responsible creature in the presence of his infinite Creator. If, then, the animal kingdom plays its part in this indirect way in the forming of man as a child of God in this 'eighth day of creation', the process must be justified by its success. The problem of animal pain is thus subordinate to that of human sin and suffering. . .

Of course, to accept that animal life is, from the animal point of view, far more good than bad, and that the animal kingdom can be seen to fulfil a role in relation to the continuing divine creation of man, is not to understand why this or that particular species of animal exists. The justification suggested has not been in terms of specific forms of animal life but in terms of a vast complex evolutionary development, with its own inner contingencies, which has produced man and which links him with the natural world. It may very well be that the material universe, and the ranges of sub-human life within it, have further significance for their Maker than simply as an environment for personal life. We can set no limit whatever to the possibly multi-dimensional complexity of the divine purpose. It may be that God fulfils many different intentions at once and that innumerable strands of the divine activity intersect in the universe in which we live. But if there are any such further meanings of our environment, they are unknown to us. We can glimpse only that aspect of God's purpose for His world that directly concerns ourselves. And we can, I think, see in this a possible reason for the existence of the whole sentient nature in which our own life is embedded.

AUSTIN FARRER
Providence and Compassion

Animals suffer an appalling amount of pain, on any showing; and it is often said that the agonies undergone by brute beasts are the most difficult of all facts to reconcile with a divine providence . . .

But is it? The issue we have to consider lies in the simple question, whether animals would be better off, if they had no pains at all.

From *Love Almighty and Ills Unlimited*, Fontana Library of Theology and Philosophy (London: Collins, 1966), pp. 84–105.

Stated thus baldly, the question sounds outrag[e]
animal in pain is in worse case than an animal wi
poor, limping beast with a poisoned paw; there i
free in the forest. We do not have to ask which i
better not to be injured or diseased. But would i
diseased or injured, not to feel it? . . .

To cut the matter short, we may boldly say that pain, and the re-
medial action which normally springs from it, are as vital as any functions of animal consciousness. Without them no living species above
the most elementary would have the faintest chance of survival. . .

No one wishes to dispute that the working of animal pain has the
rough effect of defending the species and promoting evolutionary development. The question is whether God does more for the individual's
well-being, in the allotment of suffering, than the mere average work
of the nerves will effect.

Our answer must be that in all things, and not only in the distri-
bution of pain, God does more for the individual creature than would
result from any calculations of natural law. In the study of nature, our
science concentrates on rules or uniformities, and only concerns itself
with particular examples in so far as they illustrate or test a rule. But
general laws are not the real forces which compose the universe. . .

When, therefore, God so imperceptibly and subtly directs natural
forces as we have argued that he must, if ever the world is to be made,
he does not work with laws, or generalities, or averages; these are but
fictions of the human understanding. He works with, and in, the real
constituents of nature: particular processes, energies, or systems however minute, and to our way of thinking inconsiderable. As we rise
to the higher levels of created being, this truth is still more evident,
and certainly far easier to grasp. In bringing about the evolution of a
biological species, God works through the multitude of individual
creatures, by the sum of whose destinies the evolutionary change is
realised.

The evolutionary theorist may be exclusively interested in the development of new kinds; God is not. How should we accuse divine
wisdom of that worst human folly, which loses the end in the elaboration of the means; which, for example, views history as nothing
but an infinite series of steps leading to a still unrealised utopian dream?
Although in history one thing leads on to another, and everything (if
you think so) to some final result, the whole tract of time is a field

...ne personal dramas of a million million souls. God is no less con-
...erned for the individual, than for the future of the species. The life
and activity of the single thrush or squirrel or grasshopper is a work
of God . . .

So God cares for the sparrow. Each bird is his particular creation,
her vital effort a unique drama of his composition. But no natural
regularities are violated, no natural averages falsified, no natural actions
perceptibly supplemented by his creative work. Important among the
factors moulding the creature and shaping her life will be pains and
pleasures. They are in the hands of God, but his hands are hidden in
the workings of nature; and any *a priori* expectations we may set up,
about what a loving Providence is bound to do in bending natural
effects to kind purposes, will certainly be disappointed. The relation
of natural force to divine will is an enormous theme, which we have
not been able to evade, but have been still less able to explore. We
have propounded dogmatically what we could not establish argumen-
tatively; but we trust that, even without the supporting arguments,
our conclusions will have commended themselves to the reason.

"To the reason, perhaps," our readers may reply, "but scarcely to
the heart. The God you describe is an artist in creaturely existence;
he is not the lover of his creatures. The care you attribute to him is
a care over, not a caring for . . ."

The objection builds upon the distinction between two sorts of care;
and our answer must begin by reducing it. Does not it break down
entirely, as soon as we apply it to God? We can show that this is so
by taking each sort of care in turn, and seeing how it coincides with
the other sort. To begin, then, with "care over." The sculptor can
have no care for the portrait-bust, and yet can have a motive to take
care over it, because he wants it, either for himself or for others. He
wants it to be the expression of his aesthetic perception or artistic
skill; for without such an expression, he cannot exercise these noble
activities. He wants it to give others aesthetic vision or contemplative
pleasure; for without such a medium he cannot communicate these
pure delights. He wants it to sell, and gain his bread; for with nothing
to put on the market, he cannot live.

Whereas God does not want his creatures for any ulterior aim; he
wants them to be, for their sakes, not his. Not, indeed, only for the
sake of each creature, taken severally; he wants it also to serve or feed
or delight or propagate others; but it ministers to these aims indirectly,

and by being itself first. Since then God's care over the sparrow's coming to be, and over its continuance in its being, is motived by his
desire that it should achieve and enjoy its existence, this care over it
is also a caring for it; as happens among us, when genuinely disinter-
ested elders educate the young. Their care over the making men of
them is at the same time a caring for them.

We have now to prove the equation the other way round, starting
with "caring for." Let it be assumed that God cares for the sparrow.
What form will his caring take? He will lovingly and heedfully benefit
her. And how? By his creative action, by his continual sustenance
and direction of her natural life. And this, as we have previously
agreed, will be imperceptible to us, except in so far as it is manifest
in the working of nature.

When Christ appealed to God's feeding of the ravens, or his clothing
of the grass, he was not citing special providences. The tale of Elijah
asserted that God had once made ravens carry miraculous loaves to
feed the prophet. The Sermon on the Mount does not mean anything
like the provision of miraculous loaves through prophetic hands, to
feed the ravens. They are fed through the common ecology of nature.
The things on which they feed flourish in their feeding grounds; and
they have the wit, or the instinct, to feed on them.

To turn to our problem. The God of nature gives his animal creatures
pains out of love for them, to save their lives; he makes the way of
destruction distasteful to them, as a parent makes the path of danger
distasteful to a child, by little punishments. Again, out of love for
them, God moves his creatures to shun their pains and mend their
harms, so far as their sense or capacity allows. And at last, when they
must acknowledge defeat, as every perishable creature must, he relieves
them of the power and will to struggle, of the pain on stimulus of
which they can no longer usefully act, and of the being they can no
longer hopefully defend.

One of the functions of pain, in species that are capable of it, is to
awaken compassion. The suffering is felt to be a common evil; and as
it moves the sufferer to get rid of the cause in himself, so it moves his
kindred to get rid of it for him. For, by the force of sympathy, they
feel it also. If there were no pain, no compassion would be excited,
and the creature would lose a valuable source of succour in harm or
danger.

We attribute pity or compassion to God. We cannot suppose that he suffers negative emotions. He does not need the compulsive pinch of sympathetic pain to make him do us good, his attitude is of a continual well-wishing expressed in a continual well-doing. But, speaking by human analogy, we use different terms to describe his love in several relations. In relation to demerit, we call it grace or favour; in relation to sin, forgiveness; in relation to suffering or misery, compassion. Were there no suffering in the creatures, there would be no sense in speaking of compassion in God.

God's compassion means, therefore, that he does not desert his creatures in those sufferings which his natural providence allots them, but is with them in providing the deliverance to which the pain excites them; which he does principally by sustaining and directing the working of their own natures; secondarily by the sympathy of their fellows in those species that are capable of it.

Men, though they are the greatest destroyers of animal life, are capable of sympathy with many species beside their own. When our compassion moves us to relieve animal suffering, we are being used by the compassion of God. Hurrying to the rescue, we feel that any being with sympathies equal or superior to ours must do the same, if he is within reach; and God is always within reach, being almighty. Why then is he not moved to prevent what we are moved to mitigate?

The question is not unamiable, but it is confused. God loves his animal creatures by being God to them, that is, by natural providence and creative power; not by being a brother creature to them, as he does for mankind in the unique miracle of his incarnation. He provides them with brother-saviours, or sometimes human saviours, through the working of compassion, and not otherwise.

If we say that God, from the motive of compassion, should have spared his creatures all suffering, we are surely talking nonsense. It is only because God allots pain that there is any object for his compassion, or any sense in speaking of it.

But the greatest fallacy in this whole field has still to be mentioned. This is the suggestion that God's assigning of pain, if admitted, provides a reason why we should harden our hearts. On the contrary; every pain God assigns is a call to us to remove the cause of it. God does not give pains that they may be passively endured; he gives them to awaken our detestation of their causes.

He provokes us to fight the causes; he cannot, within the fabric of the existing world, prevent their arising. It must never be forgotten that God is the God of hawks no less than of sparrows, of microbes no less than of men. He saves his creatures by creating in them the power to meet the ever-changing hostilities of their environment. And so, though individuals perish and species die out, there is a world of life.

A. RICHARD KINGSTON
Theodicy and Animal Welfare

Or rather, "Theodicy and Animal Neglect", for with a few noble exceptions theologians have done far more to discourage than to stimulate a concern for the lower creatures. As Westermarck reminded us, "No creed in Christendom teaches kindness to animals as a dogma of religion . . . Nor is there any such allusion in most treatises on ethics which base their teachings upon distinctly Christian tenets."[1] W. R. Inge conceded that "it is unhappily true that (in the words of A. Jameson in 1854) 'the primitive Christians by laying so much stress upon a future life, and placing the lower creatures out of the pale of hope, placed them at the same time out of the pale of sympathy, and thus laid the foundation for an utter disregard of animals.' "[2] Whether or not we agree with Inge's diagnosis of the cause of the trouble, we can hardly disagree with the historical fact that, to quote Lecky, "the inculcation of humanity to animals on a wide scale is the work of a recent and secular age";[3] or as Aldous Huxley puts it more pointedly, "It was not until the nineteenth century, when orthodox Christianity had lost much of its power over European minds, that the idea that it might be a good thing to behave humanely towards animals began to make headway".[4]

We are thus faced with a two-fold problem, first to account for the

From *Theology*, vol. LXX, no. 569 (November 1967), pp. 482–88.
[1]E. Westermarck, *The Origin and Development of the Moral Ideas*, Vol. 2, London, 1912, pp. 506–7.
[2]W. R. Inge, *Christian Ethics and Modern Problems*, London, 1930, p. 278.
[3]W. E. H. Lecky, *History of European Morals from Augustus to Charlemagne*, Vol. 2, London, 1905, p. 177.
[4]A. Huxley, *The Perennial Philosophy*, Fontana edition, 1958, p. 203.

apparent callousness of Christian theology in this respect, and secondly to enquire on what theological foundation a positive ethic of reverence for animal life should rest. This present article, however, must be confined to the former question, and indeed to one neglected aspect of it—theodicy, which I suggest may be as much to blame for the situation as the traditionally harsh interpretation of the doctrine of man's dominion over nature (with almost exclusive emphasis on Gen. 9:2–3, and 1 Cor. 9:9), or the theory that animals have no reason or "rational soul" and therefore no rights, on which *non sequitur* writers like Joseph Rickaby concluded that "we have . . . no duties of charity, nor duties of any kind, to the lower animals, as neither to sticks and stones. . . Much more in all that conduces to the sustenance of man may we give pain to brutes, as also in the pursuit of science. Nor are we bound to any anxious care to make this pain as little as may be."[5] Mercy is only recommended on the ground that cruelty to animals could dispose one to be cruel to human beings.

The charge that theodicy has also condoned cruelty to animals is based on two simple observations, first, that most theodicy fails lamentably to portray God as One whose "compassion is over all that he has made" (Ps. 145:9, RSV), and secondly and more seriously, that many Christians in their anxiety to vindicate the love of God in the face of animal suffering have done so by simply denying animal pain or else by treating it as insignificant—a solution which incredibly still finds its advocates.

I

As illustrative of the former defect we turn first to various "Fall" theodicies. Traditional Christian thought firmly linked the disharmony and apparent dysteleology of the animal world with the fall of man, because of which the whole of creation was cursed and nature became red in tooth and claw. As theodicy, needless to say, this is no longer tenable. The evidence for the existence of carnivora long before the emergence of man is indisputable. But what concerns us more particularly here is that the theory also fails the moral test. Few will dispute that "the notion that the animals were deliberately subjected by God to 'vanity', to pain, disease and cruel maltreatment by man *because of man's initial sin* can hardly be reconciled with justice; still less can it

<hr>

[5] J. Rickaby SJ, *Moral Philosophy*, London, 1908, pp. 249–50.

be harmonised with what our Lord says about God's care for the birds. . ."[6] Such divine indifference to the lower creatures would clearly be a deterrent to the cause of animal welfare. Rickaby and others would have the highest precedent for regarding them as little more than "sticks and stones". And yet, paradoxically, some who fully accepted the biblical myth as being historically true were able to weave it into a larger plan of salvation, based on an exegesis of Romans 8:21, from which they reached the opposite conclusion. Wesley, for instance, expounded the words "the creature itself also shall be delivered from the bondage of corruption into the glorious liberty of the children of God" as implying, amongst other things, that "the whole brute creation will then, undoubtedly, be restored, . . . As a recompense for what they once suffered, while under the 'bondage of corruption,' . . . they shall enjoy happiness suited to their state, without alloy, without interruption, and without end."[7] Wesley then asserts that some important results follow from this, e.g. it furnishes us with "a full answer to a plausible objection against the justice of God, in suffering numberless creatures that never had sinned to be so severely punished", and further it serves a "more excellent end" in that it "may encourage us to imitate Him whose mercy is over all his works". It "may soften our hearts towards the meaner creatures, knowing that the Lord careth for them".[8] Much as we may wish to retain this example of theodicy providing a supernatural sanction for kindness to animals we must admit that it is extremely doubtful if the Pauline text (especially in view of what he says in 1 Cor. 9:9) will bear the weight Wesley puts upon it; nor is it at all clear that a future paradise for animals would really vindicate the Creator for having caused them so much undeserved suffering in this life.

It is presumably the inadequacy of the fall of man explanation which has led several recent writers to base their theodicy, somewhat tentatively, on the ancient idea of a pre-mundane fall of the angels, suggesting a link between this alleged angelic rebellion and the disorder of nature. "One of the results, we may suppose", writes Dom Illtyd Trethowan "was a disorganisation of the material universe, over which, according to a reasonable theory, the angels had charge."[9] Or take C.

[6]O. F. Clarke, *God and Suffering*, Derby, 1964, p. 132.
[7]Wesley's *Works*, Vol. 6, London, 1872, pp. 249–50.
[8]Ibid., p. 251.
[9]Dom L. Trethowan, *An Essay in Christian Philosophy*, London, 1954, p. 128.

S. Lewis who argues in terms of one fallen being—Satan: "It seems to me . . . a reasonable supposition, that some mighty created power had already been at work for ill on the material universe . . . before ever man came on the scene . . . If there is such a power, as I myself believe, it may well have corrupted the animal creation before man appeared."[10] He adds that "It may have been one of man's functions to restore peace to the animal world".[11]

Despite this insight, and despite the advantage of acquitting God of having directly created a dysteleological universe, the theory is still hard to credit—especially in an age in which we tend to demythologize the devil and all his works. With John Hick I must agree that the rebellion of finitely perfect beings enjoying full fellowship with God seems incomprehensible. "The basic and inevitable criticism", he writes, "is that the idea of an unqualifiedly good creature committing sin is self-contradictory and unintelligible."[12] Quite apart from this we must point out that if God entrusted to fallible (even if "perfect") angelic beings such absolute control over creation that it was within their power to "brutalize" the animal kingdom for all time, then he cannot be exonerated from all culpability for what allegedly happened. Must we not go further and say that such action would indicate either incompetence or the fact that the sufferings of the lower creatures are unimportant in the eyes of the Creator! The fall of the angels, in brief, provides neither a sound theodicy nor a stimulus to animal welfare. It might be added here that a third fall theory, that of a World-Soul or Life-Force, by which N. P. Williams sought to account for "the cruelty that ravages the animal world" fares no better, being open to precisely the same objection as that brought against the corruption of perfect angels.

Christians have also adopted more philosophical types of theodicy, of which we note just two examples used by St. Augustine. First, there is the view that when seen from the true, the divine, perspective, the universe is wholly good and beautiful. With specific reference to animals devouring one another he writes: "Since then, . . . some perish to make way for others that are born in their room, and the less succumb to the greater . . . this is the appointed order of things transitory. Of this order the beauty does not strike us, because by our mortal

---

[10]C. S. Lewis, The Problem of Pain, Fontana edition, 1957, pp. 122–23.
[11]Ibid., p. 124.
[12]J. Hick, Evil and the God of Love, London, 1966, pp. 68–69.

frailty we are so involved in a part of it, that we cannot perceive the whole, in which these fragments that offend us are harmonized with the most accurate fitness and beauty."[13] That many a problem disappears when seen from a higher perspective is of course unquestionable, yet reason and conscience alike insist that it is not just shortsightedness which creates a problem out of animal suffering. It is the maturity, not the deficiency of man's moral sense and spirituality that makes him disturbed about this issue. A more serious criticism is that the theory not only fails to account for pain, it tends to perpetuate it. If animal, or for that matter human, suffering is but a part of a perfect portrait then there is not much incentive to spoil it by humanitarian interference.

Augustine also employed the Platonic principle of plenitude—the idea that all possible forms of existence have to be realized before creation can be complete. Hence "there are some things better than others; and for this purpose are they unequal, in order that they might all exist".[14] As theodicy this has obvious limitations. It may help to account for the variety of forms of existence, why God did not only create archangels, but the notion of a predetermined fixed number of species, apart from the problem of the verifiability or falsifiability of the idea, does not seem to square with reality. From the standpoint of our present enquiry we must also comment that whilst a charity which overflows in the bestowal of life on every type of creature is most praiseworthy, this does not hold when they include parasites, viruses, etc. The stress on creative love seems more than cancelled by the content of creation.

Since, then, the ethical implications of these (and other) types of theodicy are not conducive to a concern for animal welfare, we may be relieved rather than regret their inherent defectiveness.

II

Most people associate the theory of animal automatism with Descartes, but in fact it was Malebranche, not Descartes, who said that animals eat without pleasure and cry without pain. Descartes himself, whilst holding that animal bodies function mechanically, did not deny them feeling. His followers, however, took the theory of automatism to its limits, using it as an excuse for their tortures, "They kicked about

[13]Augustine, *The City of God*, xii, 4.
[14]Ibid., xi, 22.

their dogs and dissected their cats without mercy, laughing at any compassion for them, and calling their screams the noise of breaking machinery."[15] And to their shame there were theologians who embraced the same philosophy, regarding it as an indispensable safeguard of man's spirtuality, of original sin, etc., and not least of theodicy. Bayle complained that " 'Tis pity that the Opinion of *Descartes* should be so hard to Maintain, and so far from Likelyhood; for it is otherwise very Advantageous to Religion, and this is the only reason which hinders some People from quitting it".[16] Elaborating on this he records that "Father *Poisson* of the Oratory has profoundly Treated the Argument, which is grounded upon this Principle of St *Augustin*, *That God being just, Misery is a necessary Proof of Sin;* from whence it follows, That Beasts not having sinned are not subject to Misery: But they would be subjected to it, if they had any feeling; therefore they have none."[17] The moral consequences of such thinking become evident a few lines later. "Is this the part of a wise Agent? The Souls of Beasts never sinned, and yet they are subject to Pain and Misery, and to all the Irregular Desires of Creatures, which have sinned. How do we treat Beasts? We make them tear one another in pieces for our Diversion; we Kill them for our Nourishment, and Ransack their Bowels during their Lives, to satisfy our Curiosity: and we do all this by vertue of the Dominion that God has given us over them. What a disorder is it, That an Innocent Creature should be subject to the Caprices of a Criminal one? There's no Casuist that believes that there is any sin in baiting of Bulls, or in hunting or fishing, to destroy Animals, or in killing of Flies, as *Domitian* did. Is it not Cruelty and Injustice to subject an Innocent Soul to so many Miseries? The Opinion of *Cartesius* frees us from all these Difficulties."

It would be gratifying to be able to record that this kind of teaching has long since been discarded by Christian writers, but unfortunately this is not the case. In the chapter on theodicy in his latest book Canon F. Van Steenberghen suggests that we are "the victims of a serious illusion" when we interpret animal cries as an expression of pain. "It appears to me that an examination of instinctive animal behaviour reveals a very interesting and, indeed, very mysterious, psychism, but one that is *devoid of consciousness of any kind* and, for

---

[15]J. P. Mahaffy, *Descartes*, London, 1901, p. 118.
[16]*Bayle's Dictionary*, Vol. 4, London, 1710, pp. 2604–5.
[17]Ibid., p. 2605a.

that reason, of free will. If this is indeed the case, the problem of animal 'suffering' is an empty one, as 'unconscious suffering' is a contradiction in terms."[18] To buttress this denial of animal consciousness he prefaces his argument with the testimony that "with the entire body of traditional philosophers, I believe that being conscious implies being spiritual . . . It implies, therefore, being a *person* . . ." and he contends that all who disagree with him must treat animals as persons. We must surely reply that sensitivity cannot be equated with personality, in any human sense, nor can it be determined by mere dogma. Its reality is only too evident from animal behaviour and from the structure of their nervous systems. Some excellent studies have in fact been published by the Universities' Federation for Animal Welfare on the extent of animal consciousness of pain.

British theodicy, although not formally denying animal suffering, has often virtually done so by reducing its intensity almost to zero. It is of course true that their suffering cannot always be estimated by human standards. The lower mammals certainly seem to have less capacity for feeling pain than we have, nor, we presume, does imagination add to their agony with dread anticipation of further pain or the fear of disablement, insecurity or death. And yet when we find a certain passage from an article by Theodore Wood, about a crab calmly continuing its meal on a smaller crab whilst itself being leisurely devoured by a larger one, being quoted by writer after writer, we begin to feel uneasy about the limits of this reductionist procedure. The innuendo is that the crab is typical of all the lower creatures; but who can imagine a lion calmly . . . Some, indeed, explicitly state that animal pain is insignificant. C. E. Raven, having cited the crab incident, writes a little later that "it may be doubted whether there is any real pain without a frontal cortex, a fore-plan in mind, and a love which can put itself in the place of another; and these are attributes of humanity."[19] More recently Dom Illtyd Trethowan, having rejected the possibility of accounting for animal suffering in terms of a "fall", concludes: "So it looks as though we should have to fall back on the suggestion thrown out in an earlier chapter—that the brutes do not suffer as we do; we know too little about their psychology for it to present us with any real problem."[20] The truth is that veterinary sci-

[18]F. Van Steenberghen, *Hidden God*, Trans. by T. Crowley, Louvain, 1966, p. 252.
[19]C. E. Raven, *The Creator Spirit*, London, 1927, p. 120.
[20]Dom I. Trethowan, op. cit., p. 92.

entists are by no means as ignorant of animal pain as he supposes, nor can we evade the problem so easily. In general we must note that in practical terms it makes very little difference whether we say that animal pain is insignificant or non-existent; the net result of this method of vindicating God against the charge of creating a cruel world is by implication to make the world more cruel for his creatures. By explaining away the fact of animal suffering we directly or indirectly deepen it. Perhaps there is room in Christian thought for what Buddha would have called a "noble silence".

III

Having indicated how theodicy has helped to make Christianity harsh towards animals (if not the "hell of animals" as some non-Christians have labelled it), I must end by stressing that there are, of course, several writers on the problem of evil who are fully aware that no theodicy is tenable which fails to show God's mercy over all his works. Ideally it should entail caring for his creatures; it should lead to the conclusion that "when our compassion moves us to relieve animal suffering, we are being used by the compassion of God".[21] I only wish that this statement by Austin Farrer were not so unconvincingly supported. His argument is a paradox rather than a proof: "it is only because God allots pain that there is any object for his compassion." "Every pain God assigns is a call to us to remove the cause of it." "It must never be forgotten that God is the God of hawks no less than of sparrows, of microbes no less than of men."

Our search clearly must continue for a theodicy which really does justice both to the Creator and to all his creatures, which points to a God of love and pinpoints our duty to love.

[21] A. Farrer, *Love Almighty and Ills Unlimited*, Fontana edition, 1966, pp. 103–4.

Part Three

◆

THE
QUESTION
OF ANIMAL
REDEMPTION

Introduction to Part Three

We observed in our previous section how the discussion of animal pain raised in turn the question of redemption for animals. It would certainly not be possible to claim that the idea of redemption, salvation, or a future afterlife for animals has always found favour within Christianity. It is all the more significant, therefore, that the first pages of this section find this idea represented by the biblical writers in a variety of ways. Because of the fundamental closeness between animals and humans presupposed by much Old Testament theology, it is not surprising that the Psalmist should declare that '(m)an and beast thou savest, O Lord.' Isaiah clearly envisages a new world for humans and animals inaugurated by the Messiah. Ecclesiastes speculates whether humans have any pre-eminence over animals when it comes to life after death. St Paul in his letter to the Roman Church hopes for the redemption of all the non-human creation subject (not of its own will) to futility and death. The great passages in Ephesians and Colossians speak of a world-embracing reconciliation wrought by God in Christ. And the Book of Revelation speaks of a new heaven and a new earth involving the destruction of pain and death.

Scholastic tradition, however, has insisted upon the rationality of the human soul which alone qualifies humanity for eternal life. St Augustine, in our first selection, postulates how humans are uniquely capable of 'enjoying eternal peace' in the 'Heavenly City.' The rational part of man enables him to engage in reflection: 'so that he may thus exhibit that ordered agreement of cognition and action which we call the peace of the rational soul.' Herein lies the essential difference between animals and humans. Salvation consists in giving fullest rein to the highest God-given faculty in man, namely rationality, and obtaining freedom from the 'animal body' which weighs down the soul. Bishop Joseph Butler agrees with Augustine that death does not involve the 'disssolution or destruction of living agents' but, unlike Augustine, sees no good reason for supposing that the souls of animals are not also, like humans, immortal. In the same way that an individual can and does undergo massive changes throughout his or her individual life-time and yet remains the same person, Butler insists that we are mistaken in our common belief that our sensible change of form at death is equivalent to destruction. To the objection that these ob-servations 'are equally applicable to brutes,' Butler replies that this is no objection at all for it is 'invidious and weak' to suppose the contrary. To the argument that animals are not rational, Butler replies that we do not know the 'latent' capacities of brutes and in any case a 'great part of the human species go out of the present world before they come to the exercise of these capacities in any degree at all.'

The next four selections—from St Irenaeus, St John of the Cross, Edward Quinn and St Athanasius—concern themselves with the world-affirming, or cosmic, implications of Christ's reconciling work. In contrast to Augustine, St Irenaeus maintains that salvation does not involve the rejection of flesh but its transformation. He criticises those who opt for a purely 'spiritual' conception of salvation as treating 'the whole providence of God as though it were of no account.' As humans are part of the created order, so in the eucharist it is the created order itself which is infused with the life of the divine. Irenaeus insists upon a really new earth, the 'substance or essence' of which is the earth as we now know it. St John of the Cross, too, holds out for a world-embracing redemption. As Irenaeus argued that the Word of God 'sums up all things in Himself,' St John postulates that the incarnation in-volves the lifting up of *all* creatures. When God became man, he 'ex-alted all creatures in him, since in uniting Himself with man He united Himself with the nature of them all.' Thus for St John the act of reconciliation is also the raising up of all creatures to new life in Christ. '(W)e can say that he left them all clothed with beauty and dignity . . . derived from and communicated by that infinite supernatural beauty of the image of God.'

This idea is further explored by Edward Quinn who develops the Catholic notion of a continuity between nature and grace. Drawing on Rahnerian ideas and especially on Rahner's theory of the resur-rection as a new relationship with the world, he questions the classical view that only humans are going to heaven. Quinn looks forward to the point at which God becomes 'all in all, that is the real dawn of the new creation . . . especially for those who have consciously shared to the end the helplessness of Christ'; an idea similarly propounded by St Athanasius who develops the doctrine of Christ as the Logos through whom all things exist. The Logos, maintains Athanasius, is 'present in all things and extends his power everywhere, illuminating all things visible and invisible, containing and enclosing them in himself.' All these four writers oppose the essentially anthropocentric view that humans alone are destined for eternity. Redemption does not involve the abandonment of creation in favour of incorporeal souls, but creation's holistic transfiguration. Christ is the 'Saviour of the Universe' maintains Athanasius.

Calvin, on the other hand, sets his face against too much speculation about the fate of beasts. While he does not deny that non-human creatures are to be 'renewed'—in the fashion suggested by St Paul in his letter to the Romans—he believes that we confront here the limits of biblical revelation. 'Some shrewd but unbalanced commentators ask whether all kinds of animals will be immortal,' complains Calvin, and asks, 'If we give free rein to these speculations, where will they finally carry us?' Such reserve, however, is not exhibited by John Wesley. In his famous sermon on 'The General Deliverance' he takes St Paul at his word and argues that all creation will be delivered from its suffering and futility. 'Nothing can be more express: away with vulgar prejudices, and let the plain word of God take place' he fulminates. Whilst the Creator does not equally regard the lower creatures, their suffering is nevertheless grievous to him. Redemption, argues Wesley, is the means by which the Lord of all 'will make large amends' for the miseries they have had to undergo.

This question of divine justice is also dealt with in the three final selections from Keith Ward, Paul Tillich and C. S. Lewis. Ward argues that the Christian 'paradigm' of afterlife is the resurrected body of Jesus, an example of how suffering is transfigured by joy. From this perspective, he is adamant that any being which suffers pain must find that pain eventually transfigured by joy. 'I am quite agnostic as to how this is to happen; but that it must be asserted to be true follows from the doctrine that God is love, and would not therefore create any being whose sole destiny was to suffer pain.' Tillich offers a comparable argument. 'The function of the bearer of the New Being is not only to save individuals and to transform man's historical existence but to renew the universe.' Christ's work is therefore inclusive of all orders and worlds of existence in which there is, what Tillich calls, 'existential estrangement.' These worlds 'cannot be without the operation of saving power within them.' Divine justice requires the salvation of all worlds in which there is estrangement and some awareness of it.

Whether animals are 'aware' or 'conscious' of what Tillich calls 'estrangement' is developed in a further direction in the last piece from C. S. Lewis. He doubts whether animals can be conscious of their 'selves' in a way that is true of human subjects. And if they have no full sense of 'self,' how can their 'selves' be redeemed? Unlike Ward, therefore, he does not advocate the immortality of sentient beings *per se*. Neither does he see how animals could be 'recompensed' if there is no enduring 'self' to be so 'recompensed.' 'If the life of a newt is merely a succession of sensations, what should we mean by saying that God may recall to life the newt that died today?' Nevertheless, Lewis argues that some tame animals do acquire a sense of 'self' in relation to, and through being with, their owners, and may conceivably possess immortality because of this.

We may summarise the main issues raised by this section as follows: (1) Is possession of a rational soul essential to salvation, and can animals be said to be devoid of rationality? (2) Is the reconciling work of Christ inclusive or exclusive of the created order, and/or non-human creatures? (3) Does the incarnation involve in some sense the whole creation or just human beings? (4) If animals are to be redeemed, what does their redemption consist of? (5) Is the issue of animal redemption a question of theological speculation or is it implicit in the Bible and in Christian doctrine? (6) Does a morally acceptable view of God's justice require immortality for animals? and (7) Can animals possess a sufficient sense of self which may be essential for immortality?

The Bible
On Afterlife and Cosmic Redemption

Psalm 36:6b
> Man and beast thou savest, O Lord.

Ecclesiastes 3:19–21
> For the fate of the sons of men and the fate of beasts is the same;
> as one dies, so dies the other. They all have the same breath, and
> man has no advantage over the beasts; for all is vanity. All go to
> one place; all are from the dust, and all turn to dust again. Who
> knows whether the spirit of man goes upward and the spirit of the
> beast goes down to the earth?

Isaiah 11:6–8
> The wolf shall dwell with the lamb, and the leopard shall lie down
> with the kid, and the calf and the lion and the fatling together,
> and a little child shall lead them. The cow and the bear shall feed;
> their young shall lie down together; and the lion shall eat straw like
> the ox. The suckling child shall play over the hole of the asp, and
> the weaned child shall put his hand on the adder's den.

Romans 8:18–23
> I consider that the sufferings of this present time are not worth
> comparing with the glory that is to be revealed to us. For the creation
> waits with eager longing for the revealing of the sons of God; for
> the creation was subjected to futility, not of its own will but by the
> will of him who subjected it in hope; because the creation itself will
> be set free from its bondage to decay and obtain the glorious liberty
> of the children of God. We know that the whole creation has been
> groaning in travail together until now; and not only the creation,

but we ourselves, who have the first fruits of the Spirit, groan inwardly as we wait for adoption as sons, the redemption of our bodies.

Ephesians 1:9–10

For he has made known to us in all wisdom and insight the mystery of his will, according to his purpose which he set forth in Christ as a plan for the fulness of time, to unite all things in him, things in heaven and things on earth.

Colossians 1:15–20

He is the image of the invisible God, the first-born of all creation; for in him all things were created, in heaven and on earth, visible and invisible, whether thrones or dominions or principalities or authorities—all things were created through him and for him. He is before all things, and in him all things hold together. He is the head of the body, the church; he is the beginning, the first-born from the dead, that in everything he might be pre-eminent. For in him all the fulness of God was pleased to dwell, and through him to reconcile to himself all things, whether on earth or in heaven, making peace by the blood of his cross.

Revelation 21:1–4

Then I saw a new heaven and a new earth; for the first heaven and the first earth had passed away, and the sea was no more. And I saw the holy city, new Jerusalem, coming down out of heaven from God, prepared as a bride adorned for her husband; and I heard a great voice from the throne saying, "Behold, the dwelling of God is with men. He will dwell with them, and they shall be his people, and God himself will be with them; he will wipe away every tear from their eyes, and death shall be no more, neither shall there be mourning nor crying nor pain any more, for the former things have passed away."

ST AUGUSTINE

The Peace of the Rational Soul

We see, then, that all man's use of temporal things is related to the enjoyment of earthly peace in the earthly city; whereas in the Heavenly City it is related to the enjoyment of eternal peace. Thus, if we were irrational animals, our only aim would be the adjustment of the parts of the body in due proportion, and the quieting of the appetites—only, that is, the repose of the flesh, and an adequate supply of pleasures, so that bodily peace might promote the peace of the soul. For if bodily peace is lacking, the peace of the irrational soul is also hindered, because it cannot achieve the quieting of its appetites. But the two together promote that peace which is a mutual concord between soul and body, the peace of an ordered life and of health. For living creatures show their love of bodily peace by their avoidance of pain, and by their pursuit of pleasure to satisfy the demands of their appetites they demonstrate their love of peace of soul. In just the same way, by shunning death they indicate quite clearly how great is their love of the peace in which soul and body are harmoniously united.

But because there is in man a rational soul, he subordinates to the peace of the rational soul all that part of his nature which he shares with the beasts, so that he may engage in deliberate thought and act in accordance with his thought, so that he may thus exhibit that ordered agreement of cognition and action which we called the peace of the rational soul. For with this end in view he ought to wish to be spared the distress of pain and grief, the disturbances of desire, the dissolution of death, so that he may come to some profitable knowledge and may order his life and his moral standards in accordance with this knowledge. But he needs divine direction, which he may obey with resolution, and divine assistance that he may obey it freely, to prevent him from falling, in his enthusiasm for knowledge, a victim to some fatal error, through the weakness of the human mind. And so long as he is in this mortal body, he is a pilgrim in a foreign land, away from

From *Concerning the City of God against the Pagans*, ET by Henry Bettenson, introduction by David Knowles (Harmondsworth: Penguin Books, 4th ed., 1980), pp. 872–78.

God; therefore he walks by faith, not by sight. That is why he views all peace, of body or of soul, or of both, in relation to that peace which exists between mortal man and immortal God, so that he may exhibit an ordered obedience in faith in subjection to the everlasting Law. . .

. . . [F]or this peace is the perfectly ordered and completely harmonious fellowship in the enjoyment of God, and of each other in God. When we arrive at that state of peace, there will be no longer a life that ends in death, but a life that is life in sure and sober truth; there will be no animal body to 'weigh down the soul' in its process of corruption; there will be a spiritual body with no cravings, a body subdued in every part to the will.

BISHOP JOSEPH BUTLER
The Immortality of Brutes

[W]e cannot argue from the reason of the thing that death is the destruction of living agents, because we know not at all what death is in itself, but only some of its effects, such as the dissolution of flesh, skin, and bones. And these effects do in no wise appear to imply the destruction of a living agent. And besides, as we are greatly in the dark upon what the exercise of our living powers depends, so we are wholly ignorant what the powers themselves depend upon—the powers themselves, as distinguished not only from their actual exercise, but also from the present capacity of exercising them, and as opposed to their destruction; for sleep, or, however, a swoon, shows us not only that these powers exist when they are not exercised, as the passive power of motion does in inanimate matter, but shows also that they exist when there is no present capacity of exercising them; or that the capacities of exercising them for the present, as well as the actual exercise of them, may be suspended, and yet the powers themselves remain undestroyed. Since, then, we know not at all upon what the

From *The Analogy of Religion Natural and Revealed to the Constitution and Course of Nature*, introduction by Henry Morley (London: George Routledge and Sons, 3rd edition, 1887), pp. 12–21.

existence of our living powers depends, this shows, further, there can no probability be collected from the reason of the thing that death will be their destruction; because their existence may depend upon somewhat in no degree affected by death—upon somewhat quite out of the reach of this king of terrors. So that there is nothing more certain than that the reason of the thing shows us no connection between death and the destruction of living agents. Nor can we find anything throughout the whole analogy of nature to afford us even the slightest presumption that animals ever lose their living powers, much less, if it were possible, that they lose them by death; for we have no faculties wherewith to trace any beyond or through it, so as to see what becomes of them. This event removes them from our view. It destroys the *sensible* proof, which we had before their death, of their being possessed of living powers, but does not appear to afford the least reason to believe that they are then, or by that event, deprived of them.

And our knowing that they were possessed of these powers up to the very period to which we have faculties capable of tracing them, is itself a probability of their retaining them beyond it. And this is confirmed, and a sensible credibility is given to it, by observing the very great and astonishing changes which we have experienced—so great that our existence in another state of life, of perception, and of action, will be but according to a method of providential conduct the like to which has been already exercised even with regard to ourselves; according to a course of nature the like to which we have already gone through . . .

And thus our finding that the dissolution of matter, in which living beings were most nearly interested, is not their dissolution, and that the destruction of several of the organs and instruments of perception and of motion belonging to them is not their destruction, shows demonstratively that there is no ground to think that the dissolution of any other matter or destruction of any other organs and instruments will be the dissolution or destruction of living agents, from the like kind of relation. And we have no reason to think we stand in any other kind of relation to anything which we find dissolved by death.

But it is said these observations are equally applicable to brutes, and it is thought an insuperable difficulty that they should be immortal, and by consequence capable of everlasting happiness. Now this manner of expression is both invidious and weak, but the thing intended by it is really no difficulty at all, either in the way of natural or moral consideration. For, first, suppose the invidious thing, designed in such a manner of expression, were really implied as it is not in the least in the natural immortality of brutes—namely, that they must arrive at great attainments and become rational and moral agents, even this would be no difficulty, since we know not what latent powers and capacities they may be endued with. There was once, prior to experience, as great presumption against human creatures as there is against the brute creatures arriving at that degree of understanding which we have in mature age. For we can trace up our own existence to the same original with theirs. And we find it to be a general law of nature that creatures endued with capacities of virtue and religion should be placed in a condition of being, in which they are altogether without the use of them for a considerable length of their duration, as in infancy and childhood. And great part of the human species go out of the present world before they come to the exercise of these capacities in any degree at all. But then, secondly, the natural immortality of brutes does not in the least imply that they are endued with any latent capacities of a rational or moral nature. And the economy of the universe might require that there should be living creatures without any capacities of this kind. And all difficulties as to the manner how they are to be disposed of are so apparently and wholly founded in our ignorance, that it is wonderful they should be insisted upon by any but such as are weak enough to think they are acquainted with the whole system of things. There is then absolutely nothing at all in this objection, which is so rhetorically urged, against the greatest part of the natural proofs or presumptions of the immortality of human minds.

ST IRENAEUS
All Things in Christ

I

For the Creator of the world is truly the Word of God: and this is our Lord, who in the last times was made man, existing in this world, and who in an invisible manner contains all things created, and is inherent in the entire creation, since the Word of God governs and arranges all things; and therefore He came to his own in a visible manner, and was made flesh, and hung upon the tree, that He might sum up all things in Himself.

II

Those who deny that the flesh can be saved and are scornful about its regeneration, alleging that it is not capable of becoming incorruptible, are utterly mistaken. They treat the whole providence of God as though it were of no account. If the flesh is not saved then, obviously, neither did the Lord redeem us with his blood, nor is the cup of the Eucharist the communion of his blood, nor the bread which we break the communion of his body. Blood does not exist except in veins and flesh and everything else that goes to make a man. Being made just such flesh as this, the Word of God redeemed us by his blood. Thus his Apostle says: 'In whom we have redemption through his blood, even the remission of our sins.'

We are his members and we draw our nourishment from the created order. He himself bestows the creation upon us. He causes his sun to rise and the rain to fall according to his will. He affirmed that that cup, which is part of the created order, is his blood which was shed. With it he infuses our blood. He has assured us that that bread, which is part of the created order, is his body. With it he builds up our bodies.

The first selection is from "Against Heresies", in *The Writings of Irenaeus*, 2 vols., ET by A. Roberts and W. H. Rambaut, Ante-Nicene Christian Library (Edinburgh: T. & T. Clark, no date), vol. I, v, 18, 3, pp. 105–6; the second and third selections are from "Resurrection and Restoration", Book 5, Chapter 2, and Book 5, Chapter 36, all in A. D. Galloway (ed.), *Basic Readings in Theology* (London: Allen & Unwin, 1964), pp. 21–22.

So, when the cup which is mixed and the bread which is made receive the Word of God, and the Eucharist becomes the body of Christ, and the substance of our flesh is sustained and increased by them, how can they say that the flesh is not capable of receiving the gift of God, which is eternal life?—Why, when the flesh is nourished by the body and blood of Christ and is a member of him? As the blessed Apostle Paul also says in his letter to the Ephesians, 'For we are members of his body, of his flesh, and of his bones.' He does not say this with reference to some kind of spiritual, invisible man, for a spirit has neither bones nor flesh. He is referring to the constitution of an actual man, made up of flesh and nerves and bones. It is this flesh which is nourished by the cup which is his blood and receives growth from the bread which is his body . . .

III

Since men really exist, their renewal must be something that really exists—not a departure into nothingness, but an actual advance in the real world. It is not the substance or essence of creation that is brought to an end. (For he who established it is true and constant.) But 'the fashion of this world passeth away'—that is to say, those aspects in which transgression has been committed, for in them man grows old. For this reason the present fashion of the world has been made temporary, since God has foreknowledge of everything . . .

But when this present fashion passes away and man is renewed and flourishes to the point of incorruptibility so that he can no longer grow old, there shall be the new heaven and the new earth. In this new heaven and earth, the new humanity will remain perpetually in communion with God. As this will continue without end, Isaiah says: 'For as the new heaven and the new earth, which I make, remain before me, saith the Lord, so shall your seed and your name remain.' As the Presbyters say: Then those who are judged worthy of a life in heaven shall go there, others shall enjoy the delights of paradise, others shall have the splendour of the city. For the Saviour shall be seen everywhere according as those who see him shall be worthy . . .

ST JOHN OF THE CROSS
Beautifying the Creatures

According to Saint Paul, the Son of God is the brightness of His glory and the figure of His substance. It must be known, then, that God looked at all things in this image of His Son alone, which was to give them their natural being, to communicate to them many natural gifts and graces and to make them finished and perfect, even as He says in Genesis, in these words: 'God saw all the things that He had made and they were very good.' To behold them and find them very good was to make them very good in the Word, His Son. And not only did He communicate to them their being and their natural graces when He beheld them, as we have said, but also in this image of His Son alone He left them clothed with beauty, communicating to them supernatural being. This was when He became man, and thus exalted man in the beauty of God, and consequently exalted all the creatures in him, since in uniting Himself with man He united Himself with the nature of them all. Wherefore said the same Son of God: *Si ego exaltatus fuero a terra, omnia traham ad me ipsum.* This is: I, if I be lifted up from the earth, will draw all things to Myself. And thus, in this lifting up of the Incarnation of His Son, and in the glory of His resurrection according to the flesh, not only did the Father beautify the creatures in part, but we can say that He left them all clothed with beauty and dignity.

But, besides all this, speaking now somewhat according to the sense and the affection of contemplation, in the vivid contemplation and knowledge of the creatures, the soul sees with great clearness that there is in them such abundance of graces and virtues and beauty wherewith God endowed them, that, as it seems to her, they are all clothed with marvellous natural beauty, derived from and communicated by that infinite supernatural beauty of the image of God, Whose beholding of them clothes the world and all the heavens with beauty and joy; just as does also the opening of His hand whereby, as David

From *The Complete Works*, edited and ET by A. E. Peers, 3 vols. in one ed. (Wheatampstead, Hertfordshire: Anthony Clarke, 1974), vol. II, V, pp. 48–9.

says: *Imples omne animal benedictione.* That is to say: Thou fillest every animal with blessing. And therefore the soul, being wounded in love by this trace of the beauty of her Beloved which she has known in the creatures, yearns to behold that invisible beauty . . .

EDWARD QUINN

Animals in Heaven?

"Fido is wagging his tail in heaven to-night". According to Evelyn Waugh, this was the greeting sent out from Forest Lawn to the owners on the anniversaries of their pets buried in the cemetery. No one, of course, asked if the owners would also deserve a place in heaven if they had killed their dogs by overfeeding or whether the latter would have the joy of interrupting the heavenly choirs by their barking. But the false assumption behind this attitude was perhaps less the hope of reunion with animal friends than the idea of a heaven where we shall all congregate cozily with our pets and former neighbours. If some of us do not relish the prospect of an eternal menagerie, can we never-theless in all charity welcome the company of human beings who never hurt us but often threaten to bore us to death?

Even from traditional theology we get the impression that we shall not be troubled with bores, but equally that our joy in the beatific vision will be solitary and even then frustrated by the delay in the restoration of the body or by a reunion with the soul to which it will be no more than a glorified appendage. We look for the restoration of the whole personality, redeemed in Christ and therefore in Christ's company and in the company of those we have loved on earth. The lonely person in particular asks if the affection of his or her pet, ex-pressed in an outstretched paw, in a purring response, is not somehow transfigured also and not forever extinguished.

The fact that there is a continuity between nature and grace has always been recognised in Catholic theology. Is not the continuity between the old and the new creation equally obvious? In the new

From *New Blackfriers*, vol. 65, no. 767 (May 1984), pp. 224–26.

creation the old is transfigured and not annihilated. And the whole of nature is now moving—not by any means smoothly and easily, but with absolute certainty—towards that transfiguration. This has nothing to do with scientific theories about the beginning and end of the world, the one big-bang or successive big-bangs, with one universe or successive universes, with any particular evolutionary theory, with the possibility even of new forms of intelligent life. It is in this universe in which we now live that the preparation takes place for the renewal of the creature. And here man is one with the rest of nature.

If the primrose by the river's brim seems to him to be no more than a primrose, it has still made its impact. Wild nature transformed into strange and frightening shapes by natural upheavals forms a background to both animal and human life and can be tamed by the instinctive action of animals and the deliberate choice of man. There is mutual interaction between men and animals. Androcles' lion is at least a symbol of a real kinship between the two. Children, more basically creatures of sense than adults, can do amazing things with their pets. Soon, however, the small boy displays his intellectual ability and recognizes an intruder into the nursery as a cat, in the light of a universal notion he has formed based on an earlier experience of cats. But the cat already established in the household recognizes only by instinct the newcomer of its own breed. And the boy has become aware of man's leadership in nature. Even in his solitary prayer man is the world's representative before God.

It is through man that nature is first touched by God's grace. God's grace as merely proffered or as actually accepted in man is the prelude to the glory of the new creation. In torment and agony, joyfully and serenely, mistakenly, sinfully, aptly and virtuously, aided or frustrated by other creatures, man gives new shapes to nature. Over all God rules: makes saints out of weak humans, but tolerates amazing cruelties; sometimes draws good out of evil, but seems mostly to leave the horror and evil in the world strangely untouched by his glory.

We are bewildered and hurt by the apparently unnecessary suffering of the innocent, by the torment inflicted on animals deliberately by man or simply by natural disasters, by natural beauty distorted by human violence or in an inevitable movement towards the end of all things. Some part of the whole process is constantly interrupted by death.

This is the point at which God becomes all in all, that is the real

dawn of the new creation for those who have yielded to God's om-
nipotence, especially for those who have consciously shared to the
end the helplessness of Christ. Can this heaven be for human beings
only? Is it not the creation where God himself prevails, God's side of
the whole mysterious universe? Pain ceases, because we are no longer
left to the contingencies of nature or to the irresponsibility of unre-
deemed man. And God's light is shed on the world's mysteries, great
and small. In her poem "To a Daisy" Alice Meynell aptly describes
this transition from the love of half understood creatures in this world
to the insight we shall gain from God's light in eternity:

> Slight as thou art, thou art enough to hide
> Like all created things, secrets from me,
> And stand a barrier to eternity.
> And I, how can I praise thee well and wide
> From where I dwell—upon the hither side?
> Thou little veil for so great mystery,
> When shall I penetrate all things and thee,
> And then look back? For this I must abide,
> Till thou shalt grow and fold and be unfurled
> Literally between me and the world.
> Then I shall drink from in beneath a spring,
> And from a poet's side shall read his book.
> O daisy mine, what will it be to look
> From God's side even of such a simple thing?

Shall we not understand even better the lovableness of the animals
we have comforted in the present world and grasp the mystery of the
wild glare in the eyes of those we could not tame? If we are to see the
tiger's Creator, shall we not also penetrate the distant deeps and skies,
the forests of the night, and face without fear the burning eyes of the
creature now forever free?

ST ATHANASIUS
Christ as the Saviour of the Universe

For if, now that the cross has been set up, all idolatry has been overthrown, and by this sign all demonic activity is put to flight, and only Christ is worshipped, and through him the Father is known, and opponents are put to shame while he every day invisibly converts their souls—how then, one might reasonably ask them, is this still to be considered in human terms, and should one not rather confess that he who ascended the cross is the Word of God and the Saviour of the universe? These people seem to me to be suffering the same kind of delusion as if one were to depreciate the sun when it is hidden by clouds, but wonder at its light when he sees the whole world illuminated by it. For as light is beautiful, yet the author of light, the sun, is more beautiful, likewise, as it is something divine that the whole world is filled with knowledge of him, the author and instigator of such an achievement must be God and the Word of God . . .

By Word I do not mean the word involved and innate in every creature, which some are accustomed to call seminal; it has no life of its own neither can it reason or think, but it acts merely by an extrinsic art according to the skill of him who set it in the creature. Nor do I mean the word of human kind which is composed of syllables and expressed in the air. But I mean the living and acting God, the very Word of the good God of the universe, who is other than created things and all creation; he is rather the sole and individual Word of the good Father, who has ordered all this universe and illuminates it by his providence. He is the good Word of the good Father, and it is he who has established the order of all things, reconciling opposites and from them forming a single harmony. He, the power of God and wisdom of God, turns the heaven, has suspended the earth, and by his own will has set it resting on nothing. Illuminated by him, the sun gives light to the world, and the moon receives its measure of light. Through him water is suspended in the clouds, rains water the

From *Contra Gentes and De Incarnatione*, edited and ET by Robert W. Thomson (Oxford: The Clarendon Press, 1971), pp. 111–19.

earth, the sea is confined, and the earth is covered with verdure in all kinds of plants. And if any unbeliever were to inquire about these remarks if there is in fact a Word of God, such a one would be mad to doubt about the Word of God. But from what he can see he has proof that everything came into existence through the Word and wisdom of God, and that nothing would subsist unless it had been created by a Word, the divine Word, as has been explained.

As Word he is not composed of syllables like those of men, as I have said, but he is the express image of his Father. Men are composed of parts and created from nothing; their word is compound and dissolvable. But God exists, and is not composite; therefore his Word exists, and is not composite, but is the one, only-begotten, good God, proceeding from the Father as from a good source, who orders and contains the universe. And the cause why the Word of God really came to created beings is truly wonderful, and shows that things should not have occurred otherwise than as they are. For the nature of created things, having come into being from nothing, is unstable, and is weak and mortal when considered by itself; but the God of all is good and excellent by nature. Therefore he is also kind. For a good being would be envious of no one, so he envies nobody existence but rather wishes everyone to exist, in order to exercise his kindness. So seeing that all created nature according to its own definition is in a state of flux and dissolution, therefore to prevent this happening and the universe dissolving back into nothing, after making everything by his own eternal Word and bringing creation into existence, he did not abandon it to be carried away and suffer through its own nature, lest it run the risk of returning to nothing. But being good, he governs and establishes the whole world through his Word who is himself God, in order that creation, illuminated by the leadership, providence, and ordering of the Word, may be able to remain firm, since it shares in the Word who is truly from the Father and is aided by him to exist, and lest it suffer what would happen, I mean a relapse into non-existence, if it were not protected by the Word. 'For he is the image of the invisible God, the first-born of all creation, because through him and in him subsist all things, visible and invisible, and he is the head of the church', as the servants of the truth teach in the holy writings.

It is thus the omnipotent and perfectly holy Word of the Father himself who is present in all things and extends his power everywhere, illuminating all things visible and invisible, containing and enclosing them in himself; he leaves nothing deprived of his power, but gives life and protection to everything, everywhere, to each individually and to all together. The principles of all perceptible substance, the hot and cold, the moist and dry, he mixes together, ensuring that they do not oppose each other but produce a single euphonious harmony. Through him and his power fire does not fight with the cold, nor the moist with the dry; but these elements which by themselves are opposed, come together like friends and kin, give life to the visible world, and become the principles of existence for bodies. By obedience to this Word of God things on earth receive life and things in heaven subsist. Through him all the sea and the great ocean keep their movement within their proper limits, and all the dry land is covered with verdure in all kinds of different plants, as I said above. And lest I dwell too long by naming each visible entity, there is nothing existing or created which did not come into being and subsist in him and through him, as the theologian says: *'In the beginning was the Word, and the Word was with God, and the Word was God. All things were made by him, and without him nothing was made.'*

Just as a musician, tuning his lyre and skilfully combining the bass and the sharp notes, the middle and the others, produces a single melody, so the wisdom of God, holding the universe like a lyre, draws together the things in the air with those on earth, and those in heaven with those in the air, and combines the whole with the parts, linking them by his command and will, thus producing in beauty and harmony a single world and a single order within it, while he himself remains unmoved with the Father but by his intrinsic being moves everything as seems good to the Father. The surprising thing about his divinity is the fact that by one and the same command he links and orders everything together according to its individual nature, not by intervals but all at once: the straight and the curved, the upper, middle and lower, the moist, the cold, the hot, the visible, and the invisible. For all together by the same command of his, the straight moves in a straight line, the circular in a circle, the middle in its way; the hot is heated and the dry dried; everything according to its own nature is given life and subsistence by him; and through him a wonderful and truly divine harmony is produced.

JOHN CALVIN

Speculation About Animals

[Romans 8:]21 *In hope that the creation itself also shall be delivered.*
[St Paul] shows how the creature has been made subject to vanity *in
hope.* But the time will come when it will one day be delivered, as
Isaiah testifies and Peter still more clearly confirms.

We may, it is true, infer from this how dreadful is the curse which
we have deserved, since all innocent creatures from earth to heaven
are punished for our sins. It is our fault that they struggle in corruption.
The condemnation of the human race is thus imprinted on the heavens,
the earth, and all creatures. Again, this passage shows us to how
great an excellence of glory the sons of God are to be exalted, and
all creatures shall be renewed to magnify it and declare its splendour.

Paul does not mean that all creatures will be partakers of the same
glory with the sons of God, but that they will share in their own
manner in the better state, because God will restore the present fallen
world to perfect condition at the same time as the human race. It is
neither expedient nor right for us to inquire with greater curiosity into
the perfection which will be evidenced by beasts, plants, and metals,
because the main part of corruption is decay. Some shrewd but unbalanced commentators ask whether all kinds of animals will be immortal. If we give free rein to these speculations, where will they finally
carry us? Let us, therefore, be content with this simple doctrine—
their constitution will be such, and their order so complete, that no
appearance either of deformity or of impermanence will be seen.

22. *For we know.* He repeats the same proposition in order to pass
over to our own case, although what he now says has the effect and
form of a conclusion. Because the creatures are subject to corruption,
not through their natural desire, but by God's appointment, and also
because they have a hope of being freed hereafter from corruption, it

From *Calvin's Commentaries: The Epistles of Paul the Apostle to the Romans and to the Thessalonians,*
edited by D. W. Torrance and T. F. Torrance, ET by Ross Mackenzie (London and Edinburgh:
Oliver and Boyd, 1961), pp. 173–74.

follows that they groan like a woman in labour until they have been delivered. This is a most appropriate comparison to inform us that the groaning of which he speaks will not be in vain or without effect. It will finally bring forth a joyful and happy fruit. In short, the creatures are not content with their present condition, and yet they are not so distressed as to pine away irremediably. They are, however, in labour, because they are waiting to be renewed to a better state. By saying that they *groan together*, he does not mean that they are bound together by common anxiety, but he connects them with us as our companions. The particle *until now*, or, *to this day*, serves to reduce the wearisome nature of the dullness which we experience each day. If the creatures have continued their groaning for so many ages, our softness or in-dolence will be inexcusable if we faint in the brief course of our shadowy life.

JOHN WESLEY
The General Deliverance

But will "the creature," will even the brute creature, always remain in this deplorable condition? God forbid that we should affirm this; yea, or even entertain such a thought! While "the whole creation groaneth together," (whether men attend or not,) their groans are not dispersed in idle air, but enter into the ears of Him that made them. While his creatures "travail together in pain," he knoweth all their pain, and is bringing them nearer and nearer to the birth, which shall be accomplished in its season. He seeth "the earnest expectation" wherewith the whole animated creation "waiteth for" that final "manifestation of the sons of God;" in which "they themselves also shall be delivered" (not by annihilation; annihilation is not deliverance) "from the" present "bondage of corruption, into" a measure of "the glorious liberty of the children of God."

From *Sermons on Several Occasions*, vol. II, introduction by John Beecham (London: Wesleyan Conference Office, 1874), pp. 281–86.

Nothing can be more express: away with vulgar prejudices, and let the plain word of God take place. They "shall be delivered from the bondage of corruption into glorious liberty,"—even a measure, according as they are capable,—of "the liberty of the children of God."

A general view of this is given us in the twenty-first chapter of the Revelation. When He that "sitteth on the great white throne" hath pronounced, "Behold, I make all things new;" when the word is fulfilled, "The tabernacle of God is with men, and they shall be his people, and God himself shall be with them, and be their God;"—then the following blessing shall take place (not only on the children of men; there is no such restriction in the text; but) on every creature according to its capacity: "God shall wipe away all tears from their eyes. And there shall be no more death, neither sorrow, nor crying, neither shall there be any more pain: for the former things are passed away."

To descend to a few particulars: the whole brute creation will then, undoubtedly, be restored, not only to the vigour, strength, and swiftness which they had at their creation, but to a far higher degree of each than they ever enjoyed. They will be restored, not only to that measure of understanding which they had in paradise, but to a degree of it as much higher than that, as the understanding of an elephant is beyond that of a worm. And whatever affections they had in the garden of God, will be restored with vast increase; being exalted and refined in a manner which we ourselves are not now able to comprehend. The liberty they then had will be completely restored, and they will be free in all their motions. They will be delivered from all irregular appetites, from all unruly passions, from every disposition that is either evil in itself, or has any tendency to evil. No rage will be found in any creature, no fierceness, no cruelty, or thirst for blood. So far from it, that "the wolf shall dwell with the lamb, the leopard shall lie down with the kid; the calf and the young lion together; and a little child shall lead them. The cow and the bear shall feed together; and the lion shall eat straw like the ox. They shall not hurt nor destroy in all my holy mountain." (Isaiah xi. 6, &c.)

Thus, in that day, all the vanity to which they are now helplessly subject will be abolished; they will suffer no more, either from within or without; the days of their groaning are ended. At the same time, there can be no reasonable doubt, but all the horridness of their appearance, and all the deformity of their aspect, will vanish away, and be exchanged for their primeval beauty. And with their beauty their happiness will return; to which there can then be no obstruction. As there will be nothing within, so there will be nothing without, to give them any uneasiness: no heat or cold, no storm or tempest, but one perennial spring. In the new earth, as well as the new heavens, there will be nothing to give pain, but everything that the wisdom and goodness of God can create to give happiness. As a recompence for what they once suffered, while under the "bondage of corruption," when God has "renewed the face of the earth," and their corruptible body has put on incorruption, they shall enjoy happiness suited to their state, without alloy, without interruption, and without end.

But though I doubt not that the Father of All has a tender regard for even his lowest creatures, and that, in consequence of this, he will make them large amends for all they suffer while under their present bondage; yet I dare not affirm that he has an *equal regard* for them and for the children of men. I do not believe that

> "He sees *with equal eyes*, as Lord of all,
> A hero perish, or a sparrow fall."

By no means. This is exceeding pretty; but it is absolutely false. For though

> "Mercy, with truth and endless grace,
>   O'er all his works doth reign,
> Yet chiefly he delights to bless
>   His favorite creature, man."

God regards his meanest creatures much; but he regards man much more.

KEITH WARD
Sentient Afterlife

[T]o say that God is infinitely good or loving is not to say that every created thing, considered in itself, must be supremely good. It is to say that God is the moral standard and goal for all creatures, the source of all values and the guarantor that all things will ultimately work together for good; that personal values will not be thwarted. One must abandon the Leibnizian picture of God considering every possible world and choosing to create the best, as though there was a fixed realm of possibilities and God was necessitated by his own goodness to select only one set of them. One must start from the world one has, and say that this is the world God has made, and that a moral purpose will be realised in it; that, taken as a whole, it is of intrinsic value, though not necessarily the greatest possible intrinsic value. One might be tempted to say that parts of the world could have been better—less painful, perhaps—than they are. That is true; but it would always be true, in any finite world, that some particulars could be better than they are. For to be finite implies having a limit, and some limits could always be less severe than they are. Perhaps, then, one protests only that the amount of suffering in the world seems disproportionately high. However, what is the standard of comparison here? One must remember that the Christian belief is that there is an existence after earthly life which is so glorious that it makes any earthly suffering pall in comparison; and that such eternal life is internally related to the acts and sufferings of worldly life, so that they contribute to, and are essential parts of, the sort of glory which is to come. The Christian paradigm here is the resurrection body of Jesus, which is glorious beyond description, but which still bears the wounds of the cross.[1] So the sufferings of this life are not just obliterated; they are transfigured by joy, but always remain as contributory factors to make us the sort of individual beings we are eternally.

From *The Concept of God* (Oxford: Basil Blackwell, 1974), pp. 222–24.
[1]Jn. 20, 27.

This must be true for the whole of creation, insofar as it has sentience at all. If there is any sentient being which suffers pain, that being—whatever it is and however it is manifested—must find that pain transfigured by a greater joy. I am quite agnostic as to how this is to happen; but that it must be asserted to be true follows from the doctrine that God is love, and would not therefore create any being whose sole destiny was to suffer pain. In the case of persons, the truth of this claim requires the existence of a continuous personal life after death. The Christian will then say that his sufferings, whatever they are, help to make him the unique individual he is. To wish for a better world is to wish for one's non-existence, as the person one is. Often one may indeed wish for that; but the Christian would say that, if one could clearly see the future which is prepared for one, such doubts and fears would disappear; and the resurrection of Jesus is given to confirm this faith.

Perhaps, then, one would not really desire that only the best possible world should exist; for then one, as the precise person one is, would not be a member of it. We cannot assign a reason why this particular world exists; but we can say that it comes solely from God, whose being contains the possibilities of all the good and evil things alike which we see around us. The appropriate response to this knowledge is, like Job, to bow in acceptance before the unfathomable ground of being.[2] Perhaps all possible worlds, an infinite number of them, do exist; we do not know; we only know that this one, not the best or the worst (if those superlatives make any sense), exists. And we believe, as Christians, of this world that, taken as a whole, taking into account life after death, it is better that it exists than not; and that every sentient creature in it which wills to do so will find an appropriate fulfilment within which, as an integral part, its own sufferings will contribute to the unique character of its final joy . . .

. . . And we think of God as sharing in the pain and sorrow of creation, as well as its joy and happiness, and thus, by his omniscience, as participating in the creative expression of his own reality which is creation.

[2] Job 42, 1–6.

PAUL TILLICH
Redemption of Other Worlds

In discussing the character of the quest for and the expectation of the Christ, a question arises which has been carefully avoided by many traditional theologians, even though it is consciously or unconsciously alive for most contemporary people. It is the problem of how to understand the meaning of the symbol "Christ" in the light of the immensity of the universe, the heliocentric system of planets, the infinitely small part of the universe which man and his history constitute, and the possibility of other "worlds" in which divine self-manifestations may appear and be received. Such developments become especially important if one considers that biblical and related expectations envisaged the coming of the Messiah within a cosmic frame. The universe will be reborn into a new eon. The function of the bearer of the New Being is not only to save individuals and to transform man's historical existence but to renew the universe. And the assumption is that mankind and individual men are so dependent on the powers of the universe that salvation of the one without the other is unthinkable.

The basic answer to these questions is given in the concept of essential man appearing in a personal life under the conditions of existential estrangement. This restricts the expectation of the Christ to historical mankind. The man in whom essential man has appeared in existence represents human history; more precisely, as its central event, he creates the meaning of human history. It is the eternal relation of God to man which is manifest in the Christ. At the same time, our basic answer leaves the universe open for possible divine manifestations in other areas or periods of being. Such possibilities cannot be denied. But they cannot be proved or disproved. Incarnation is unique for the special group in which it happens, but it is not unique in the sense that other singular incarnations for other unique worlds are excluded. Man cannot claim that the infinite has entered the finite to overcome its existential estrangement in mankind alone. Man cannot claim to occupy the only possible place for Incarnation. Although statements

From *Systematic Theology*, vol. II, *Existence and the Christ* (London: SCM Press, 1978), pp. 95–96.

about other worlds and God's relation to them cannot be verified experientially, they are important because they help to interpret the meaning of terms like "mediator," "savior," "Incarnation," "the Messiah," and "the new eon."

Perhaps one can go a step further. The interdependence of everything with everything else in the totality of being includes a participation of nature in history and demands a participation of the universe in salvation. Therefore, if there are non-human "worlds" in which existential estrangement is not only real—as it is in the whole universe—but in which there is also a type of awareness of this estrangement, such worlds cannot be without the operation of saving power within them. Otherwise self-destruction would be the inescapable consequence. The manifestation of saving power in one place implies that saving power is operating in all places. The expectation of the Messiah as the bearer of the New Being presupposes that "God loves the universe," even though in the appearance of the Christ he actualizes this love for historical man alone.

C. S. LEWIS

Animal Resurrection

The real difficulty about supposing most animals to be immortal is that immortality has almost no meaning for a creature which is not "conscious" in the sense explained above. If the life of a newt is merely a succession of sensations, what should we mean by saying that God may recall to life the newt that died to-day? It would not recognise itself as the same newt; the pleasant sensations of any other newt that lived after its death would be just as much, or just as little, a recompense for its earthly sufferings (if any) as those of its resurrected—I was going to say "self", but the whole point is that the newt probably has no self. The thing we have to try to say, on this hypothesis, will not even be said. There is, therefore, I take it, no question of immortality for

From *The Problem of Pain*, Fontana Books (London: Collins, 8th ed., 1967), pp. 125–28.

creatures that are merely sentient. Nor do justice and mercy demand that there should be, for such creatures have no painful experience. Their nervous system delivers all the *letters* A, P, N, I, but since they cannot read they never build it up into the word PAIN. And all animals *may* be in that condition.

If, nevertheless, the strong conviction which we have of a real, though doubtless rudimentary, selfhood in the higher animals, and specially in those we tame, is not an illusion, their destiny demands a somewhat deeper consideration. The error we must avoid is that of considering them in themselves. Man is to be understood only in his relation to God. The beasts are to be understood only in their relation to man and, through man, to God . . . Now it will be seen that, in so far as the tame animal has a real self or personality, it owes this almost entirely to its master. If a good sheepdog seems "almost human" that is because a good shepherd has made it so. I have already noted the mysterious force of the word "in". I do not take all the senses of it in the New Testament to be identical, so that man is *in* Christ and Christ *in* God and the Holy Spirit *in* the Church and also *in* the in-dividual believer in exactly the same sense. They may be senses that rhyme or correspond rather than a single sense. I am now going to suggest—though with great readiness to be set right by real theo-logians—that there may be a sense, corresponding, though not iden-tical, with these, in which those beasts that attain a real self are *in* their masters. That is to say, you must not think of a beast by itself, and call that a personality and then inquire whether God will raise and bless *that*. You must take the whole context *in* which the beast acquires its selfhood—namely "The-goodman-and-the-goodwife-ruling-their-children-and-their-beasts-in-the-good-homestead". That whole context may be regarded as a "body" in the Pauline (or a closely sub-Pauline) sense; and how much of that "body" may be raised along with the goodman and the goodwife, who can predict? So much, pre-sumably, as is necessary not only for the glory of God and the beatitude of the human pair, but for that particular glory and that particular beatitude which is eternally coloured by that particular terrestrial ex-perience. And in this way it seems to me possible that certain animals may have an immortality, not in themselves, but in the immortality of their masters . . .

My picture of the good sheepdog in the good homestead does not, of course, cover wild animals nor (a matter even more urgent) ill-treated domestic animals. But it is intended only as an illustration drawn from one privileged instance—which is, also, on my view the only normal and unperverted instance—of the general principles to be observed in framing a theory of animal resurrection.

Part Four

♦

REVERENCE, RESPONSIBILITIES AND RIGHTS

Introduction to Part Four

With the possible exception of St Paul writing about oxen, it seems clear that the Bible includes animals—to some degree—within the community of moral obligation. The various humane regulations in Jewish Law regarding the treatment of animals—some of which are enumerated at the beginning of this section—are a reflection of a growing conviction that animals are owed some of the basic obligations which we extend to humans beings. Thus even apparently innocuous injunctions from Deuteronomy concerning which animals should plough together, or which should not be muzzled, are essentially welfare regulations designed to respect the distinctive lives of the animals involved. It is difficult not to see a reflection of the Deuteronomic injunction to rescue animals fallen into a pit, in Jesus' dispute about whether it is lawful to heal on the Sabbath. For Jesus justifies his own actions of healing on the Sabbath with the express view that 'it is lawful to do good on the Sabbath' as his accusers do good by rescuing suffering animals.

But the question remains: *How much* do we owe the animals? Should we show them reverence and respect? Do we have definite duties towards them? Do animals have certain basic rights?

Albert Schweitzer begins our section by insisting upon the need for reverence for life as a 'basic principle of the moral.' 'A man is truly ethical,' he maintains, 'only when he obeys the compulsion to help all life which he is able to assist, and shrinks from injuring anything that lives.' For Schweitzer this basic obligation extends throughout the whole created order and not just to animals. 'Life is sacred' for Schweitzer whether it is sentient or non-sentient, animal or vegetable. Karl Barth accepts that Schweitzer may well be right to lament our 'astonishing indifference' to our fellow creatures, but equally insists that animals can only claim to be a 'secondary responsibility' for human beings. Barth argues that while animals and plants do not 'belong' to man, 'they are provided for his use.' Because God reveals himself to man and makes common cause with him, Barth concludes that it is right to posit 'a higher necessity' in the case of human life.

The question whether animals are made for human use is also dominant in the next selection from St Thomas Aquinas. Aquinas denies that it is wrong for humans to kill animals because there 'is no sin in using a thing for the purpose for which it is.' In the same way that there is no wrong in animals using plants, there is nothing wrong with humans using animals. God has ordained that the lower orders of creation should serve the higher in this way, suggests Aquinas. Neither, according to Aquinas, is there any duty to love animals. Only in so far as there is some human interest involved, is it wrong to injure or kill animals or right to be charitable to them. Humphry Primatt, in contrast, argues that the important issue is not what kind of species a being may be, but whether it can feel pain. 'Pain is pain, whether it be inflicted on man or on beast,' maintains Primatt, 'and the creature that suffers it, whether man or beast, being sensible of the misery of it whilst it lasts, suffers evil.' Thus mercy is a duty. Superiority of rank 'can give no right to inflict unnecessary pain.'

The view of St Thomas is again defended in the next selection from Henry Davis. Davis is adamant that animals 'have no rights.' We have 'no duties of justice or charity towards them' only insofar as some relevant human factor is involved. Wanton cruelty to animals *may* be wrong—not because it is an offence to the animals concerned—but because it may make humans callous. Andrew Linzey attacks this position. He holds that the tradition of denying rights to animals, especially apparent in scholastic catholicism, is responsible for contemporary abuse of animals. Linzey argues that we can quite legitimately base animal rights on God's own rights as Creator. Thus Linzey advances the concept of 'Theos-rights' for animals. 'When we speak of animal rights we conceptualise what is objectively owed to animals by virtue of their Creator's right.' In sum: 'Animals can be wronged because their Creator can be wronged in his creation.'

Richard Griffiths takes issue with the theory of animal rights in two ways. First, he opposes sentiency (understood as the capacity to experience pain) as a basis for moral rights arguing that this constitutes a 'naturalistic fallacy.' Second, he maintains that rights arguments lead to a *reductio ad absurdum* in which 'everything should have rights.' Tom Regan replies to both objections. He argues that rights theories are based on appeals to consistency, so that it would be morally inconsistent to oppose some actions (such as the wanton infliction of pain) on humans without also opposing the same actions performed on other beings which are similarly capable of being harmed. To the second objection that animal rights theory might involve recognising the rights of plants, Regan insists that consistency involves 'making the same moral judgement in morally relevant cases.' There is 'no plausible basis' for believing that plants experience pain, and 'every good reason to believe that this is true in the case of . . . animals.'

The final piece in our section is by Stephen Clark. He distinguishes between 'positive' and 'negative' rights. Perhaps, he surmises, animals have no 'positive' rights in an absolute sense. Suppose, he suggests, that they 'have no right to claim any share of the world's or of our resources, because they are unable to *claim* such a share.' It still does not follow, according to Clark, that animals have no rights at least in a 'negative' sense. 'A drowning man has no absolute, unfocussed *right* to life' but 'it does not follow that he had no right not-to-be-pushed which is simply to say that no-one else had or has the right so to push him.'

We may summarise the main issues in this section as follows: (1) Should the lives of all living creatures be respected? (2) Do we have any *direct* duties to animals, even when there is no human interest involved? (3) What *kind of* duties do we have towards animals, for example, to prevent suffering, to refrain from killing, and/or to respect their natural lives? (4) Do animals have rights? and (5) On *what basis* should we recognise the rights of animals—for example, because God has rights in his creation, because they are sentient, and/or because they have 'negative' rights?

The Bible
On the Right Treatment of Animals

Exodus 21:28–32

"When an ox gores a man or a woman to death, the ox shall be stoned, and its flesh shall not be eaten; but the owner of the ox shall be clear. But if the ox has been accustomed to gore in the past, and its owner has been warned but has not kept it in, and it kills a man or a woman, the ox shall be stoned and its owner also shall be put to death. If a ransom is laid on him, then he shall give for the redemption of his life whatever is laid upon him. If it gores a man's son or daughter, he shall be dealt with according to this same rule. If the ox gores a slave, male or female, the owner shall give to their master thirty shekels of silver, and the ox shall be stoned."

Deuteronomy 22:1–4

"You shall not see your brother's ox or his sheep go astray, and withhold your help from them; you shall take them back to your brother. And if he is not near you, or if you do not know him, you shall bring it home to your house, and it shall be with you until your brother seeks it; then you shall restore it to him, and so you shall do with his ass; so you shall do with his garment; so you shall do with any lost thing of your brother's which he loses and you find; you may not withhold your help. You shall not see your brother's ass or his ox fallen down by the way, and withhold your help from them; you shall help him to lift them up again."

Deuternomy 22:6–7

"If you chance to come upon a bird's nest, in any tree or on the ground, with young ones or eggs and the mother sitting upon the young or upon the eggs, you shall not take the mother with the young; you shall let the mother go, but the young you may take to yourself; that it may go well with you, and that you may live long."

Deuteronomy 22:10
"You shall not plough with an ox and an ass together."

Deuteronomy 25:4
"You shall not muzzle an ox when it treads out the grain."

Proverbs 12:10
A righteous man has regard for the life of his beast, but the mercy of the wicked is cruel.

Matthew 12:9–13
And he went on from there, and entered their synagogue. And behold, there was a man with a withered hand. And they asked him, "Is it lawful to heal on the sabbath?" so that they might accuse him. He said to them, "What man of you, if he has one sheep and it falls into a pit on the sabbath, will not lay hold of it and lift it out? Of how much more value is a man than a sheep! So it is lawful to do good on the sabbath." Then he said to the man, "Stretch out your hand." And the man stretched it out, and it was restored, whole like the other.

1 Corinthians 9:9–10
For it is written in the law of Moses, "You shall not muzzle an ox when it is treading out the grain." Is it for oxen that God is concerned? Does he not speak entirely for our sake? It was written for our sake, because the ploughman should plough in hope and the thresher thresh in hope of a share in the crop.

ALBERT SCHWEITZER
The Ethic of Reverence for Life

Ethics consist, therefore, in my experiencing the compulsion to show to all will-to-live the same reverence as I do to my own. There we have given us that basic principle of the moral which is a necessity of thought. It is good to maintain and to encourage life; it is bad to destroy life or to obstruct it . . .

The basic principle of the moral which is a necessity of thought means, however, not only an ordering and deepening, but also a widening of the current views of good and evil. A man is truly ethical only when he obeys the compulsion to help all life which he is able to assist, and shrinks from injuring anything that lives. He does not ask how far this or that life deserves one's sympathy as being valuable, nor, beyond that, whether and to what degree it is capable of feeling. Life as such is sacred to him. He tears no leaf from a tree, plucks no flower, and takes care to crush no insect. If in summer he is working by lamplight, he prefers to keep the window shut and breathe a stuffy atmosphere rather than see one insect after another fall with singed wings upon his table.

If he walks on the road after a shower and sees an earthworm which has strayed on to it he bethinks himself that it must get dried up in the sun, if it does not return soon enough to ground into which it can burrow, so he lifts it from the deadly stone surface, and puts it on the grass. If he comes across an insect which has fallen into a puddle, he stops a moment in order to hold out a leaf or a stalk on which it can save itself.

He is not afraid of being laughed at as sentimental. It is the fate of every truth to be a subject for laughter until it is generally recognized. Once it was considered folly to assume that men of colour were really men and ought to be treated as such, but the folly has become an accepted truth. To-day it is thought to be going too far to declare that constant regard for everything that lives, down to the lowest mani-

From *Civilization and Ethics*, ET by C. T. Campion, Unwin Books (London: Adam & Charles Black, 1967 ed.), pp. 214–22.

festations of life, is a demand made by rational ethics. The time is coming, however, when people will be astonished that mankind needed so long a time to learn to regard thoughtless injury to life as incompatible with ethics.

Ethics are responsibility without limit towards all that lives.

As a general proposition, the definition of ethics as a relationship within a disposition to reverence for life, does not make a very moving impression. But it is the only complete one. Compassion is too narrow to rank as the total essence of the ethical. It denotes, of course, only interest in the suffering will-to-live. But ethics include also feeling as one's own all the circumstances and all the aspirations of the will-to-live, its pleasure, too, and its longing to live itself out to the full, as well as its urge to self-perfecting.

Love means more, since it includes fellowship in suffering, in joy, and in effort, but it shows the ethical only in a simile, although in a simile that is natural and profound. It makes the solidarity produced by ethics analogous to that which nature calls forth on the physical side, for more or less temporary purposes between two beings which complete each other sexually, or between them and their offspring.

Thought must strive to bring to expression the nature of the ethical in itself. To effect this it arrives at defining ethics as devotion to life inspired by reverence for life. Even if the phrase reverence for life sounds so general as to seem somewhat lifeless, what is meant by it is nevertheless something which never lets go of the man into whose thought it has made its way. Sympathy, and love, and every kind of valuable enthusiasm are given within it. With restless living force reverence for life works upon the mind into which it has entered, and throws it into the unrest of a feeling of responsibility which at no place and at no time ceases to affect it. Just as the screw which churns its way through the water drives the ship along, so does reverence for life drive the man . . .

What does reverence for life say about the relations between man and the animal world?

Whenever I injure life of any sort, I must be quite clear whether it is necessary. Beyond the unavoidable, I must never go, not even with what seems insignificant. The farmer, who has mown down a thousand flowers in his meadow as fodder for his cows, must be careful on his way home not to strike off in wanton pastime the head of a single flower by the roadside, for he thereby commits a wrong against life without being under the pressure of necessity.

Those who experiment with operations or the use of drugs upon animals, or inoculate them with diseases, so as to be able to bring help to mankind with the results gained, must never quiet any misgivings they feel with the general reflection that their cruel proceedings aim at a valuable result. They must first have considered in each individual case whether there is a real necessity to force upon any animal this sacrifice for the sake of mankind. And they must take the most anxious care to mitigate as much as possible the pain inflicted. How much wrong is committed in scientific institutions through neglect of anæsthetic, which to save time or trouble are not administered! How much, too, through animals being subjected to torture merely to demonstrate to students generally known phenomena! By the very fact that animals have been subjected to experiments, and have by their pain won such valuable results for suffering humanity, a new and special relation of solidarity has been established between them and us. From that springs for each one of us a compulsion to do to every animal all the good we possibly can. By helping an insect when it is in difficulties, I am only attempting to cancel part of man's ever new debt to the animal world. Whenever an animal is in any way forced into the service of man, every one of us must be concerned with the sufferings which for that reason it has to undergo. None of us must allow to take place any suffering for which he himself is not responsible, if he can hinder it in any way. He must not soothe his conscience with the reflection that he would be mixing himself up in something which does not concern him. No one must shut his eyes and regard as non-existent the sufferings of which he spares himself the sight. Let no one regard as light the burden of his responsibility. While so much ill-treatment of animals goes on, while the moans of thirsty animals in railway trucks sound unheard, while so much brutality prevails in our slaughter-houses, while animals have to suffer in our kitchens painful death from unskilled hands, while animals have to endure intolerable treatment from heartless men, or are left to the cruel play of children, we all share the guilt.

KARL BARTH
A Reply to Schweitzer

Albert Schweitzer has not wholly unjustly complained of the narrowness and reserve with which even naturalistic ethics has hitherto limited its attention to the address and dedication of man to man and human society. "Just as the housewife who has scrubbed the room is careful to see that the door is shut lest the dog should come in and ruin the finished job with its footprints, so European thinkers are on their guard lest animals should intrude into ethics." As against this ethics must venture the thought that "dedication must be extended not only to man but also to creatures, and in fact to all life that exists in the world and enters the sphere of man. Ethics must rise to the notion that man's relation to man is only an expression of the relation in which he stands to being and the world generally." . . . And then again the general sentence from whose many repetitions and variations there emerges the one and so far the only concrete demand: "Ethics is infinitely extended responsibility to everything that lives."

We may leave the general statement and ask what is to be said of the concrete demand. We certainly cannot dismiss it as "sentimental." Nor may we take the easy course of questioning the practicability of the instructions given, let alone the wider consequences and applications. The directness of the insight and feeling revealed (not unlike those of Francis of Assisi), and the constraint expressed, are stronger than all such criticism. Those who can only smile at this point are themselves subjects for tears. How do we really justify ourselves if we differ from Schweitzer in this matter? For while the problem of treating life with respect becomes very obscure beyond its human form, it does not cease to be a problem. If we are really listening in relation to the human life of ourselves and others, we cannot feign deafness with regard to animal and vegetative life outside the human sphere. It is surely to Schweitzer's credit, even if on the basis of an unacceptable

From *Church Dogmatics*, vol. III, part 4, *The Doctrine of Creation*, ET by A. T. Mackay, T. H. L. Parker, H. Knight, H. A. Kennedy, and J. Marks (Edinburgh: T. & T. Clark, 1978), pp. 349–51.

general presupposition, that he has warned us so warmly and earnestly to consider this question. There always have been men who in respect of non-human life have no greater knowledge but do have deeper and more vivid presentiments and intuitions and therefore feel more acute and detailed obligations than the great majority. It is told of one of the most enlightened of the younger generation of German theologians immediately after the First World War that he once discovered near Bamberg a weir on whose grating certain snails were always being caught and perishing, and that this made such an impression on him that from time to time he felt compelled to travel to Bamberg to help at least some of these creatures. And who is to say whether this kind of bizarre action is not in the long run at least as noble and respectable as the books in which men like F. T. Vischer, J. W. Widmann and Carl Spitteler, objecting strongly to the divine activity, dilate on the suffering of animals and commend themselves as thoughtful poets? But why should we not also hear the poets in this matter and take their insight to heart? It is hardly an accident that in those who speak along these lines there is usually something strange and even excessive. It may be connected with the fact that here we find ourselves at the extreme limit of what can be said and also done. What we hear along these lines obviously cannot be understood as doctrine, principle and precept, nor can the strange statements of Schweitzer on what man will do or not do in this matter if he is "truly ethical." It is a further help to our understanding that Schweitzer himself did not finally take up service as a veterinary surgeon but set a fine example of medical work among the natives of the Ogowe. His statements are simply a protest against our astonishing indifference and thoughtlessness in this matter. Whatever the solutions proposed, the problem itself is important. It may well be insoluble and barely tangible, but it is genuine and cannot be ignored. We have to ask how we are to treat the strange life of beasts and plants which is all around us. In the blessing of Noah and his sons we read in Gen. 9: "And the fear of you and the dread of you shall be upon every beast of the earth, and upon every fowl of the air, upon all that moveth upon the earth, and upon all the fishes of the sea; into your hand are they delivered." It is surely obvious that the possession of such power confers upon man a very definite responsibility towards non-human life . . .

Our starting-point must be that in this matter too, as a living being in co-existence with non-human life, man has to think and act responsibly. The responsibility is not the same as he has to his own life and that of his fellow-men. Only analogically can we bring it under the concept of respect for life. It can only follow the primary responsibility at a distance. If we try to bring animal and vegetable life too close to human, or even class them together, we can hardly avoid the danger of regarding and treating human life, even when we really want to help, from the aspect of the animal and vegetable, and therefore in a way which is not really apposite. But why should we not be faced here by a responsibility which, if not primary, is a serious secondary responsibility?

The special responsibility in this case rests primarily on this, that the world of animals and plants forms the indispensable living background to the living-space divinely allotted to man and placed under his control. As they live, so can he. He is not set up as lord over the earth, but as lord on the earth which is already furnished with these creatures. Animals and plants do not belong to him; they and the whole earth can belong only to God. But he takes precedence of them. They are provided for his use. They are his "means of life." The meaning of the basis of this distinction consists in the fact that he is the animal creature to whom God reveals, entrusts and binds Himself within the rest of creation, with whom He makes common cause in the course of a particular history which is neither that of an animal nor a plant, and in whose life-activity He expects a conscious and deliberate recognition of His honour, mercy and power. Hence the higher necessity of his life, and his right to that lordship and control. He can exercise it only in the responsibility thus conferred upon him.

ST THOMAS AQUINAS
The Lawful Treatment of Animals

QUESTION 64, ARTICLE 1
Whether It Is Unlawful to Kill Any Living Thing

We proceed thus to the First Article:

Objection 1. It would seem unlawful to kill any living thing. For the Apostle says (Rom. xiii. 2): *They that resist the ordinance of God purchase to themselves damnation.* Now Divine providence has ordained that all living things should be preserved, according to Ps. cxlvi. 8, 9, *Who maketh grass to grow on the mountains . . . Who giveth to beasts their food.* Therefore it seems unlawful to take the life of any living thing.

Obj. 2. Further, Murder is a sin because it deprives a man of life. Now life is common to all animals and plants. Hence for the same reason it is apparently a sin to slay dumb animals and plants.

Obj. 3. Further, In the Divine law a special punishment is not appointed save for a sin. Now a special punishment had to be inflicted, according to the Divine law, on one who killed another man's ox or sheep (Exod. xxii. I). Therefore the slaying of dumb animals is a sin.

On the contrary, Augustine says (*De Civ. Dei* i. 20): *When we hear it said, 'Thou shalt not kill,' we do not take it as referring to trees, for they have no sense, nor to irrational animals, because they have no fellowship with us. Hence it follows that the words, 'Thou shalt not kill' refer to the killing of a man.*

I answer that, There is no sin in using a thing for the purpose for which it is. Now the order of things is such that the imperfect are for the perfect, even as in the process of generation nature proceeds from imperfection to perfection. Hence it is that just as in the generation of a man there is first a living thing, then an animal, and lastly a man, so too things, like the plants, which merely have life, are all alike for animals, and all animals are for man. Wherefore it is not unlawful if man use plants for the good of animals, and animals for the good of man, as the Philosopher states (*Polit.* i. 3).

From *Summa Theologica,* literally translated by the English Dominican Fathers (Benziger Brothers, 1918), Part II, Question 64, Article 1, and Question 65, Article 3.

Now the most necessary use would seem to consist in the fact that animals use plants, and men use animals, for food, and this cannot be done unless these be deprived of life: wherefore it is lawful both to take life from plants for the use of animals, and from animals for the use of men. In fact this is in keeping with the commandment of God Himself: for it is written (Gen. i. 29, 30): *Behold I have given you every herb . . . and all trees . . . to be your meat, and to all beasts of the earth:* and again (*ibid.* ix. 3): *Everything that moveth and liveth shall be meat to you.*

Reply Obj. 1. According to the Divine ordinance the life of animals and plants is preserved not for themselves but for man. Hence, as Augustine says (*De Civ. Dei* i. 20), *by a most just ordinance of the Creator, both their life and their death are subject to our use.*

Reply Obj. 2. Dumb animals and plants are devoid of the life of reason whereby to set themselves in motion; they are moved, as it were by another, by a kind of natural impulse, a sign of which is that they are naturally enslaved and accommodated to the uses of others.

Reply Obj. 3. He that kills another's ox, sins, not through killing the ox, but through injuring another man in his property. Wherefore this is not a species of the sin of murder but of the sin of theft or robbery.

QUESTION 65, ARTICLE 3
Whether Irrational Creatures also Ought to Be Loved out of Charity

We proceed thus to the Third Article:

Objection 1. It would seem that irrational creatures also ought to be loved out of charity. For it is chiefly by charity that we are conformed to God. Now God loves irrational creatures out of charity, for He loves *all things that are* (Wis. xi. 25), and whatever He loves, He loves by Himself Who is charity. Therefore we also should love irrational creatures out of charity.

Obj. 2. Further, Charity is referred to God principally, and extends to other things as referable to God. Now just as the rational creature is referable to God, in as much as it bears the resemblance of image, so too, are the irrational creatures, in as much as they bear the resemblance of a trace. Therefore charity extends also to irrational creatures.

Obj. 3. Further, Just as the object of charity is God, so is the object of faith. Now faith extends to irrational creatures, since we believe that heaven and earth were created by God, that the fishes and birds were brought forth out of the waters, and animals that walk, and plants, out of the earth. Therefore charity extends also to irrational creatures.

On the contrary, The love of charity extends to none but God and our neighbour. But the word neighbour cannot be extended to irrational creatures, since they have no fellowship with man in the rational life. Therefore charity does not extend to irrational creatures.

I answer that, According to what has been stated above (Q. XIII., A. I) charity is a kind of friendship. Now the love of friendship is twofold: first, there is the love for the friend to whom our friendship is given, secondly, the love for those good things which we desire for our friend. With regard to the first, no irrational creature can be loved out of charity; and for three reasons. Two of these reasons refer in a general way to friendship, which cannot have an irrational creature for its object: first because friendship is towards one to whom we wish good things. While properly speaking, we cannot wish good things to an irrational creature, because it is not competent, properly speaking, to possess good, this being proper to the rational creature which, through its free-will, is the master of its disposal of the good it possesses. Hence the Philosopher says (*Phys.* ii. 6) that we do not speak of good or evil befalling suchlike things, except metaphorically. Secondly, because all friendship is based on some fellowship in life; since *nothing is so proper to friendship as to live together,* as the Philosopher proves (*Ethic* viii. 5). Now irrational creatures can have no fellowship in human life which is regulated by reason. Hence friendship with irrational creatures is impossible, except metaphorically speaking. The third reason is proper to charity, for charity is based on the fellowship of everlasting happiness, to which the irrational creature cannot attain. Therefore we cannot have the friendship of charity towards an irrational creature.

Nevertheless we can love irrational creatures out of charity, if we regard them as the good things that we desire for others, in so far, to wit, as we wish for their preservation, to God's honour and man's use; thus too does God love them out of charity.

Wherefore the *Reply* to the *First Objection* is evident.

Reply Obj. 2. The likeness by way of trace does not confer the capacity for everlasting life, whereas the likeness of image does: and so the comparison fails.

Reply Obj. 3. Faith can extend to all that is in any way true, whereas the friendship of charity extends only to such things as have a natural capacity for everlasting life; wherefore the comparison fails.

HUMPHRY PRIMATT
The Duty of Mercy

Love is the great Hinge upon which universal Nature turns. The Creation is a transcript of the divine Goodness; and every leaf in the Book of Nature reads us a lecture on the wisdom and benevolence of its great Author. The Philosopher, inured to study and contemplation, untainted with pride, and unbiased by prejudice, sees and acknowledges this truth as incontestable, that the Supreme Being is wise, and just, and good, and merciful . . . I shall therefore take it for granted, that as God is wise and good, all his works and appointments must be the effects of wisdom and goodness.

Upon this principle, every creature of God is good in its kind; that is, it is such as it ought to be. For to suppose otherwise, is to arraign the divine Wisdom for making it such as it is. And as every creature is good in its kind, and did not make itself what it is, but is such as it is solely by the will and appointment of God,—it follows, that whatever its perfections or defects may be, they cannot be owing to any merit or demerit in the creature itself, being, not prior, but consequential to its creation. There is not therefore in nature any foundation for pride on account of perfection, nor for contempt on account of defect. . .

. . . At the top of the scale of terrestrial animals we suppose *Man;* and when we contemplate the Perfections of *Body,* and the Endowments of *Mind,* which, we presume, He possesses above all the other animals, we justly suppose Him there constituted by his Maker. But, in this *highest* rank, we may observe degrees and differences, not only as to *stature, beauty, strength,* and *complexion,* but also as to those very

From *The Duty of Mercy and the Sin of Cruelty to Brute Animals* (Edinburgh: T. Constable, 2nd. ed., 1834), pp. 9–21.

Powers of the Mind, which so eminently distinguish Men from brutes. Yet, in *one* particular we all agree alike, from the most perfect to the most dull and deformed of men, and from him down to the vilest brute, that we are all susceptible and sensible of the misery of *Pain;* an evil, which, though necessary in itself, and wisely intended as the spur to incite us to self-preservation, and to the avoidance of destruction, we nevertheless are naturally averse to, and shrink back at the apprehension of it. Superiority of rank or station exempts no creature from the sensibility of pain,—nor does inferiority render the feelings thereof the less exquisite. Pain is pain, whether it be inflicted on man or on beast; and the creature that suffers it, whether man or beast, being sensible of the misery of it whilst it lasts, suffers *Evil;* and the sufferance of evil, unmeritedly, provokedly, where no offence has been given; and no good end can possibly be answered by it, but merely to exhibit power or gratify malice, is *Cruelty* and Injustice in him that occasions it.

I presume there is no *Man of feeling,* that has any idea of *Justice,* but would confess upon the principles of reason and common *sense,* that if he were to be put to *unnecessary* and *unmerited* pain by another man, his tormentor would do him an act of *injustice;* and from a sense of the injustice in his *own* case, now that He is the sufferer, he must naturally infer, that if he were to put *another* man of feeling to the same unnecessary and unmerited pain which He now suffers, the injustice in himself to the other would be exactly the same as the injustice in his tormentor to Him. Therefore the man of feeling and justice will not put another man to unmerited pain, because he will not do that to another, which he is unwilling should be done to himself. Nor will he take any advantage of his own superiority of *strength,* or of the accidents of *fortune,* to abuse them to the oppression of his inferior; because he knows that in the article of *feeling* all men are equal; and that the differences of strength or station are as much the gifts and appointments of God, as the differences of understanding, colour, or stature. Superiority of rank or station may give ability to communicate happiness, and seems so intended; but it can give no right to inflict unnecessary or unmerited pain. A *wise* man would impeach his own wisdom, and be unworthy of the blessing of a good understanding, if he were to infer from thence that he had a right to despise or make game of a *fool,* or put him to any degree of pain. The folly of the fool ought rather to excite his compassion, and demands the wise man's care and attention to one that cannot take care of himself.

It has pleased God the Father of all men, to cover some men with white skins, and others with black skins; but as there is neither merit nor demerit in complexion, the *white* man, notwithstanding the barbarity of custom and prejudice, can have no right, by virtue of his *colour*, to enslave and tyrannize over a *black* man; nor has a *fair* man any right to despise, abuse, and insult a *brown* man. Nor do I believe that a *tall* man, by virtue of his *stature*, has any legal right to trample a *dwarf* under his foot. For, whether a man is wise or foolish, white or black, fair or brown, tall or short, and I might add, *rich* or *poor*, for it is no more a man's choice to be poor, than it is to be a fool, or a dwarf, or black, or tawny,—such he is by God's appointment; and, abstractedly considered, is neither a subject for pride, nor an object of contempt. Now, if amongst men, the differences of their powers of the mind, and of their complexion, stature, and accidents of fortune, do not give any one man a right to abuse or insult any other man on account of these differences; for the same reason, a man can have no natural right to abuse and torment a beast, merely because a beast has not the *mental* powers of a man. For, such as the man is, he is but as God made him; and the very same is true of the beast. Neither of them can lay claim to any intrinsic *Merit*, for being such as they are; for, before they were created, it was impossible that either of them could deserve; and at their creation, their shapes, perfections or defects were invariably fixed, and their bounds set which they cannot pass. And being such, neither more nor less than God made them, there is no more demerit in a beast being a beast, than there is merit in a man being a man; that is, there is neither merit nor demerit in either of them.

A *Brute* is an animal no less sensible of pain than a Man. He has similar nerves and organs of sensation; and his cries and groans, in case of violent impressions upon his body, though he cannot utter his complaints by speech, or human voice, are as strong indications to us of his sensibility of pain, as the cries and groans of a *human* being, whose language we do not understand. Now, as pain is what we are all averse to, our own sensibility of pain should teach us to commiserate it in others, to alleviate it if possible, but never wantonly or unmeritedly to inflict it. As the differences amongst men in the above particulars are no bars to their feelings, so neither does the difference of the *shape* of a brute from that of a man exempt the brute from feeling; at least, we have no ground to suppose it. But shape or figure is as much the appointment of God, as complexion or stature. And if the difference of complexion or stature does not convey to one man a right to despise and abuse another man, the difference of shape between a man and a brute, cannot give to a man any right to abuse and torment a brute.

HENRY DAVIS
Animals Have No Rights

Animals have no rights; they can give us nothing freely nor understand our claims. We have no duties of justice or charity towards them, but as they are God's creatures, we have duties concerning them and the right use we make of them. In the treatment of animals we may not give way to rage or impatience, nor invade our neighbour's right of ownership in them, nor may we give way to cruelty in the treatment of animals, nor wantonly misuse or abuse them, for this disposes us to dull the fine edge of pity and to be cruel to human beings. God, therefore, for this reason, forbade the Jews to muzzle the threshing ox (Deut. 25, 4) or to seethe the kid in its mother's milk (Deut. 14, 21)[1] To be wantonly cruel to beasts is to increase one's tendency to cruelty, but reasonable sport is not cruelty for its own sake, and the pain of animals may be permitted, as may also their suffering in vivisection, for the sake of useful experiment and the increase of knowledge. The contrary tendency of lavishing affection on beasts—not wrong in itself—may lead, and often does lead to the neglect of one's duty to a neighbour in need, and to an altogether

---

From *Moral and Pastoral Theology*, vol. II, *Commandments of God; Precepts of the Church* (London: Sheed and Ward, 5th ed. 1946), pp. 258–59.
[1]The version: "in its mother's fat" is defensible, but does not affect the argument; cf. also the application of the text by S. Paul (1 Cor. 9, 9; 1 Tim. 5, 8). The meaning of Deut. 14, 21 may be that God forbade the magical and superstitious rite of sprinkling the fruit trees in spring with the milk (or fat) in which the kid had been boiled, or sacrifice to the Phœnician deity of fertility.

false sentimentality.[2] Nevertheless, S. Thomas well says, since brute animals can feel, there can arise in man a feeling of pity towards animals in pain, and thereby man is disposed to feel pity for fellow-men; therefore, God wishing to recall the Jewish people—naturally prone to cruelty—to a sense of pity, forbade certain appearances of cruelty in respect of dumb animals. One who seethes the kid in its mother's milk that he may eat its flesh would appear heartless in using for his own convenience what, by nature, was intended for the nourishment of the offspring.

Justice, being a virtue that regards actual rights, requires an exact balancing, so that absolute equality between what is due and what is given is to be established and maintained. It has, therefore, an objective mean which no other virtue has; all other moral virtues regard the reasonable use of appetites, and they are a mean between two extremes. The theological virtues are not a mean between extremes, for we cannot exceed in Faith, Hope, or Charity. The mean of justice in, v.g., buying and selling, is the exact just price, which is the same for every man; whereas such virtues as temperance or fortitude will incline men to different acts, and their virtuous mean has reference, not to external objects, but to the man himself, so that the mean is a rational not an objective mean, and what would be temperate or brave in one man could be excessive or foolhardy in another, and what would be temperate at one time could be the contrary at another.

ANDREW LINZEY
The Theos-Rights of Animals*

For Catholic theology, steeped as it is in scholasticism, animals have no moral status. If we have any duties to them, they are indirect, owing to some human interest involved. Animals are not rational like

[2]cf. S. Th., S., 1, 2, q. 102, a. 6, ad 8: 2. 2, q. 25, a. 3, where he says that though there can be no true love of friendship—which implies a real communication of favours—between man and brute animals, nevertheless, we can love irrational creatures in so far as we can wish them to be preserved in existence for God's honour and man's use.

*From Christianity and the Rights of Animals (London: SPCK and New York: Crossroad, 1987), pp. 68–69 and 94–98.

human beings and therefore cannot possess immortal souls. Even the most hard-boiled scholastic would now probably admit that animals feel *some* pain but, if so, their pain is not regarded as morally relevant or truly analogous to human pain. In consequence, animals have no rights. 'Zoophilists often lose sight of the end for which animals, irrational creatures were created by God, viz., the service and use of man,' argues the *Dictionary of Moral Theology*. 'In fact, Catholic moral doctrine teaches that animals have no rights on the part of man.'

It is in this context that we have to understand the present discussion, both philosophical and theological, about animal rights. It is the persistence of scholastic Catholicism which inevitably makes rights the issue it is. When one considers the wealth of positive insight and prescription within the Christian tradition about animals, it is surely disconcerting that these negative influences should have held, and continue to hold, such prominence. The issue of animal rights is not some concession to secular thinking within theological circles but simply the latest stage of a debate that began hundreds of years ago. John Foster, writing in 1856 (against William Wyndham's opposition to early animal welfare legislation), complains of our being taught 'from our very infancy, that the pleasurable and painful sensations of animals are not worth our care; that it is not of the smallest consequence what they are made to suffer, so that they are not rendered less serviceable to us by their suffering . . . that in short they have *no rights* as sentient beings, existing for their own sakes as well as for ours'. If today people concerned for animals prefer the term 'animal rights' to 'animal lovers' or 'animal welfare', they are, consciously or unconsciously, linking themselves to a historic debate which is by no means concluded. It is not without significance that the 'National Catholic Society for Animal Welfare' in the United States has now become the 'International Society for Animal Rights' . . .

The argument that Christians should continue to utilize rights language and extend its use to animals needs to be subject to three qualifications. The first is that Christians should not claim that rights theory is the *only* theory of moral obligation. To the objection that rights theory may in some ways be deficient or inadequate, we have to reply that no one theory can possibly do justice to the complete range of themes and insights from within the Christian tradition. If this sounds like something less than a complete endorsement of rights, then it needs to be considered whether any moral theory, either of divine command or human duty, can claim to be the only possible one from a theological perspective. What we are characterizing in Christian moral theory is nothing less than the will of God. Divine will is undubitably complex, even subtle and possibly developing. When we opt for the language of theos-rights, we do it with necessary reserve and caution, not because this theory is necessarily more difficult than any other, but because *all* moral theory is theologically problematic. Whenever we move from any straightforward indentification of God's will with a particular imperative in a specific situation to the work of characterization, that is, to characterizing and systematizing God's will in general terms, then we are faced with the continual danger of over-simplification. Of course God's will can be simple, but it can also be remarkably mysterious. Even Karl Barth, that robust defender of divine commands, accepts that it is not an easy task for Christian ethics to tell us what God's will is. By our intellect and language we are always, through characterization, *approximating* God's will for his creation. Though theos-rights may be the best way of characterizing the divine imperative, it does not follow that we must hold that such theory is in every way adequate or that in God's good time some new form of theo-moral characterization may not better it. Doubtless our own moral reasoning, however inspired, is like the rest of creaturely life itself, in need of redemption.

The second qualification is that rights language cannot claim to be comprehensive. I mean by this that it cannot exclude other forms of moral language and insight. Talk of generosity, respect, duty, sacrifice and mercy as well as rights is essential. It may be that animal rightists have so stressed the importance of rights as a concept that they have neglected talk of compassion and respect. It may be, but for Christians my hope is that we can take such language for granted . . . One function of rights language is to provide checks and markers *en route* to living a less exploitative way of life with other creatures. This is surely a valuable function, but by itself does not provide a wholistic or sufficiently positive interpretation of the divine imperative. In other words, Christian ethics is not simply about preventing the worst but promoting the good. For the elaboration, definition and pursuit of the good with animals we require more terms than rights language can provide. It may be in some situations that we should accord animals more than that which rights theory may strictly give them, and err, if we do, on the generous side. For generosity is surely an important notion and rights language must be careful not to limit it even if we cannot persuade ourselves that it has the status of a declared 'ought'. To those who feel that we should not just respect the rights of say, sparrows, but actually seek loving, caring relationships with them, the rights view offers no obstacle. To those who feel called to especially heroic acts of mercy and self-sacrifice towards particular kinds of animals, the rights view again advances no objection. There will always be people, inspired by the life of Christ and the many saints, who feel moved to morally heroic, sacrificial acts. But, of course, it is not to these people that rights language is normally directed. In short: in fighting for the positive good of animals and humans, Christians will need to utilize a varied vocabulary. All that is claimed here is that rights language should be part of the necessary armoury.

Thirdly, we need to reiterate that the rights of which we speak are properly and solely God's rights. He alone wills that givenness of life which makes them possible; he alone charges man with the stewardship of them; and he alone can in the end properly guarantee them. One conclusion follows from this: as our knowledge of God increases by the power of the Spirit, so may our knowledge of the nature of his will and therefore our understanding of his rights. Some theologians regard rights terminology as far too static a way of describing God's relationship with what is, after all, a dynamic and open creation. But theos-rights are not necessarily as static as may be their secular counterparts. The possibility of change is inherent in the fact that our understanding of God develops, whether for better or worse. It may be that God's Spirit has much more to show us about the nature and variety of valuable beings in his universe. Again it may be that God's Spirit will move us to a new understanding of our place in the universe such as to make previous controversies about individual salvation in the Reformation period appear trivial by comparison. It may be or may not be. In either case it is our responsibility to recognize God's rights in creation and to champion them.

The question may not unreasonably be posed: What then is the overwhelming advantage of rights theory which justifies it in spite of these serious qualifications? The answer may be obvious. Rights language insists that we envisage the claims of animals in analogous terms to those of other, human, beings. This is why [some, perhaps many,] hesitate or reject animal rights: they deny that the claims of other Spirit-filled breathing beings can be in any real sense analogous to human claims. In the issue of animal rights, perhaps more than any other, Christians confront the limitations of their own scholastic history. Scholasticism has for centuries regarded animals as 'things'. The consequence is unsurprising: animals have been treated as things. For all the intellectual sophistication of the arguments against animal rights, one quite practical consideration is frequently dominant. *To accept that animals have rights must involve accepting that they should be treated differently from the way most of them are treated at present.* Explicitly acknowledging that animals have rights involves accepting that they have a fundamental moral status. If they have no such status, they cannot make claims; and if they have no claims, they can have no rights. Perhaps in the light of their traditions, it is easier for Christians to see the historic significance of the debate about rights than many of their secular contemporaries. Those who deny rights to the non-human do well to ponder the history of what rightlessness has meant for animals; if the opposing arguments do not convince, it is invariably because they do not want to accept that most animals are treated unjustly.

Here is the rub. To grant animals rights is to accept that they can be wronged. According to theos-rights what we do to animals is not simply a matter of taste or convenience or philanthropy. When we speak of animal rights we conceptualize what is objectively owed to animals as a matter of justice by virtue of their Creator's right. Animals can be wronged because their Creator can be wronged in his creation. Some philosophers are still adamant that it is possible to provide a theoretical framework for the better treatment of animals without recourse to the notion of rights. It may be possible in this way to provide for something better, but how much remains historically open. Perhaps through utilitarian calculation it may be possible to prevent some of the worst possible from happening to animals, but will their status be fundamentally changed thereby? Language and history are against those who want the better treatment of animals and who also want to deny the legitimacy of the language of rights. For how can we reverse centuries of scholastic tradition if we still accept the cornerstone of that tradition, namely that all but humans are morally rightless? If the foregoing appears to invoke the dubious need for penitence in formulating ethical theory, it can only be replied that repentance is a cardinal duty for Christians. If calculation of the consequences is to be allowed some say in moral assessments, then we have to accept that Christians have good reason for looking at what their own theology has created and, in the light of this, theologizing afresh.

But apart from this obvious practical need to reverse centuries of neglect, theos-rights makes sense of a whole range of crucial theological insights—three in particular. The first is the sheer giveness of created reality. Unless God is really indifferent to creation, those beings whose lives are filled with his Spirit have special value and therefore require special protection. The second is the need to witness to the electing power of God in his covenant relationship. Man and animals form a moral community, not only because of their common origin, but because God elects them within a special relationship with himself. Catholic scholasticism has denied the possibility of a moral community with brutes. 'Nothing irrational can be the object of the Christian virtue of neighbourly love, charity', writes Bernard Häring. 'Nothing irrational,' he tells us, 'is capable of the beautifying friendship with God'. What scholasticism here neglects or disputes, theos-rights assumes. Because men and brutes are elected by God, we form one covenanted community of Spirit-filled beings before him. Thirdly, the perspective of theos-rights gives meaning to the long tradition of rating man's God-like powers in creation. According to theos-rights, humans must exercise power, but only towards God's end. The unique significance of man in this respect consists in his capacity to perceive God's will and to actualize it within his own life. Man is 'to commit himself to the divine task', argues Edward Carpenter, 'of lifting up creation, redeeming those orders of which he forms part, and directing them towards their end'.

Those who deny theos-rights to animals need to show how it is that they can give sufficient reality to these insights without participating in the moral neglect of the non-human which still characterizes continuing elements within the Christian tradition.

RICHARD GRIFFITHS
A Critique of Animal Rights

Animal rightists often refer to a passage from Jeremy Bentham: 'The day may come when the rest of the animal creation may acquire those *rights* which never could have been withheld from them but by the hand of tyranny . . . the question is not can they *reason?* Nor can they *talk?* But, can they *suffer?*'[1] It was inevitable that once the Utilitarians made pleasure and pain the criteria for moral judgments all sentient beings should be granted moral status and the right to be free from unnecessary suffering. It is a measure of the debt owed to Bentham that the modern animal welfare movement has a strongly utilitarian cast. And this has stood it in good stead, because this kind of moral reasoning (the good is that which produces the least pain and the most pleasure) is what most people use.

I think that the rightist's case is at its strongest when this argument is used. Many animals feel pain, and seek to avoid it. Most men of western cultures instinctively shrink from hurting animals wantonly, and so the welfare movement makes effective use of harrowing photographs of animals being hunted, experimented on, slaughtered, and so on. Is this emotional reaction to animal pain ethically sound? Frey has pointed out that the ethical relevance of sentiency is assumed by animal rightists.[2] But it is not at all obvious why the capacity to feel pain should be the basis for extending rights from men to animals. The fact that pain is a universal human experience does not make it a valid basis for the possession of human rights. What if a person is congenitally insensitive to pain? Would he forfeit his rights?

We need to remember that rightists do not use sentiency as a basis for conferring the right merely to be free of unnecessary pain, but for conferring a wide range of rights, including the right not to be *humanely* slaughtered for food. Even if it were granted that all pain is intrinsically

From *The Human Use of Animals* (Nottingham: Grove Books, 1982), pp. 15–18.
[1]Bentham, *Introduction to the Principles of Morals and Legislation* (London, 1789), Ch. XVII Para. 4. footnote.
[2]D. Paterson and R. D. Ryder (eds.), *Animals' Rights—A Symposium* (Fontwell, Sussex: Centaur Press, 1979), pp. 109–110.

evil . . . I do not see that this would make it an adequate bridge whereby a wide range of rights could be extended to animals. Further, pain is not the only experience with intrinsic moral value: if other experiences have moral value, why should they not be used to confer rights—why pick on sentiency?

Suffering is a subjective experience. It is essentially private, and therefore difficult to study . . . Some animals can undoubtedly suffer . . . Even so, there is as yet no reliable way of measuring *how much* an animal is suffering. This is important, because the right to freedom from suffering is not to freedom from *all* suffering, but from *disproportionate* or *unjust* suffering. To determine this involves calculating the amount of suffering involved. And this [is] impossible within the limits required.

ANIMAL RIGHTS AND THE NATURALISTIC FALLACY

David Hume has pointed out that there is a logical fallacy involved when a person attempts to deduce moral conclusions from non-moral premises: he ignores the logical gulf between statements of fact and moral judgments, between 'is' and 'ought'. If Hume (and those who have adopted his stance) is correct, then there is a fallacy involved when the animal rightist says, 'Man *is* evolved from lower forms of life, therefore lower forms of life *ought* to be treated in certain ways'; or, 'Some animals *are* intelligent, therefore they *ought* to possess rights'; or, 'Animals *are* capable of suffering, therefore they *ought* to be spared it'. In fact all naturalistic philosophies (and Utilitarianism, which is the dominant philosophy of the animal welfare movement, is one of them) tend to commit the naturalistic fallacy.

The fallacy is a *logical* one. There may be excellent *moral* reasons why I should not do what another dislikes, but the statement, 'I ought not to cause him pain', cannot be deduced logically from, 'He dislikes pain'. So, although the naturalistic fallacy does not negate naturalistic ethics entirely, it does show that ethics cannot be grounded exclusively in the facts of human (or animal) experience. These facts may be relevant to the application of moral principles, but the principles themselves cannot be drawn from them alone. . .

With regard to . . . sentiency, while it is granted that many animals are . . . sentient, I have already tried to show that it is next to impossible to know how . . . sentient they are. The bald facts that they can . . . feel does not in itself achieve much: what we need to know is . . . how much they feel if we are going to have the facts that are needed for our ethics. It seems to be a common assumption among animal welfarists that we know a good deal more facts about animal psychology and pathology than is actually the case. Ethics cannot be built on opinions or theories alone.

WHERE DO RIGHTS END?

Animal rightists tend to dismiss the criticism that their arguments are open to *reductio ad absurdum* with the comment that such an attack is not worth arguing against. This is a mistake on their part, because those who use this attack use it in all seriousness, and suspect that the welfarists have no reasoned answer to give. In fact, welfarists do seem to find it a problem to prove why it is that not everything should have rights. The point is best illustrated by reference to an article by Brigid Brophy, an old campaigner for animal rights. 'Plants', she says, 'are individuals, they are sensitive, and they certainly demonstrate an instinctual will to live—that is, they assert in instinctual terms a right to live'. But, she adds, plants do not have a central nervous system, and goes on: 'I think what I think is that, providing it is not threatening our life, we have no right to extinguish an individuality that has been formed by negotiating the world by the agency of a nervous system.' Why draw the line here? What has a central nervous system to do with rights? Miss Brophy seems to have erected an entirely arbitrary sticking point in order to avoid bringing everything into the class of right-possessors. She does not offer any sound reason for picking on possession of a nervous system as a basis for the extension of rights to animals.

The weakness of her argument indicates the problem that once the distinctive nature of man, compared with the animals, is lost in the attempt to extend rights from man to the animals, any attempt to exclude anything with life (or even anything that exists) from holding rights looks rather arbitrary. And yet the welfarist is forced to use something which can act as a 'sticking point' otherwise his position becomes ridiculous. He also runs another risk: as soon as his 'sticking point' has been erected, he must be careful not to relegate everything beyond it to a kind of moral limbo where duty ceases because rights can no longer be claimed.

TOM REGAN
A Reply to Griffiths

Logic has its limits. For example, by itself logic cannot establish that our alphabet has twenty six letters. But once one concedes this much, then logic does speak out sternly against the assertion that the last letter, Z, is the thirty fourth letter, or that, as the last one, it is the eighteenth. Logically speaking, people are inconsistent when they affirm what cannot possibly be true; so anyone who affirms both that our alphabet has twenty six different letters and that the last one, Z, is the eighteenth (or the twenty fourth, etc.) is inconsistent. Among mortal sins, inconsistency is not the worst; among intellectual failings, it is not the least. No one who seeks truth speaks in its favor.

Arguments for animal rights often are rooted in appeals to consistency. Richard Griffiths seems not to have seen this. Unlike Cartesian critics of animal rights, Griffiths concedes what surely is true, that many nonhuman animals suffer pain. That much conceded, he then asks whether it logically follows that those animals have a right not to be made to suffer. Because he believes that "values" do not logically follow from "facts", Griffiths thinks that this kind of argument for animal rights fails to pass muster.

On this point Griffiths is correct. And if proponents of animal rights could do no better than this, Griffiths could rest content in the belief that he has refuted them. But they can, and he can't.

Imagine that a human being has been fiercely beaten, almost to the point of death. Imagine, further, that this individual posed no threat to others and was guilty of no wrong. The beating, we are to suppose, was unprovoked and undeserved.

These are the (supposed) facts. And from these facts alone, of course, it does not follow logically that any wrong has been done. Nor does logic by itself, apart from these facts, yield this result. And yet all of us, it is safe to assume, would agree that the beating was wrong. Why it was, remains to be discussed, and our agreement at this basic level— our agreeing, that is, that the beating was wrong—might give rise to deep, protracted disagreements at other levels, including the one where we explore why it was wrong. But thought begins where it can, and in this case there is no better place to begin than with our shared judgment: The beating was wrong.

Now, suppose the victim of the beating was not a human being but a horse or a dog. If there was some morally relevant difference between horses and dogs, on the one hand, and human beings, on the other, it would be possible logically to affirm that the beating was wrong when the victim was a human being and deny this in those cases when the victim was a dog or horse. But it is not possible to cite a morally relevant difference. The mere fact of species difference is insufficient, and the importance many people attach to some human capacities— for example, higher level intellectual or aesthetic traits—is similarly deficient. If we suppose that the human victim happened to be severely mentally handicapped, we would not be tempted to alter our judgment about the wrongness of the beating. How much less, then, can we avoid this same judgment in those cases when the victim, whether horse or dog, has the same or greater intellectual and other capacities as the unfortunate human.

Griffiths might protest: Although we do know that horses and dogs suffer, we do not know *how much* they do. This seems true, at least up to a point. But it is no less true, up to that same point, when we consider the extent of human suffering. How much do the newborn suffer? Or children of a year or less? Or the permanently retarded? Who can know with certainty? And yet the existence of our ignorance in this matter would not lead us to qualify our moral judgment about the beating, if the victim was a human infant or baby, or a permanently (and severely) retarded human being. If we are to be consistent, there-fore, our uncertainty about animal suffering, to the extent that this uncertainty is valid, cannot make any greater (or lesser) difference. That uncertainty, in a word, turns out to be morally indecisive, if not irrelevant.

It is out of respect for logical consistency, therefore, that we come to recognize the necessity of making the same judgments about the morality of how nonhuman animals are treated in the imagined case as we do when a human being is the victim. Rationally considered, we are no more at liberty to make different judgments in this situation than we can when, having acknowledged that out alphabet has twenty-six different letters, we are asked to assign a numerical place to the last one, Z. Of course, by itself the preceding does not prove that it is wrong to beat horses or dogs. And neither does it prove that it is wrong to do this in the case of human beings. What it does prove is that if it is wrong to do this in the latter case, then it is wrong to do it in relevantly similar circumstances in the former cases too.

Even less does the preceding prove that humans or other animals have rights. Whether either or both do is a long, difficult story that can't be recounted here. On this occasion we must be content to make the following observations.

To say that a way of behaving is wrong is not to say why it is. Now, one way of trying to illuminate why it is wrong to beat a human being, in the ways imagined, is to couch the explanation in the language of moral rights. For example, one might believe that human beings have a fundamental moral right to be treated with respect and that for one to be beaten in the imagined ways is wrong because it violates this fundamental right.

Suppose this is correct—a very large supposition, to be sure! It then is possible to ask whether this way of accounting for the moral wrong done when the victim of the beating is a human being can be extended to those cases when the victims are nonhuman animals. Assuming that it can—and I, for one, believe it can—then we again have an argument from consistency which shows, if it is sound, that the case for animal rights is at least as compelling as the case for human rights. Because Griffiths fails adequately to apprehend the arguments from consistency at work in the literature he discusses critically, his criticisms skim the surface and do not plumb the depths of the best arguments for animal rights.

Griffiths likely will lodge a second protest at this point. Whereas the point of his previous objection was that arguments for animal rights prove too little, the point of the present objection is that they prove too much. If animals have rights, why is the same not true of plants? And if the same is true of plants, then the animal rights' position succumbs to a *reductio* of its own devising.

But Griffiths surely is mistaken here. The reason we would give for objecting to the beating administered to a human victim is not that that individual is alive and biologically intact; the reasons, rather, are that the beating hurts, and that the victim has done nothing to provoke or deserve the injury. To the extent that we respect consistency, therefore, we will recognize the necessity of making the same moral judgment in morally relevant cases. Thus will we make this same judgment when the victim is a horse or dog. And thus will we refrain from making this same judgment when the "victim" is an asparagus or ge-ranium. For there is no plausible basis for believing that these plants experience pain (are hurt) when they are "beaten", and every good reason to believe that this is true in the case of these animals. Contrary to Griffiths, therefore, the animal rights argument, rooted in appeals to consistency, does not lead to the unhappy result that "everything should have rights".

STEPHEN R. L. CLARK
Positive and Negative Rights

Suppose that non-human animals are such that no compact can be made with them: nothing can be reasonably expected of them whether of commission or omission. Suppose that they cannot be given 'moral credit' for any of their actions, or rather for their behaviour: does it follow that they are owed no respect at all? Surely the reverse—it is impertinent to be angry or indignant with beasts, as also with babies, and for that very reason they must be given greater toleration. I will assume for a moment that animals are still to be reckoned sentient: what is lacking in them is any capacity to act on principle, any capacity to call something their own or another's on the basis of agreed codes of conduct. I do not believe that this can be true in any clear sense—the very songs of birds are, in a sense, declarations of an agreed prop-erty—but I am willing to concede that there are important differences, or may be: animals perhaps cannot decide to *exchange* their 'property', though even this is debatable. It is likely enough, though I suspect often false, that they do not stop to think. Must they then be denied all rights? Are they fair game? Positive rights, let us suppose, they do not have: they have no *right* to claim any share of the world's or of our resources, because they are unable to *claim* such a share. They may of course seek to get it, but they cannot be said to be *claiming* it, because (we are supposing) they have no notion of a claim.

Now on absolute terms it is plausible to say that nothing has any

From *The Moral Status of Animals* (Oxford: The Clarendon Press, 1977), pp. 27–29.

positive rights: all is gift, whether to us, or to jackdaws, or to the young lions that seek their prey from God. But such a philosophy is obviously not the best basis upon which to erect our present tyranny . . .

But let us agree that we are not required to go out of our way to supply the necessities of animals, that they have no positive claim on us . . . Does it follow because a beggar has no *right* to our money (if he has not, and if in any clear sense it *is* ours) that we are therefore in the right if we take away what little he seems to have? Surely not: and neither does it follow from the 'rightlessness' of animals in the present sense that we have or should be expected to have any rights to their flesh or their service, or are in the right if we torment them . . .

Let no one think that factory farms are something strange and new: they are but the logical conclusions of our old iniquity. An iniquity that even Barth recognizes: 'Man must not murder an animal. He can only kill it, knowing that it does not belong to him, but to God, and that in killing it he surrenders it to God in order to receive it back from Him as something he needs and desires.' Barth's error is to suppose more necessary than is.

In short, perhaps animals can make no rightful claim on land, on food, on the air they breathe, on human care, on their own bodies. It does not follow that *we* can make any claim on them that our fancy pictures. If they have no positive rights, yet they have negative. A drowning man has no absolute, unfocused *right* to life, nor even (in law) a right to be rescued by whoever passes by: it does not follow that he had no right not-to-be-pushed-in—which is simply to say that no-one else had or has the right so to push him.

Part Five

◆

PRACTICAL ISSUES

Introduction to Part Five

We turn finally to the practical issues. Our opening biblical selection focuses on animal sacrifices and killing for food. The Bible appears to offer us contrasting insights into the morality and efficacy of animal sacrifice. On the one hand, Genesis and Exodus in particular, see the institution of animal sacrifice as the result of divine command, as a means of moral reparation. On the other hand, some of the Psalms and the Prophetic books are uneasy with the practice, partly we may suppose because of its inefficacy and partly because of its inappropriateness. When we turn to the New Testament, however, we find Jesus departing from sacrificial practice. Jesus and his followers do not sacrifice animals. The incident in the Temple might well indicate a moral rejection of the sacrificial system in total. In any case Jesus certainly appears to insist, like the Prophets before him, upon the primacy of offering love as a moral sacrifice rather than the blood of animals.

Again when it come to the morality of killing for food, the biblical material is also ambiguous. Genesis 1 envisages man living in peace with creation and a vegetarian diet is commanded. Genesis 9, however, allows man to eat animals after the fall and the flood on the condition that the blood (symbolising the life given by God) is not also consumed. The Prophetic writers, such as Isaiah and Hosea, clearly see carnivourousness as a departure from God's original intention and look forward to a future time when creation will live at peace again. When we turn to the New Testament, we find the Deuteronomic view that certain classes of animals are 'unclean' is upturned by St Peter's vision where he is commanded to 'kill and eat' but also told that 'What God has cleansed, you must not call common.' Paradoxically the vision underlines the value of God's creatures whilst allowing Peter to kill

147

them. Jesus certainly ate fish and possibly meat (depending upon the view taken of the Passover meal), while John the Baptist was probably a vegetarian.

I. ANIMAL EXPERIMENTATION

Lord Soper begins by offering a general critique of experimentation from a Christian standpoint, but on the central issue of whether pain can sometimes justifiably be inflicted on animals seems to come down on the affirmative side. 'I would not rule out the necessity, in certain circumstances, of even imposing a certain amount of pain on animals, if and when it seemed to be the only realisable method' of benefitting humanity. A much stronger view is taken by John Canon McCarthy who reflects the traditional Roman Catholic position that animals have no rights. In consequence whilst 'useless or unnecessary' experimentation is to be opposed, it is 'lawful' to inflict even 'severe pain' in research that may help humanity. In short: accidental abuses there may be, but the practice is basically justifiable.

In utter contrast, C. S. Lewis argues that the practice of vivisection is 'sinister' and should be abolished. After establishing that the infliction of unnecessary pain is an 'evil,' he maintains that 'no argument for experiments on animals can be found which is not also an argument for experiments on inferior men.' Lewis is particularly troubled by the knowledge that vivisection is performed by non-Christians who see the human species as simply the cleverest of the anthropoids in which case there can be no morally relevant distinction between animals and humans, and both will ultimately fall victim to 'non-moral utilitarianism.' Cardinal Manning also agrees that vivisection should be abolished. His treatment of this subject is radically unlike other Roman Catholic approaches. Although he accepts that animals are not 'moral persons' and that we do not have direct duties to them because of this, Manning argues that we have a prior duty to the Creator of animals. 'Our obligation and moral duty is to Him who made them, and if we wish to know the broad outline of our obligation . . . I say at once that it is His nature, and His perfections, and, among those perfections, one is most profoundly that of eternal mercy.' God, according to Manning, gave humans dominion in order that they may show his mercy over lesser creatures. Vivisection, however, is 'torture.'

II. FUR-TRAPPING

The statement by the Anglican and Roman Catholic Bishops in Northern Canada expresses 'solidarity with the aboriginal peoples of the North who are engaged in a struggle to save fur trapping as a way of life.' The anti-fur movement is, according to the Bishops, threatening to destroy their ancient way of life and with it their own 'deeply felt cultural and spiritual traditions.' In addition they argue that aboriginal hunters are 'ecologically responsible,' practising conservation wherever possible. In reply, Andrew Linzey complains that the Bishops simply do not address the enormous amount of suffering that trapping causes fur-bearing creatures every year. Linzey argues that cultural identity is important but cannot be regarded as morally sufficient to justify prolonged and widespread suffering. It is an open question, according to Linzey, whether 'the exploitation of crimes by indigenous cultures is in fact the result of our exploitation of them for commercial profit.'

III. HUNTING FOR SPORT

Two Catholic saints offer opposing views on hunting. St Francis de Sales describes hunting as one of those 'innocent recreations that we may always make good use of.' Hunting, like other amusements such as tennis or backgammon, is morally innocent. Not so, according to the Utopians of St Thomas More's imagining. The joys of hunting are described in *Utopia* as 'senseless delights.' The killing of animals 'for pleasure' is regarded as morally reprehensible. This last point is developed at length by Edward Carpenter in his analysis of the moral aspect of hunting. Whilst it is true that 'natural' life has a parasitical element to it, Christians should regard this as a result of the 'fallenness' of creation. Consequently, according to Carpenter, the task of Christians should be to cooperate in the process of redemption which involves lifting up 'the whole order of creation into a higher estate . . . more noble, more divine.' Hunting represents a lack of reverence and moral irresponsibility. James Whisker, on the other hand, surveys the practice of hunting in the Judaeo-Christian tradition and comes to the opposite conclusion. 'One who wishes to condemn hunting as immoral,' he concludes, 'must look to authorities other than traditional religious works for support.' Not one passage in the Bible condemns hunting, maintains Whisker. 'The entire Judaeo-Christian synthesis suggests that it is quite correct for man to hunt if he wishes to do so.'

IV. INTENSIVE FARMING

Ruth Harrison begins by illustrating the psychological suffering that animals may have to undergo in intensive systems of farming. Traditional definitions of cruelty, she argues, are insufficient as a means of measuring the inevitable deprivations that most farm animals experience in large systems of farming. A new kind of farming which involves respect for animals is required. This idea is developed by E.F. Schumacher who insists that animals must be regarded as ends-in-themselves rather than as simply means-to-our-ends. To support this view he draws upon the Judaeo-Christian tradition as offering a sense that animals have an irreducible value in themselves and form part of a wholly valuable creation. 'It is a metaphysical error,' he argues, 'likely to produce the gravest practical consequences, to equate 'car' and 'animal' on account of their utility.'

Karl Barth, however, drives us back to the basic question whether man's lordship over the animal 'consists in his self-evident freedom to take its life in the service of his own ends.' His answer is basically in the affirmative, although he maintains that man must always act with responsibility and 'under the pressure of necessity.' Barth's justification of killing for food invokes the Old Testament notion of sacrifice and the idea of man as high priest of creation. 'The killing of animals,' he argues, 'when performed with the permission of God and by His command, is a priestly act of eschatological character.' Moreover, '(i)t can be accomplished with a good conscience only as we glance backward to creation and forward to the consummation as the boundaries of the sphere in which alone there can be any question of its necessity.'

And yet Barth does not deny the moral basis of vegetarianism. '(I)t is not only understandable but necessary that the affirmation of this whole possibility should always have been accompanied by a radical protest against it.' Vegetarianism, it seems, is God's will, but not yet. It represents 'a wanton anticipation of what is described by Isaiah 11 and Romans 8 as existence in the new aeon for which we hope.'

V. KILLING FOR FOOD

Barth's ambiguous espousal of vegetarianism brings us naturally to our final section. Is it God's will that man should be a leaf-eating herbivore or a flesh-eating omnivore? Leo Tolstoy begins our section by describing his own conversion to vegetarianism. He argues that killing for food is simply unnecessary for good health. Indeed it is injurious to spiritual health too because humans 'violate' their own spiritual capacities by suppressing 'sympathy and pity towards living creatures.' Living free of the slaughter-house is a 'first-step' towards moral perfection. Alec Vidler, however, has no such scruples. Once a vegetarian, he has now converted back. 'I never succeeded in convincing myself that eating animals is wrong.' Vidler now judges that we may use animals for our 'service and sustenance' as 'the Bible says so clearly.' Jesus ate fish, and St Peter and St Paul ate meat. 'What was good enough for Peter and Paul is good enough for you and me,' argues Vidler.

Calvin goes further. Commenting on Genesis 9, he sees nothing less than a divine command to be flesh eaters. In doing so we do not act as 'tyrants' but in good faith. Indeed 'tyranny' is on the other boot. 'For it is an unsupportable tyranny, when God the Creator of all things, has laid open to us the earth and the air, in order that we may thence take food as from his storehouse, for these to be shut up from us by mortal man, who is not able to create even a snail or a fly.' In short: what God has pronounced 'lawful' we must not judge 'unlawful.' Our final piece comes down on the side of the animals. Stephen Clark, with equal force, berates the 'tyranny' of an 'intellectual elite' who want to treat their sentient, but intellectual inferiors, 'as trash.' 'Honourable men may honourably disagree about some details of the human treatment of the non-human,' he argues, 'but vegetarianism is now as necessary a pledge of moral devotion as was the refusal of emperor-worship in the early Church.' Starker still: 'Those who still eat flesh when they could do otherwise have no claim to be serious moralists.'

We may summarise the main issues in this final section as follows: (1) Can the infliction of pain on animals be justified in experimentation, trapping, hunting or farming? (2) Can the killing of animals be justified for food, clothes or pleasure? and (3) Can deprivations of the natural life of animals be justified in, for example, intensive farming?

The Bible
On Animal Sacrifices and Killing for Food

ANIMAL SACRIFICES

Genesis 8:20–21

Then Noah built an altar to the Lord, and took of every clean animal and of every clean bird, and offered burnt offerings on the altar. And when the Lord smelled the pleasing odour, the Lord said in his heart, "I will never again curse the ground because of man, for the imagination of man's heart is evil from his youth; neither will I ever again destroy every living creature as I have done."

Exodus 12:1–8

The Lord said to Moses and Aaron in the land of Egypt, "This month shall be for you the beginning of months; it shall be the first month of the year for you. Tell all the congregation of Israel that on the tenth day of this month they shall take every man a lamb according to their fathers' houses, a lamb for a household; and if the household is too small for a lamb, then a man and his neighbour next to his house shall take according to the number of persons; according to what each can eat you shall make your count for the lamb. Your lamb shall be without blemish, a male a year old; you shall take it from the sheep or from the goats; and you shall keep it until the fourteenth day of this month, when the whole assembly of the congregation of Israel shall kill their lambs in the evening. Then they shall take some of the blood, and put it on the two doorposts and the lintel of the houses in which they eat them. They shall eat the flesh that night, roasted; with unleavened bread and bitter herbs they shall eat it."

Psalm 50:7–11

> "Hear, O my people, and I will speak,
>   O Israel, I will testify against you.
>   I am God, your God.
> I do not reprove you for your sacrifices;
>   Your burnt offerings are continually before me.
> I will accept no bull from your house,
>   nor he-goat from your folds.
> For every beast of the forest is mine,
>   the cattle on a thousand hills.
> I know all the birds of the air,
>   and all that moves in the field is mine."

Isaiah 1:11–17

"What to me is the multitude of your sacrifices?" says the Lord. "I have had enough of burnt offerings of rams and the fat of fed beasts; I do not delight in the blood of bulls or of lambs, or of he-goats. When you come to appear before me, who require of you this trampling of my courts? Bring no more vain offerings; incense is an abomination to me. New moon and sabbath and the calling of assemblies—I cannot endure iniquity and solemn assembly. Your new moons and your appointed feasts my soul hates; they have become a burden to me, I am weary of bearing them. When you spread forth your hands, I will hide my eyes from you; even though you make many prayers, I will not listen; your hands are full of blood. Wash yourselves; make yourselves clean; remove the evil of your doings from before my eyes; cease to do evil, learn to do good; seek justice, correct oppression; defend the fatherless, plead for the widow."

Mark 11:15–16

And they came to Jerusalem. And he entered the temple and began to drive out those who sold and those who bought in the temple, and he overturned the tables of the money-changers and the seats of those who sold pigeons; and he would not allow any one to carry anything through the temple.

Mark 12:32–34a

And the scribe said to him, "You are right, Teacher; you have truly said that he is one, and there is no other but he; and to love him with all the heart, and with all the understanding, and with all the strength, and to love one's neighbour as oneself, is much more than all whole burnt offerings and sacrifices." And when Jesus saw that he answered wisely he said to him, "You are not far from the kingdom of God."

KILLING FOR FOOD

Genesis 1:29–30

And God said, "Behold, I have given you every plant yielding seed which is upon the face of all the earth, and every tree with seed in its fruit; you shall have them for food. And to every beast of the earth, and to every bird of the air, and to everything that has the breath of life, I have given every green plant for food." And it was so.

Genesis 9:1–4

And God blessed Noah and his sons, and said to them, "Be fruitful and multiply, and fill the earth. The fear of you and the dread of you shall be upon every bird of the air, upon everything that creeps on the ground and all the fish of the sea; into your hand they are delivered. Every moving thing that lives shall be food for you; and as I gave you the green plants, I give you everything. Only you shall not eat flesh with its life, that is, its blood."

Deuteronomy 14:3–8

"You shall not eat any abominable thing. These are the animals you may eat: the ox, the sheep, the goat, the hart, the gazelle, the roebuck, the wild goat, the ibex, the antelope, and the mountain-sheep. Every animal that parts the hoof and has the hoof cloven in two, and chews cud, among the animals, you may eat. Yet of those that chew the cud or have the hoof cloven you shall not eat these: The camel, the hare, the rock badger, because they chew the cud but do not part the hoof, are unclean for you. And the swine, because it parts the hoof but does not chew the cud, is unclean for you. Their flesh you shall not eat, and their carcasses you shall not touch."

Isaiah 11:9

They shall not hurt or destroy in all my holy mountain; for the earth shall be full of knowledge of the Lord as the waters cover the sea.

Hosea 2:18

"And I will make for you a covenant on that day with the beasts of the field, the birds of the air, and the creeping things of the ground; and I will abolish the bow, the sword, and war from the land; and I will make you lie down in safety."

Acts 10:9–16

The next day, as they were on their journey and coming near the city, Peter went up on the housetop to pray, about the sixth hour. And he became hungry and desired something to eat; but while they were preparing it, he fell into a trance and saw the heaven opened, and something descending, like a great sheet, let down by four corners upon the earth. In it were all kinds of animals and reptiles and birds of the air. And there came a voice to him, "Rise, Peter; kill and eat." But Peter said, "No, Lord; for I have never eaten anything that is common or unclean." And the voice came to him again a second time, "What God has cleansed, you must not call common." This happened three times, and the thing was taken up at once to heaven.

I. Animal Experimentation

DONALD SOPER
The Question of Vivisection

'Do you agree with vivisection?'
Like all the questions that hold within themselves answers which
can be arrived at in general as well as in precise terms, and also issues
which are marginal, and therefore much less susceptible of simple answers, this question of vivisection must be broken down into a number
of separable issues.

First of all, it is obviously wrong to make use of animals as an escape
from, or as an alternative to, the more zealous and careful use of other
methods of obtaining medical knowledge or of assessing medical opinions and convictions, without taking the necessary trouble which
should and would otherwise be necessary. Vivisection is often the lazy
scientist's way of arriving at conclusions by ignoring the pain and,
indeed, the dignity of the animal world and concentrating entirely
upon his own selfish—and maybe at the same time humanitarian—
interests.

I am quite sure that vivisection as a cheap and lazy method of making
use of animals where other methods would be tedious and difficult is
unjustified.

Secondly, I am equally sure that there are some uses to which we
are entitled to put the animal creation (and to which, indeed, we do
put the animal creation) which come within the general framework

From *Tower Hill, 12.30* (London: Epworth Press, 1963), pp. 92–93.

of vivisection and are as permissible as putting a horse between the shafts, or taking a cow and separating it from its calf in order to obtain more milk for human beings. To make use of animals in ways which do not involve cruelty or the impoverishment of their natural life is permissible, and in this particular regard vivisection seems to be no more objectionable than any other form of utilization of the animal world in the service of man.

Within the third category comes the whole question as to whether or not certain discoveries can be made only by imposing first of all on animals the kind of stresses and strains that otherwise would have to be imposed on human beings in the first instance. This is a highly complex problem, and I would not rule out the necessity, in certain circumstances, of even imposing a certain amount of pain on animals, if and when it seemed to be the only realizable method of obtaining such results. I cannot presume to be an authority in this field, but it does seem to me that we must leave a certain area of dubiety in the answer to include those compromises which are as necessary in this field as in every other. I think the general answer, therefore, must be that when man arrogates to himself the capacity to use animals in his service, irrespective of their own natural rights (and this, incidentally, has been a dogma of the Roman Catholic Church for long enough and is, in my judgement, basically irreconcilable with Christian teaching) it is to be condemned by the Christian. But there are marginal issues included within the general condemnation which cause many people to be extravagantly sentimental and to shy away from the word 'vivisection' as if it contained within itself, in all its forms, something which is abhorrent.

A little more understanding on both sides would be of immense benefit, but I think that, in general terms, the Christian answer must be as I stated.

It would be too facile to endeavour to sum this matter up in a sentence or so, but, as an indication of the kind of approach to such a summing up which I believe sooner or later we shall be able to arrive at, let me suggest that Dr Schweitzer's great claim that all life should be based on respect for personality has been too narrowly interpreted as being confined entirely to the personality of human beings. I believe that this creed 'respect for personality' must be applied to the whole of creation. I shouldn't be surprised if the Buddhists are nearer to an understanding of it than we are. When we apply this principle, we shall be facing innumerable problems, but I believe we shall be on the right track which leads finally to the end of violence and the achievement of a just social order which will leave none of God's creatures out of that Kingdom which it is our Father's good pleasure to give us.

JOHN CANON McCARTHY
Justified Use of Animals

Vivisection means the practice of using living animals for surgical and medical experimentation. Living animals are operated on, or are inoculated with various types of germs in order to observe symptoms and to test remedies, especially in the medical, pathological and biological spheres—remedies which will afterwards be applied for the prevention or cure of human disease. Basically, then, the practice of vivisection really implies that living animals are used for the welfare of man. And it is perfectly lawful that they should be so used. There is a hierarchy in created nature.[1] In the designs of God, animals were created to serve the use and benefit of human beings. 'What is man that thou art mindful of him? . . . Thou has set him over the works of thy hands. Thou hast subjected all things under his feet, all sheep and oxen, the beasts also of the fields, the birds of the air and the fishes of the sea.'[2] Accordingly, it can be said at once that vivisection is not, in itself, unlawful.

At the same time it must immediately be added that vivisection can be regarded as lawful only in so far as the experimentation carried out may be calculated to serve a really useful purpose.[3] In other words, Catholic doctrine does not condone useless or unnecessary experimentation on living animals. And, in the carrying out of the various experiments, all needless and excessive pain or cruelty should be

From *Problems in Theology*, vol. II, *The Commandments* (Dublin: Browne and Nolan Limited, 1960), pp. 155–57.
[1]Cf. St. Thomas, S.T., 2, 2, 64, a 1; *Summa Contra Gentiles*, 1, iii.c. cxii.
[2]Ps. viii, 5–9, cf. Gen. i, 26.

avoided. Thus, in painful experimentation, if it is possible, without notably interfering with the value of the tests, to drug or anaesthetize the animals, this procedure should be followed.

It is clear, then, that Catholic teaching on vivisection holds a middle way between two extremes. We have, firstly, the excessive sentimentalism of those antivivisectionists who would ban *all* experimentation on living animals. At the other extreme we have the sadistic view of those who apparently regard living animals as the fitting object of all kinds of unnecessary and cruel experimentation and exploitation. The antivivisectionist ignores the fundamental principle, mentioned earlier, that, in God's arrangement, animals are created to serve human needs. The antivivisectionist seems to be more interested in preventing animal suffering than in alleviating and curing human pain. He is generally illogical. He will eat animal flesh—though death is rarely inflicted without pain. He may even hunt, shoot or fish—for pleasure. He sometimes speaks of the rights of animals. This is an inaccurate expression. Animals lack reason and personality, and, therefore, they cannot be the subject of strict rights.[4] But it is wrong to regard living animals as fair game for any and every form of human experimentation and cruelty. Animals, indeed, have no strict rights, but they have feeling and sensation and can clearly suffer grievously from punishment and pain. It is unethical, and every normal human instinct revolts from the practice, to inflict needless suffering on any of God's creatures.

Briefly then, experimentation on living animals, even though they may suffer severe pain in the process, is lawful to the extent that it is necessary for a genuinely scientific purpose which may benefit humanity. It is unlawful to inflict any unnecessary suffering on animals either in the course of vivisection experiments or otherwise. How is this sin of wanton cruelty to animals to be classified? It is not a sin of injustice. Nor is it, *per se*, a mortal sin. Some writers say that it is a violation of no particular virtue, but is opposed to the general obligation of acting in accordance with rational principles.[5] We think,

---

[4]Cf. Prümmer, *Th. Mor.*, ii, n. 1: 'Ex dictis sequitur, ut animalibus non competant iura quia non sunt praedita facultatibus *moralibus*. Ergo numquam aliquis committit iniustitiam proprie dictam contra animal. Quare theologi solent breviter dicere: Animalia sunt quidem obiectum, sed non subiectum iuris.' Cf. Davis, *Moral and Pastoral Theology*, ii, pp. 258, 259.

[5]Cf. Prümmer, op. cit., ii, 14: 'Crudeliter tractare et vexare animalia (sine sufficienti ratione) est peccaminosum, tum quia rectae rationi repugnat, tum quia homo in tali tortura saepe quaerit voluptatem plane perversam.'

however, that cruelty to animals may well be classed as a violation of the virtue of temperance[6]—or more specifically as a violation of mildness and clemency which are potential parts of the cardinal virtue of temperance. *Apropos* of this, St. Thomas[7] points out that indulgence in cruelty to animals often leads men to ill-treat their fellows, and this, he considers, is one reason why cruelty to animals is forbidden. It is a question of fact whether unnecessary suffering is sometimes inflicted in vivisection experiments.[8] There may, indeed, be such abuses. If so, they are regrettable and should be eradicated. But we cannot condemn vivisection *in toto* because of abuses accidentally associated with it; *abusus non tollit usum.*

C. S. LEWIS
A Case for Abolition*

It is the rarest thing in the world to hear a rational discussion of vivisection. Those who disapprove of it are commonly accused of "sentimentality", and very often their arguments justify the accusation. They paint pictures of pretty little dogs on dissecting tables. But the other side lie open to exactly the same charge. They also often defend the practice by drawing pictures of suffering women and children whose pain can be relieved (we are assured) only by the fruits of vivisection. The one appeal, quite as clearly as the other, is addressed to emotion, to the particular emotion we call pity. And neither appeal proves anything. If the thing is right—and if right at all, it is a duty—then pity for the animal is one of the temptations we must resist in order to perform that duty. If the thing is wrong, then pity for human suffering

[6]Cf. Noldin, *De Praeceptis*, n. 346.
[7]*Summa Contra Gent.*, loc. cit.: 'Si quae vero in sacra Scriptura inveniantur prohibentia aliquid crudelitatis in animalia bruta committi . . . hoc fit vel ad removendum hominis animum a crudelitate in homines exercenda, ne aliquis exercendo crudelia circa bruta, ex hoc procedat ad homines.'
[8]Noldin, loc. cit., writes: 'Negari nequit vivisectiones complurium medicorum honestos limites multum excedere atque in veram torturam animalium degenerasse.'
*From "Vivisection", first published as a pamphlet by the New England Anti-Vivisection Society (1947) and in *Undeceptions: Essays on Theology and Ethics*, edited by Walter Hooper (London: Geoffrey Bles, 1952), pp. 182–86.

is precisely the temptation which will most probably lure us into doing that wrong thing. But the real question—*whether* it is right or wrong—remains meanwhile just where it was.

A rational discussion of this subject begins by inquiring whether pain is, or is not, an evil. If it is not, then the case against vivisection falls. But then so does the case for vivisection. If it is not defended on the ground that it reduces human suffering, on what ground can it be defended? And if pain is not an evil, why should human suffering be reduced? We must therefore assume as a basis for the whole discussion that pain is an evil, otherwise there is nothing to be discussed.

Now if pain is an evil then the infliction of pain, considered in itself, must clearly be an evil act. But there are such things as necessary evils. Some acts which would be bad, simply in themselves, may be excusable and even laudable when they are necessary means to a greater good. In saying that the infliction of pain, simply in itself, is bad, we are not saying that pain ought never to be inflicted. Most of us think that it can rightly be inflicted for a good purpose—as in dentistry or just and reformatory punishment. The point is that it always requires justification. On the man whom we find inflicting pain rests the burden of showing why an act which in itself would be simply bad is, in those particular circumstances, good. If we find a man giving pleasure it is for us to prove (if we criticize him) that his action is wrong. But if we find a man inflicting pain it is for him to prove that his action is right. If he cannot, he is a wicked man.

Now vivisection can only be defended by showing it to be right that one species should suffer in order that another species should be happier. And here we come to the parting of the ways. The Christian defender and the ordinary "scientific" (i.e., naturalistic) defender of vivisection, have to take quite different lines.

The Christian defender, especially in the Latin countries, is very apt to say that we are entitled to do anything we please to animals because they "have no souls". But what does this mean? If it means that animals have no consciousness, then how is this known? They certainly behave as if they had, or at least the higher animals do. I myself am inclined to think that far fewer animals than is supposed have what we should recognize as consciousness. But that is only an opinion. Unless we know on other grounds that vivisection is right we must not take the moral risk of tormenting them on a mere opinion. On the other hand, the statement that they "have no souls" may mean that they have no moral responsibilities and are not immortal. But the absence of "soul" in that sense makes the infliction of pain upon them not easier but harder to justify. For it means that animals cannot deserve pain, nor profit morally by the discipline of pain, nor be recompensed by happiness in another life for suffering in this. Thus all the factors which render pain more tolerable or make it less totally evil in the case of human beings will be lacking in the beasts. "Soullessness", in so far as it is relevant to the question at all, is an argument against vivisection.

The only rational line for the Christian vivisectionist to take is to say that the superiority of man over beast is a real objective fact, guaranteed by Revelation, and that the propriety of sacrificing beast to man is a logical consequence. We are "worth more than many sparrows",[1] and in saying this we are not merely expressing a natural preference for our own species simply because it is our own but conforming to a hierarchical order created by God and really present in the universe whether any one acknowledges it or not. The position may not be satisfactory. We may fail to see how a benevolent Deity could wish us to draw such conclusions from the hierarchical order He has created. We may find it difficult to formulate a human right of tormenting beasts in terms which would not equally imply an angelic right of tormenting men. And we may feel that though objective superiority is rightly claimed for men, yet that very superiority ought partly to *consist in* not behaving like a vivisector: that we ought to prove ourselves better than the beasts precisely by the fact of acknowledging duties to them which they do not acknowledge to us. But on all these questions different opinions can be honestly held. If on grounds of our real, divinely ordained, superiority a Christian pathologist thinks it right to vivisect, and does so with scrupulous care to avoid the least dram or scruple of unnecessary pain, in a trembling awe at the responsibility which he assumes, and with a vivid sense of the high mode in which human life must be lived if it is to justify the sacrifices made for it, then (whether we agree with him or not) we can respect his point of view.

But of course the vast majority of vivisectors have no such theological background. They are most of them naturalistic and Darwinian. Now here, surely, we come up against a very alarming fact. The very same

[1]Matthew x. 31

people who will most contemptuously brush aside any consideration of animal suffering if it stands in the way of "research" will also, in another context, most vehemently deny that there is any radical difference between man and the other animals. On the naturalistic view the beasts are at bottom just the same *sort* of thing as ourselves. Man is simply the cleverest of the anthropoids. All the grounds on which a Christian might defend vivisection are thus cut from under our feet. We sacrifice other species to our own not because our own has any objective metaphysical privilege over others, but simply because it is ours. It may be very natural to have this loyalty to our own species, but let us hear no more from the naturalists about the "sentimentality" of anti-vivisectionists. If loyalty to our own species, preference for man simply because we are men, is not a sentiment, then what is? It may be a good sentiment or a bad one. But a sentiment it certainly is. Try to base it on logic and see what happens!

But the most sinister thing about modern vivisection is this. If a mere sentiment justifies cruelty, why stop at a sentiment for the whole human race? There is also a sentiment for the white man against the black, for a *Herrenvolk* against the non-Aryans, for "civilized" or "progressive" peoples against "savages" or "backward" peoples. Finally, for our own country, party or class against others. Once the old Christian idea of a total difference in kind between man and beast has been abandoned, then no argument for experiments on animals can be found which is not also an argument for experiments on inferior men. If we cut up beasts simply because they cannot prevent us and because we are backing our own side in the struggle for existence, it is only logical to cut up imbeciles, criminals, enemies or capitalists for the same reasons. Indeed, experiments on men have already begun. We all hear that Nazi scientists have done them. We all suspect that our own scientists may begin to do so, in secret, at any moment.

The alarming thing is that the vivisectors have won the first round. In the nineteenth and eighteenth centuries a man was not stamped as a "crank" for protesting against vivisection. Lewis Carroll protested, if I remember his famous letter correctly, on the very same ground which I have just used.[2] Dr Johnson—a man whose mind had as much *iron* in it as any man's—protested in a note on *Cymbeline* which is

[2]"Vivisection as a Sign of the Times", *The Works of Lewis Carroll*, ed. Roger Lancelyn Green (London, 1965), pp. 1089–92. See also "Some Popular Fallacies about Vivisection", ibid., pp. 1092–1100.

worth quoting in full. In Act I, scene v, the Queen explains to the Doctor that she wants poisons to experiment on "such creatures as We count not worth the hanging,—but none human".[3] The Doctor replies:

> Your Highness
> Shall from this practice but make hard your heart.[4]

Johnson comments: "The thought would probably have been more amplified, had our author lived to be shocked with such experiments as have been published in later times, by a race of men that have practised tortures without pity, and related them without shame, and are yet suffered to erect their heads among human beings."[5]

The words are his, not mine, and in truth we hardly dare in these days to use such calmly stern language. The reason why we do not dare is that the other side has in fact won. And though cruelty even to beasts is an important matter, their victory is symptomatic of matters more important still. The victory of vivisection marks a great advance in the triumph of ruthless, non-moral utilitarianism over the old world of ethical law; a triumph in which we, as well as animals, are already the victims, and of which Dachau and Hiroshima mark the more recent achievements. In justifying cruelty to animals we put ourselves also on the animal level. We choose the jungle and must abide by our choice.

You will notice I have spent no time in discussing what actually goes on in the laboratories. We shall be told, of course, that there is surprisingly little cruelty. That is a question with which, at present, I have nothing to do. We must first decide what should be allowed: after that it is for the police to discover what is already being done.

---

[3]Shakespeare, *Cymbeline*, I, v, 19–20
[4]ibid., 23
[5]*Johnson on Shakespeare: Essays and Notes Selected and Set Forth with an Introduction* by Sir Walter Raleigh (London, 1908), p. 181.

CARDINAL MANNING
Obligations to the Creator

A literary man of very great reputation, and highly celebrated for his literary powers, but not equally so for his accuracy, I believe, was present at one of our meetings, and he heard out of my mouth this statement: that inasmuch as animals are not moral persons, we owe them no duties, and that, therefore, the infliction of pain is contrary to no obligation. Now, he omitted to say that I did make that statement for the purpose only of refuting it—but he put it into my mouth, and there it is in a book that is sold to all the book-stalls in the railway stations, and I am credited to this day with that which I denounced as a hideous and, I think, an absurd doctrine. It is perfectly true that obligations and duties are between moral persons, and therefore the lower animals are not susceptible of those moral obligations which we owe to one another; but we owe a sevenfold obligation to the Creator of those animals. Our obligation and moral duty is to Him who made them, and, if we wish to know the limit and the broad outline of our obligation, I say at once it is His nature, and His perfections, and, among those perfections, one is most profoundly that of eternal mercy. And, therefore, although a poor mule or a poor horse is not indeed a moral person, yet the Lord and Maker of that mule and that horse is the highest law-giver, and His nature is a law to Himself. And, in giving a dominion over His creatures to man, He gave them subject to the condition that they should be used in conformity to His own perfections, which is His own law, and, therefore, our law. It would seem to me that the practice of vivisection, as it is now known and now exists, is at variance with those moral perfections.

Now there is one other word I will add, and that is, I believe that science consists in the knowledge of truth obtained by the processes which are in conformity with the nature of God, who, the Holy Scripture says, is the Lord of all sciences. I remember Lord Shaftesbury

From a speech to the Victoria Street Society for the Prevention of Vivisection at the Westminister Palace Hotel, 9 March 1887, in *Speeches Against Vivisection*, published as a leaflet by the National Anti-vivisection Society and Catholic Study Circle for Animal Welfare, no date.

saying at one of our meetings. 'I don't believe that science can be attained by processes which are at variance with the perfections of God', and if I have been right in what I have laid down, as it appears to me, that the infliction of torture of the most exquisite kind on the poor animals is at variance with the perfections of God for that reason, my conclusion is that science is not attained by that path, and that those who walk in it are out of the way.

But I will most heartily continue to support the proceedings of this Society, for at the present day we are under the tyranny of the word Science. I believe in science most profoundly within its own limits; but it has its own limits, and, when the word science is applied to [a] matter which is beyond those limits, I don't believe in it, and, as I believe that vivisection is susceptible of such excessive abuse—such facile abuse—such clandestine abuse—all over the land, and by all manner of people, I shall do all I can to restrain it to the utmost of my power.

II. Fur-Trapping

In Defence of Fur-Trapping

As pastoral leaders of Catholic and Anglican missions in northern Canada, we wish to express our solidarity with the aboriginal peoples of the North who are engaged in a struggle to save fur trapping as a way of life. After more than a century of missionary presence in the North, our churches have come to know how important hunting and trapping is to the aboriginal peoples. It is more than an economic source of income. It is a way of life deeply rooted in the cultural traditions of aboriginal societies in the Canadian North.

Today, this aboriginal way of life is being severely threatened by the anti-fur campaign being waged in Europe and elsewhere. In response to the massive public campaign against the seal hunt, for example, the European Economic Community placed a ban on the import of baby seal skins. As a result, the market for all seal products was destroyed. This, in turn, has had a devastating effect on many Inuit communities in the Arctic. Whole communities have suffered a dramatic drop in annual income[1] and many indigenous sealers have been forced to abandon the land as a way of life.

From *Harvesting Wildlife in the Canadian North: A Question of Cultural Survival of Aboriginal Peoples,* A joint statement of social concern by Roman Catholic and Anglican Bishops in Northern Canada, March 1986. The editors would like to thank Dr. Ethel Thurston and Michael O'Sullivan for their help in obtaining a copy of this document.

[1] In the Arctic community of Resolute, the collective income primarily generated from the seal hunt dropped from $54,000. in 1982 to $1,000. in 1983. The community income of Igloolik dropped from $46,800. in 1982 to $5,000. in 1983. In Frobisher Bay, the community income from the seal hunt declined from $23,000 to $4,000. And, in the Inuit community of Sanikilwag, the annual income fell from $6,800. to $399 during the same period.

167

The full economic and social impact from the collapse of the seal hunt and the threat to related fur trade activities has yet to be measured across the Canadian North. For many northern aboriginal peoples, hunting and trapping serves as more than a supplement for employment in the wage economy. It is a primary source of essential food stuff (fresh fish and meat) for aboriginal communities in a region where commercial food prices are by far the highest in Canada.

The sudden decline in fur trade has brought chronic levels of unemployment for most northern communities. Social welfare programs are now being severely taxed. In turn, the loss of economic self-sufficiency has generated a sense of hopelessness in many communities. Today, the suicide rate in northern communities is as high as 16 times the national average.

The activity of harvesting wildlife is also deeply embedded in the culture of aboriginal peoples. As the people themselves have often said, "Our land is our life". Through hunting and trapping, aboriginal peoples are able to practice traditional skills which serve to keep their cultures and societies alive for themselves and their children. As the leaders of several northern aboriginal organizations recently stated: "Participation in all aspects of traditional resource harvesting activities helps us to reinforce our traditional social and cultural values, and ensures the continuation of these values for succeeding generations."[2]

For aboriginal peoples, humans and animals are an integral part of the cycle of nature or the eco-system. The approach of aboriginal peoples is one of respect and reciprocity with animal life. The harvesting of wildlife is essential in the North, not only to help people survive physically and economically but also to prevent the danger of over-populated wildlife and the corresponding danger of disease.[3] Both the animal and the hunter need each other to maintain ecological balance. For the traditional harvesting process of aboriginal peoples is based on the recognition of present and future dependence on certain animal species and the need to ensure that those species survive in sufficient numbers.

Thus, the aboriginal harvesting process entails the responsible stewardship of creation. For the most part, aboriginal hunters and trappers

[2]A statement by aboriginal leaders from Canada, Alaska, and Greenland involved in Indigenous Survival Internationale (ISI). See the ISI submission to the Canadian Royal Commission on Seals and the Sealing Industry, London, England, April 9, 1985.
[3]See Thomas Coon, *Man and Animal: Building a New Relationship with Nature.*

have managed to sustain a renewable resource economy by practicing conservation in their animal harvesting each year. There have, of course, been occasions when they have been charged with over-harvesting. But the most serious threat to wildlife today is not aboriginal hunters and trappers. It is the increasing destruction of the wildlife habitat by major industrial projects.

We believe the anti-fur campaign poses a direct threat to aboriginal peoples and their way of life in the North today. Contrary to charges made by campaign activists, aboriginal peoples are not out to destroy the animal population. Deep within their cultural and spiritual traditions, aboriginal peoples have a close bond with the land and animal life. Their approach to harvesting wildlife is designed to respect and preserve these traditions. The anti-fur campaign, therefore, violates the dignity of aboriginal peoples and some of their deeply felt cultural and spiritual traditions. We find this to be morally unacceptable.

At this point, we call upon the people of Canada to actively support the aboriginal peoples in preserving and strengthening the harvesting of wildlife as an important renewable resource economy in this country. In particular, we urge the federal government to develop strategies for the expansion of the domestic market here in Canada for aboriginal fur products, and to provide assistance to aboriginal groups for the development of harvesting enterprises such as co-operative processing houses in the North. Rather than being a luxury enjoyed only by the more affluent, Canadian furs can be used for much more practical purposes such as the manufacturing of winter clothing required by the vast majority of people in this country.

Greater domestic use of Canadian furs would also reduce Canada's present high dependence on imported furs. Yet, revitalizing the domestic market alone would not be sufficient. We also urge the federal government to develop appropriate strategies for the promotion of aboriginal fur products in international markets. This includes more vigorous efforts on the part of the Canadian government to seek the removal of the EEC ban on seal products. These and related initiatives are in keeping with the constitutional responsibilities of the federal government to safeguard aboriginal rights in this country.

Finally, we urge members of the Christian community throughout Canada to join us in expressing support for, and solidarity with, aboriginal groups striving to save their cultural tradition of wildlife harvesting. Many Christian groups have already provided financial support and others have initiated public education efforts. We hope that many more Christians will join other people of good will in pressing for more effective government action on this issue. Together, we may be able to authentically assist the aboriginal peoples of the North in their struggle for cultural survival.

ANDREW LINZEY
A Reply to the Bishops

We come face to face with institutionalized suffering in the food we eat, the products we buy and also the clothes we wear. At first sight the case for the trapping of fur animals for adornment purposes will appear the weakest of all. How can adornment articles like fur coats possibly justify the sustained suffering that fur-bearing animals have to endure? If there is some dispute about the suffering of farm animals, there can be none when it comes to trapping. Almost all the methods involved are *inherently* painful.[1] And yet fur-trapping has not lacked its defenders, and Christian apologists too. A recent statement issued by the Anglican and Roman Catholic Bishops in Northern Canada expressed their 'solidarity with the aboriginal peoples of the North who are engaged in a struggle to save fur-trapping as a way of life'.[2] Their arguments appear to be threefold. The first is that trapping 'is a way of life deeply rooted in the cultural traditions of aboriginal societies in the Canadian North'.[3] The second is that sudden declines in trade, as when the European Economic Community placed a ban on the importation of baby seal skins, cause the 'loss of economic self-sufficiency' and with it 'a sense of hopelessness' and even a 'suicide rate in native communities . . . more than six times the national av-

---

From *Christianity and the Rights of Animals* (London: SPCK and New York: Crossroad Publishing, 1987), pp. 125–28.
[1] Those in any doubt should consult F. Jean Winter, *Facts about Furs* (Washington, DC: Animal Welfare Institute; Horsham, Sussex: RSPCA, 1973), which provides an excellent factual survey.
[2] 'Canada's Northern Bishops' in *Prairie Messenger* (Benedictine Monks of St Peter's Abbey, Muenster, Saskatchewan), reprinted under the heading 'Northern Bishops Seek Resurgence of Fur Trapping', *Fur Age Weekly*, 8 December 1985, p. 4. I am grateful to Ethel Thurston for this reference.
[3] ibid.

erage'.[4] The third argument is that trappers are environmentally responsible: 'The aboriginal harvesting process entails the responsible stewardship of creation' because they practise 'conservation in their animal harvesting each year'.[5]

The first argument is question-begging. The issue is not of course whether a particular way of life depends upon fur-trapping but whether fur-trapping can be justified from the outset. The second argument also begs this point. It is not difficult to understand why bishops as 'pastoral leaders' should be concerned for the welfare of the peoples they apparently represent. Unemployment, a sense of hopelessness and suicidal tendencies are matters of concern to pastors especially. But the Christian concern demonstrated by these bishops does not appear to extend to fur-bearing animals at all. They clearly do not see it as part of their responsibility to the Christian gospel to ask whether ways of life which necessarily involve suffering to other forms of life are in fact worth defending in the first place. Since it is well known that Christian missionaries all over the world have disrupted the natural life of indigenous peoples, we may fail to see how it is that defending the 'social and cultural values' of traditional life is now to be regarded as a self-evident Christian concern. Of course the bishops may reply that they are simply trying to pay back indigenous culture something of what imposed Christian culture once took from them. 'The anti-fur campaign', argue the bishops, 'violates the dignity of aboriginal peoples and some of their deeply felt cultural and spiritual traditions'.[6] One cannot help wondering whether some sense of guilt is being rationalized here for all the previous disruption that Christian missionaries have caused.

To the third argument, that trappers are also conservationists and thus obeying the Christian doctrine of stewardship, two replies are appropriate. The first is that conservation, far from being a religious duty, may be little more than enlightened self-interest for the trappers concerned if their way of life depends upon it. The second is that in stewardship thus defined we have no specific responsibilities to the individual animals concerned, save that of not making them extinct as a species. Stewardship clearly does not encompass issues such as the right of suffering creatures to be relieved of their suffering or more

[4]ibid. [Cf. the figure on p. 168 above ("16 times"). Discrepancy noted but unresolved. —A.L.]
[5]ibid.
[6]ibid.

directly the justifiability of trade which necessitates such suffering. This point is surely the most disturbing from the standpoint of theos-rights. Wild fur-bearing animals are simply assumed to be renewable for humans to 'harvest' (their word). Issues of suffering can be put to one side, if it can be shown that some human interest, represented by a way of life people wish to lead, is at stake. As an exercise in moral theology it is partisan to say the least. To argue that suffering animals count for little is one thing. To argue that the welfare of animals should be absolutely subordinated to human needs is another. But it is altogether lamentable that suffering animals should count for nothing save that of being a renewable human resource.

And yet it may be argued that humans have a right to their culture and their way of life. What would we be, it may be questioned, without our land and history and ways of life? In general, culture is valuable. But it is also the case that there can be evil cultures, or at least cher-ished traditions which perpetuate injustice or tyranny. The Greeks, for example, despite all their outstanding contributions to learning, did not appear to recognize the immorality of slavery. There can be elements within every culture that are simply not worth defending, not only slavery but also infanticide and human sacrifice. At the very least the case must be made that trading in animals is a morally ac-ceptable, as well as a culturally essential, element within that which we are concerned to preserve. In short: human traditions and ways of life may be generally worth defending, but not at any cost and certainly not when they depend upon the suffering of thousands, if not millions, of wild animals every year.

What then must we do? In the first place we must address the cultural claim by seeing how far human lives, as distinct from preferences, are actually at stake in the moral issue. 'In one twelve-month period', according to the RSPCA, 'when 38.2 million wild animals were killed for their fur, a substantial proportion were caught in traps in the USA where only 2% of trappers are professional'.[7] From a practical point of view there is a distinction between what is genuinely indigenous and what are indigenous skills exploited for our benefit. My own view is that no human lives will or need be lost by the rundown of the fur-trapping industry. Dollars may be lost, of course. Some individuals may have to face some difficult questions about where they should

---

[7]'Fur Trapping: The Lost Innocence', RSPCA (1984) p. 4.

live and how they are to be employed. *Perhaps* the human population, and therefore the ecclesiastical congregations of the North, will diminish over a period of time. But from the perspective of theos-rights these will be acceptable costs if the result is the reduction of suffering to millions of animals. No moral options are cost free. The pastoral task, and incidentally I can think of no better people than bishops to lead the way, is to help people desist from a cultural life which however otherwise laudable can only be achieved at the expense of pain and suffering to other creatures. Moreover, this policy may restore, where possible, the genuinely indigenous form of life which has been prevented by our own gain. It remains an open question how far the exploitation of crimes by indigenous cultures is in fact the result of our exploitation of them for commercial profit.

The second response is to underline the gravity of our consumer choice. Our choice to wear fur is made quite literally at the cost of a number of animals that have died in agony. The claims by the 'Ecology Section' of the International Fur Trade Federation that among other things 'acrylic fibres, which are often used in the production of fake fur, are highly inflammable and therefore constitute a fire risk', or that 'the use of the chemical industry makes heavy use of irreplaceable mineral resources for the production of fibres for synthetic fur' are signs of an industry clutching at any straw in the face of growing unpopularity.[8] The campaign against fur-wearing led by the RSPCA in 1985 resulted in a significant number of high-street stores abandoning their retail trade in fur. Consumers who effectively organize themselves can change the frequently volatile fashions in dress and adornment.

The third response is the development of effective international trading restrictions. The bishops were able to testify in their statement to the effect of the recent EEC ban on baby seal skins which resulted in the devastation of 'the market for all seal products'.[9] Restrictive legislation will not of course meet every situation, but since business is at the heart of the trade in furs, consumer demand and import controls can destroy markets as well as create them. Our hope for the indigenous peoples of the North is that they may live in peace with wild animals (as arguably many of them once did) but, if they cannot, perhaps it is better that the animals be left free to live according to *their own* way of life.

[8]'Answers to Criticism: Fake Fur Versus Real Fur', *Fur Age Weekly*, 8 December 1985.
[9]Northern Bishops, cited in ibid.

III. Hunting for Sport

ST FRANCIS DE SALES
Lawful Recreations

Some recreation is necessary to refresh mind and body. Cassian tells us that a hunter once found St John the Evangelist holding a partridge in his hand and amusing himself by stroking it. When the hunter asked him how so great a man could waste his time in such a trivial way St John replied: 'Why do you not carry your bow always taut?' 'Because,' replied the hunter, 'it would then lose its resilience, and so be rendered useless.' 'Do not be surprised then,' said the Apostle, 'if I sometimes relax my mind and take a little recreation so that afterwards I may concentrate the better.' It is certainly wrong to be so strict with oneself, so austere and unsociable, as to deny oneself, and everyone else, recreation. To go out in the fresh air, to go for a walk, to take part in cheerful and friendly conversation, to sing or play some musical instrument or other, or to go hunting, are such innocent recreations that we may always make good use of them so long as we exercise that common prudence which governs time, place, measure and order. Games in which success alone is the reward for skill and effort of mind or body, for example, tennis, ball, pall-mall, tilting, chess and backgammon are good and lawful so long as we guard against excess either in the time we spend on them or the stakes played for. To spend too much time on a game makes it an occupation rather than a recreation; instead of being refreshed we become tired and de-

From *An Introduction to the Devout Life*, ET by Michael Day (London: Burns and Oates, 1956), pp. 172–73.

pressed! Five or six hours of chess would tire our minds as much as an excessively long game of tennis would exhaust our bodies. To play for extravagant stakes tends to make the players too excited, and in any case it is unreasonable to risk too much on the skill and effort required in such unimportant games. Above all, Philothea, take care that you never become attached to such things, for this would be wrong however good the recreation in itself. I do not mean that we should not enjoy such games, for they would then cease to be a recreation, but that we must never be so set on them that we desire them too eagerly or spend too much time on them.

ST THOMAS MORE

Why Utopians Do Not Hunt

Among those who indulge such senseless delights they reckon . . . hunters and hawkers . . . what sweetness can there be, and not rather disgust, in hearing the barking and howling of dogs? Or what greater sensation of pleasure is there when a dog chases a hare than when a dog chases a dog? The same thing happens in both cases: there is racing in both if speed gives you delight.

But if you are attracted by the hope of slaughter and the expectation of a creature being mangled under your eyes, it ought rather to inspire pity when you behold a weak, fugitive, timid, and innocent little hare torn to pieces by a strong, fierce, and cruel dog. In consequence the Utopians have imposed the whole activity of hunting as unworthy of free men, upon their butchers as a craft, as I explained before, they exercise through their slaves. They regard hunting as the meanest part of the butcher's trade and its other functions as more useful and more honorable, seeing that they do much more positive good and kill animals only from necessity, whereas the hunter seeks nothing but pleasure from the killing and mangling of a poor animal. Even in the case

From *The Complete Works of St Thomas More*, vol. IV, edited by E. Surtz and J. H. Hexter (New Haven and London: Yale University Press, 1965), p. 171.

of brute beasts, this desire of looking on bloodshed, in their estimation, either arises from a cruel disposition or degenerates finally into cruelty through the constant practice of such brutal pleasure.

Although the mob of mortals regards these and all similar pursuits—and they are countless—as pleasures, yet the Utopians positively hold them to have nothing to do with true pleasure since there is nothing sweet in them by nature. The fact that for the mob they inspire in the senses a feeling of enjoyment—which seems to be the function of pleasure—does not make them alter their opinion.

EDWARD CARPENTER
Christian Faith and the Moral Aspect of Hunting

There can be no question but that the Christian, like every other person, is bound to recognize realistically that it is not only the personal order which is the scene of strife and warfare. "Nature red in tooth and claw" is not a meaningless exaggeration. In the natural world it *is* true that one order of creation preys upon another, and indeed often that the condition of continued life in one species is the death and destruction of its neighbour. The Christian is the more conscious of this situation because it stands in sharp contrast with that pattern of ultimate reality from which all his moral criteria arise. He begins with, and accepts as basic to final existence, a Trinitarian conception of God. This conception supposes that within His Divine Being there are real distinctions analogous to, though not of course identical with, the distinctions that obtain between persons. The love of the Father eternally begets the Son, and this love returns through the Spirit back to the Father. There is no "confusion" of persons; no aggression of the one "order" against the other; but all is held together in a community of mutual understanding and outgoing love. Here is the archetypal pattern of all fulfilled living throughout time and in eternity.

From "Christian Faith and the Moral Aspect of Hunting", in Patrick Moore (ed.), *Against Hunting* (London: Gollancz, 1965), pp. 134–37.

Yet the Christian cannot but recognize that the natural order in much of its instinctive life does not conform to this pattern. That this is so constitutes a deep and maybe impenetrable mystery which can become almost unbearable . . . St. Paul, for example, sees the whole creation as caught up in a kind of bondage, "groaning and travailing in pain together until now". The prophet Isaiah cries out, "Verily thou art a God that hidest thyself". Yet, while recognizing the problem, the Bible testifies to the hope that, through the Providence of God, the whole creation is to be "redeemed"—that is, to enter into liberation and fulfilment in which the pattern of strife and internecine warfare is to be transcended, and an universal order of love and understanding established . . .

There can, I think, be no doubt but that this realistic recognition of ambiguity in nature and in man, and yet at the same time the conviction that it will finally be resolved in a fully co-operative society, flow from a prior belief as to the nature of God in Himself, and therefore the kind of Kingdom that He is seeking in time to build. Why there should be this ambiguity, we cannot say, though many have speculated on it. To go into it here would mean a discussion of many things— the Christian doctrines of the Fall, temporal or pre-temporal; the possibility of some inherent limitation involved in the creation of an order moving in space and time, so that value can only arrive painfully out of, and after struggle with, disvalue. But whatever the cause or necessity, the Christian is bound to affirm that the whole movement which God initiates, directs and sustains, and with which man is invited consciously to co-operate, is designed to bring about a Kingdom: and this Kingdom is to reproduce within and between its various "orders", and at different levels of "created being", that which is eternally true of (i.e. existing in) His Triune Being. It is from out of this deep insight of faith that the Christian has a respect for all creation, and for what, in spite of its ambiguity, that creation is finally seeking after. The Bible bears witness to this insight, and shows man as having a special responsibility for the other orders living alongside of him. "Thou shalt not muzzle the ox that treadeth out the corn." "Are not two sparrows sold for a farthing? and one of them shall not fall on the ground without your Father."

Respect, then, for the various orders of creation is involved in, and is integral to, Christian Faith. The dominion that man has over them is in the nature of a stewardship, and finally all the orders belong to

God. Thus Schweitzer, moving within the thought-forms of Christian Faith, sees reverence for life as a regulative principle to which developed man must subscribe . . .

The grim and sad fact is that our very respect for life at one level involves us often in a seeming conflict with life at another. No slick principle can resolve this agonizing dilemma; no formal law can lay down the rules which the individual conscience must follow. Where do we draw the line? When do the seeming rights of one order give way to another? How do we balance higher interests against lower, and what criteria determine this standard of evaluation?

Such questions can only be answered by the sensitive and good man in given situations and when he comes to them. If what he sees as a grim necessity forces him to do violence to one order, even to "take life", he does so acutely conscious of the burdens of his ambiguous position, and recognizing that as he does so he is not registering to an absolute moral order. When he does violence to another existence, he knows that he must only do so reluctantly and with a knowledge of what he is doing. He will act in a measure sadly; and will regret the ambiguity of his position, and wish that it were otherwise. The destruction of life, sometimes in its beauty, sometimes in its "awesomeness", must always appear to him in a measure tragic, necessary though it may seem to be. Would that the world were different, and that every order of creation found itself internally and in relation to each other as in the divine "system" of Father, Son and Holy Spirit.

It is from out of *this* situation, and within such thought-forms, that hunting is seen to be, in the strictest sense of the word, deplorable. To make a sport of taking life, to do it for fun, to organize it into a form of collective enjoyment, is to fail to act responsibly and with a proper reverence for God's creation. It is to fall back into that bondage, into that predatory system of nature, from which the Christian hope has always been that not only man but the natural order itself is to be released and redeemed. Moral indignation against those who hunt is probably out of place and will not get us very far. Most of us, doubtless, indulge in far worse evils. But we may well feel a sense of sorrow for those who "know not what they are doing". Hunting represents, in dramatic form and often in colourful dress, both man's lack of sensitivity to his real condition and his unwillingness seriously to try to lift the whole order of creation into a higher estate, closer to the pattern "shown in the mount"—an estate more noble, more divine.

It is for this reason that the very existence of hunting and the pub-licity given to it—no matter how delightful the people who engage in it—do violence to Christian Faith and witness to a lower order than that redeemed creation to which Christ leads us.

JAMES B. WHISKER
The Right to Hunt

The Jewish recollection of hunting is dim in the Bible. Adam and Cain are described as farmers; Abel is a shepherd. Isaac and Jacob are contrasted with the hunting tribal leaders, for they are no longer hunt-ers. But the term *kethibh* (hunting) in Genesis suggests that at one time food (*zedah*) was obtained in this way . . .

Hunting was not condemned anywhere in the Old Testament. In-deed, Nimrod, founder of Assyria, is credited with having been "a mighty hunter before Jehovah.". . .

In Leviticus (17:13) the Hebrews are instructed to bleed any kill made in the hunt because they are forbidden to eat the blood. But beyond the proscription against eating the blood there is nothing said to prohibit hunting; indeed, it seems to be a wholly acceptable way of obtaining fresh meat. This same proscription applies to domesticated animals. Later (Lev. 17:15), it is proscribed to eat an animal which has died of natural causes, or which has been killed by other predators. In short, man is not permitted to scavenge, although he may hunt and kill animals of the forest himself.

In the Book of Proverbs (12:27) man is admonished not to waste what he has taken in the hunt. The sin of sloth is described using the example of one who hunts but does not cook (or, presumably, eat) what he has killed. The diligent person would kill and not waste the product of his successful hunt.

During the Exodus the Lord provided the people of Israel with a foodstuff called manna, but the people wanted meat as well. The Lord promised "At even(ing) ye shall eat flesh . . ." God then caused quail

From "Hunting in the Judaeo-Christian Tradition", chapter 3 in *The Right to Hunt* (Croton-on-Hudson, N. Y.: North River Press, 1981), pp. 33–40.

to appear in vast numbers, and the people ate of these, having snared them in nets and clubbed them to death (Exod. 16:13ff) . . ..

The only negative suggestion that can be made concerning hunting in the Old Testament concerns the nature of Cain's punishment for slaying Abel. The Lord told Cain that he could not become a farmer, for, "when thou tillest the ground, it shall henceforth not yield unto thee her strength; and a vagabond shalt thou be in the earth" (Gen. 4:12). A reasonable reading of the passage suggests that Cain was condemned to be a hunter, a person who could not earn his daily bread by tilling the fields. But a fair reading also suggests that the punishment consists in not having roots, not in being forced to hunt. That is, Cain was denied a place of his own, condemned to be a wanderer, and thus had to hunt; he was not made a hunter as a punishment. There was no onus attached to hunting . . .

In general, the theology of the ancient people of Israel recognized the substantial difference between man and animals. Early on, God, having created all sorts of animals and birds and fishes, gave man complete control over all that God had created. "So God created man in his own image, in the image of God he created him; male and female he created them. And God blessed them, and God said unto them, Be fruitful and multiply and replenish the earth and subdue it; and have dominion over the fish of the sea, and over the fowl of the air, and every other living thing that moveth upon the earth" (Gen. 1:27–28).

It is possible to interpret Genesis (especially 1:29–30) to conclude that originally man and all the animals were vegetarians. God gives "seed-bearing plants" and "all green plants" to both man and all animal life for food. It is not clear when this was changed, but presumably it was altered by the time of the fall of Adam from God's grace. From what we know of animal, fish, and bird life, there was never a time when only herbivores existed. The language of Genesis 1:29–30 suggests more that life ("whatsoever breatheth") could eat of vegetables and other things than that sentient life was limited exclusively to seeds and plants. The passage does not condemn the eating of flesh. It is compelling that we conclude that, whatever the condition in the Garden of Eden, by the time historical man appears, it is permissible to eat plants and flesh. This is precisely the point made in Deuteronomy: how and under what conditions which kinds of animals may be killed and their flesh incorporated in the human diet.

Old Testament religion is quite clear on the doctrine of sin. One may commit sin against one's fellow man, that is, creatures of the same order of creation; and one can commit sin against the higher power, namely, against Jehovah. The latter case is very clear, for the very first instance of sin (Gen. 3) occurred as disobedience of God's orders concerning the eating of the fruit of the tree of the knowledge of good and evil. It may be argued that, without God, sin would be impossible, even against one's fellow man. That is, we can sin against our neighbor only because God has made it a sin, by requiring a code of interpersonal conduct among men. Animals are considered only insofar as they are the possessions of men, or when the treatment of animals might have a bearing on relations among men, or between man and God . . .

The New Testament says absolutely nothing about hunting. However, it says a great deal about fishing. The best we can do is to fabricate an argument on the analogy between the taking of the life of a fish, also a living and breathing and sentient being, and the taking of animal or bird life.

Christ took bread and two fishes, "and looking up to heaven, he blessed, and brake . . . and they did all eat, and were filled"(Matt. 14:19–20). And, again, "he took seven loaves and the fishes, and gave thanks . . . and gave to his disciples, and the disciples to the multitude" (Matt. 15:36–37). In Mark (6:38–44), Christ ". . . the two fishes divided he among them all." The same command to eat of the fish available was recorded in Mark 8:7–8. Luke reports the same distributions of fish among those who listened to Jesus (Luke 9:13–16) as does John (6:11–12).

Christ ate fish on at least one instance, this being after the Resurrection. "And when he had thus spoken, he shewed them his hands and feet . . . He said unto them, have ye here any meat? And they gave him a piece of broiled fish . . . and he took it and did eat before them" (Luke 24:41–43). One may suggest that Christ asked for meat without stipulating whether it was to be of fish, fowl, or animal. Since it was traditional to slaughter a lamb at Passover, it is probable that Christ, during most of his years on earth, ate of that meat, at least once a year. Clearly, there is no proscription in the New Testament against eating fish or meat.

Christ ordered his disciples to fish on at least two occasions. Several of the twelve disciples were fishermen by profession (Mark 1:16–17;

Matt. 4:18–19), and the New Testament records no onus being attached to that profession. When a profession was held in contempt, as was the case with Judas, a tax collector, this was noted. Although Jesus took the fishermen away from fishing, making them "fishers of men," they did occasionally return to their old profession. Jesus came to his disciples, at the Sea of Tiberius, apparently after some period of absence. "Then Jesus saith unto them, Children, have ye any meat? They answered him, No. And he said unto them, cast the net on the right side of the ship, and ye shall find. They cast therefore, and now they were not able to draw it for the multitude of fishes" (John 21; Luke 5). The second instance of Christ ordering his disciples to fish occurs in Matthew (17:27): ". . . Go thou to the sea, and cast an hook, and take up the fish that first cometh up . . ."

The passage which is most often quoted as showing that Christ disapproved of hunting or killing of animals, that "not one of these [sparrows] will fall to the ground without your Father's will" (Matt. 10:29), is misused here, for it applies not to hunting, but to God's providential sovereignty over all things . . .

One who wishes to condemn hunting as immoral must look to authorities other than traditional religious works for support. The entire Judaeo-Christian synthesis suggests that it is quite correct for man to hunt if he wishes to do so. There is not a single passage that condemns hunting or hunters. Nowhere in the Bible, nor in the Book of Mormon, can one find anything negative attached to the act of hunting or to the profession or the sport of the hunter.

The only rules that are attached to hunting are those that are the general Christian principles that can be, and necessarily are, applied to all human activities. One may not negate the obligation of love and charity in pursuing any human action. One may not act in a way that brings harm or injury to his neighbor, disgrace upon himself, or which interferes with his love of God. If hunting passes these tests, that is, if it is regulated human conduct which is made obedient to accepted ethical standards, then it is permitted.

Of course, one is certainly not compelled to hunt; nor is one required to eat meat from any source. It is a voluntary action. Man may himself kill meat (hunting), or he may have it killed for him (slaughtering). These actions are permissive; but they are not prohibited.

IV. Intensive Farming

RUTH HARRISON
Ethical Issues in Intensive Farming

One of the problems is that during the last two decades the design of livestock systems has moved out of the hands of stockmen and into the hands of engineers and technicians in allied trades, men of great skill and ingenuity but with little knowledge of animals, and especially of animal behaviour. Perhaps the phrase "design of livestock systems" is misleading, for often there has been no attempt at any overall design. The systems have developed, rather haphazardly, with each firm trying to maximise the use of its own products. Innovation has followed innovation and the animals have been, in effect, the guinea pigs of constantly changing techniques and fashions.

The design of housing and equipment has been directed towards ease of management rather than the comfort and well-being of the animals. It is a matter of some concern that firms are allowed to put a product on the market without prior testing in the field. They can then proceed to sell it widely with all the pressures of high-powered salesmanship and advertising and nobody can stop them. Anyone concerned with the humanity of the product, on the other hand, has to produce evidence of pathological damage before action is even con-

From "Ethical Questions Concerning Modern Livestock Farming", in David Paterson and R. D. Ryder (eds.), *Animals' Rights—A Symposium* (Fontwell, Sussex: Centaur Press, 1979), pp. 123–29.

sidered, and this means that much suffering is likely to occur before the product is altered or taken off the market. In Sweden this situation is reversed and firms are not permitted to sell such products until they have been independently tested at the firm's expense . . .

The most important thing in law is that the suffering of the animal must be substantial and observable. It sticks to the traditionally accepted forms of cruelty: the infliction of injury, neglected festering sores, emaciation, advanced and untreated disease. It also recognises certain concepts, again easily seen, such as terrifying, beating or overloading an animal. [The British] Act covering farm animals—the 1968 *Agriculture (Miscellaneous Provisions) Act* has added "unnecessary distress" to "unnecessary pain" as an offence, and it was to be hoped that this would cover *behavioural* distress. In practice the situation is unchanged. The [British] Codes of Practice which the Minister issues for the guidance of stockmen are voluntary and are honoured more in the breach than the observance. Farms are visited by the State Veterinary Service who are always willing to investigate complaints . . .

In the spring of 1977 a case was taken by the National Society for the Abolition of Factory Farming against a firm of veal producers. It was pointed out in Court that the calves were kept in pens 22" wide by 5' deep, on wooden slats without bedding, that they could not stretch their legs freely when they were lying down, had difficulty in grooming themselves, were fed entirely on a milk substitute and denied the roughage normally given to young ruminants. It was further stated that the calves were kept in darkness apart from twice-a-day feeding. The producers were not complying with the Codes of Practice which stipulate that the width of the pen should be equal to the height of the animal at the shoulder (thereby enabling it to turn round and freely to lie down and groom) and that the level of lighting should be such that all the calves can be seen clearly.

The Chairman of the Magistrates was a West Country dairy farmer, a splendid man. He listened very carefully hour after hour to the arguments and then said he would like to see the unit. This was arranged for the following morning and he then made his judgement. He said that the system was one that obviously *could* cause suffering, but that he had not *seen* any suffering that morning.

What worried me was the emphasis, yet again, on *seeing* suffering. We were right back at having to have pathological evidence of distress.

. . . [T]he State Veterinary Service . . . carried out an extensive survey of farms in 1970 to see whether farmers were complying with the provisions of the Codes of Practice and whether any evidence of pain or distress was apparent. Their Report came up with statements like this:

On veal units:

> "In the majority of the units the calves were unable to turn round after the 6th or 7th week of life, and in their last two or three weeks of life many of them also had difficulty in grooming. We found no evidence of pain or distress in the calves attributable to these restrictions."

On pigs—and this will go down as a classic!

> "In those cases where pigs were kept in darkness or where the lighting was so reduced as to be insufficient to enable the pigs to be seen clearly we found no evidence that these systems of management were causing any pain or distress to the pigs."

Now to be fair to the State Veterinary Service I must point out that the Report was based on the veterinarians' judgement of the *physical* well-being of the animals. Perhaps they did not feel qualified to judge whether inability to groom was distressful to an animal. But today, when behavioural research on farm animals has itself become somewhat of a growth industry, and when there are special courses in behaviour for the Veterinary Service, we still get the same sort of statements quoted soothingly by the Minister in answer to anxious questioners in Parliament . . .

Genetic breeding and improved nutrition have led to younger slaughter weights and often the animals are slaughtered before distress can result in clinical symptoms which could be questioned in law. The situation is further confused by the armoury of drugs now in use on farms. These can delay and mask the effects of imperfect systems. And if we have to wait for clinical manifestations of suffering before we can take action, aren't we in effect taking the animal *beyond* the measure of stress it can endure in its short life? . . .

The well-being of the animal will be assured only if it is kept within the limits of that environmental range to which it can *adapt without suffering*. This must form the criterion for any future system . . .

The mass production systems in use today were developed in the decades of plenty—the 1950s and 1960s—when imports of feeding-stuffs and energy were cheap and plentiful, labour was leaving the land and we were faced with a steadily rising population. We thought this situation would go on for ever and ever. Now we are faced with the reverse situation. The population of Europe has stabilised and may even be starting to fall, we have massive unemployment with agri-cultural schools bursting at the seams and people desperately trying to get back onto the land. We also face dwindling reserves of energy, foodstuffs, fertilisers and water.

One situation which remains the same today as it was twenty years ago is that the meat produced goes to feeding the overfed, especially in the west, and has little to do with the hungry in the developing countries. I regard the argument that we are robbing the starving of food by feeding grain to our livestock as grossly over-simplified, yet of course there is some truth in it. What seems to me just as serious is that we tend to be fashion setters for other countries and of course our commercial salesmen try their utmost to take over potential new markets whether or not it is in the interests of the people of those countries to use their products. Whereas in India, for example, the people were in the past mostly vegetarian, increased travel has brought them in touch with western standards to which they aspire and, sadly, included in these these standards is meat eating. Some sixty per cent of the people of India are now prepared to eat meat. I say "sadly" because their country cannot support a food programme of increased meat eating. It cannot support, either, the use of battery cages which involve using precious grain for the hens, in place of the scavenging hen which did not compete for its food with the human population.

What does seem certain is that there is going to be an increasing demand globally for animal feed, and competition will increase prices so that production of food animals will have to be cut back. Obviously the first priority on land in all countries is the maintenance of sufficient supplies of basic plant foods to ensure an adequate diet for their pop-ulations. Only then can surplus land be used for animals.

These pressures—on land, the need to conserve dwindling energy supplies, the need for a fairer sharing of the world's resources—may make it easier for governments to make radical changes in the way food animals are kept . . .

If we adopt as our aim systems which give the animal an environment to which it can adapt without suffering it will not be easy to maintain very large units and mass-production techniques. It will tend to take production out of the hands of the big monopolies and back into the hands of the farmer, which is no bad thing. Farming is not, after all, a conveyor belt industry churning out nuts and bolts, it is a biological process, self-renewing, the farmer being a husbandman for the future.

E. F. SCHUMACHER
Animals Are Ends-in-Themselves

There are always some things which we do for their own sakes, and there are other things which we do for some other purpose. One of the most important tasks for any society is to distinguish between ends and means-to-ends, and to have some sort of cohesive view and agreement about this. Is the land merely a means of production or is it something more, something that is an end in itself? And when I say 'land', I include the creatures upon it.

Anything we do just for the sake of doing it does not lend itself to utilitarian calculation. For instance, most of us try to keep ourselves reasonably clean. Why? Simply for hygienic reasons? No, the hygienic aspect is secondary; we recognise cleanliness as a value in itself. We do not calculate its value; the economic calculus simply does not come in. It could be argued that to wash is uneconomic: it costs time and money and produces nothing—except cleanliness. There are many activities which are totally uneconomic, but they are carried on for their own sakes. The economists have an easy way of dealing with them: they divide all human activities between 'production' and 'consumption'. Anything we do under the head of 'production' is subject to the economic calculus, and anything we do under the heading of

From *Small Is Beautiful: A Study of Economics as if People Mattered* (London: Abacus, 1974), pp. 86–90.

'consumption' is not. But real life is very refractory to such classifications, because man-as-producer and man-as-consumer is in fact the same man, who is always producing and consuming *at the same time*. Even a worker in his factory consumes certain 'amenities', commonly referred to as 'working conditions', and when insufficient 'amenities' are provided he cannot—or refuses to—carry on. And even the man who consumes water and soap may be said to be producing cleanliness.

We produce in order to be able to afford certain amenities and comforts as 'consumers'. If, however, somebody demanded these same amenities and comforts while he was engaged in 'production', he would be told that this would be uneconomic, that it would be inefficient, and that society could not afford such inefficiency. In other words, everything depends on whether it is done by man-as-producer or by man-as-consumer. If man-as-producer travels first-class or uses a luxurious car, this is called a waste of money; but if the same man in his other incarnation of man-as-consumer does the same, this is called a sign of a high standard of life.

Nowhere is this dichotomy more noticeable than in connection with the use of the land. The farmer is considered simply as a producer who must cut his costs and raise his efficiency by every possible device, even if he thereby destroys—for man-as-consumer—the health of the soil and beauty of the landscape, and even if the end effect is the depopulation of the land and the overcrowding of cities. There are large-scale farmers, horticulturists, food manufacturers and fruit growers today who would never think of consuming any of their own products. 'Luckily,' they say, 'we have enough money to be able to afford to buy products which have been organically grown, without the use of poisons.' When they are asked why they themselves do not adhere to organic methods and avoid the use of poisonous substances, they reply that they could not afford to do so. What man-as-producer can afford is one thing; what man-as-consumer can afford is quite another thing. But since the two are the same man, the question of what man—or society—can really afford gives rise to endless confusion.

There is no escape from this confusion as long as the land and the creatures upon it are looked upon as *nothing but* 'factors of production'. They are, of course, factors of production, that is to say, means-to-ends, but this is their secondary, not their primary, nature. Before everything else, they are ends-in-themselves; they are meta-economic, and it is therefore rationally justifiable to say, as a statement of fact, that they are in a certain sense sacred. Man has not made them, and it is irrational for him to treat things that he has not made and cannot make and cannot recreate once he has spoilt them, in the same manner and spirit as he is entitled to treat things of his own making.

The higher animals have an economic value because of their utility; but they have a meta-economic value in themselves. If I have a car, a man-made thing, I might quite legitimately argue that the best way to use it is never to bother about maintenance and simply run it to ruin. I may indeed have calculated that this is the most economical method of use. If the calculation is correct, nobody can criticise me for acting accordingly, for there is nothing sacred about a man-made thing like a car. But if I have an animal—be it only a calf or a hen—a living, sensitive creature, am I allowed to treat it as nothing but a utility? Am I allowed to run it to ruin?

It is no use trying to answer such questions scientifically. They are metaphysical, not scientific, questions. It is a metaphysical error, likely to produce the gravest practical consequences, to equate 'car' and 'animal' on account of their utility, while failing to recognize the most fundamental difference between them, that of 'level of being'. An irreligious age looks with amused contempt upon the hallowed statements by which religion helped our forbears to appreciate metaphysical truths. 'And the Lord God took man and put him in the Garden of Eden'—not to be idle, but 'to dress it and keep it'. 'And he also gave man dominion over the fish in the sea and the fowl in the air, and over every living being that moves upon the earth.' When he had made 'the beast of the earth after his kind, and cattle after their kind, and everything that creepeth upon the earth after his kind', he saw that it was 'good'. But when he saw everything he had made, the entire biosphere, as we say today, 'behold, it was *very* good'. Man, the highest of his creatures, was given 'dominion', not the right to tyrannise, to ruin and exterminate. It is no use talking about the dignity of man without accepting that *noblesse oblige*. For man to put himself into a wrongful relationship with animals, and particularly those long domesticated by him, has always, in all traditions, been considered a horrible and infinitely dangerous thing to do. There have been no sages or holy men in our or in anybody else's history who were cruel to animals or who looked upon them as *nothing but* utilities, and innumerable are the legends and stories which link sanctity as well as happiness with a loving kindness towards lower creation.

It is interesting to note that modern man is being told, in the name of science, that he is really *nothing but* a naked ape or even an accidental collocation of atoms. 'Now we can define man', says Professor Joshua Lederberg. 'Genotypically at least, he is six feet of a particular molecular sequence of carbon, hydrogen, oxygen, nitrogen and phosphorous atoms.' As modern man thinks so 'humbly' of himself, he thinks even more 'humbly' of the animals which serve his needs: and treats them as if they were machines. Other, less sophisticated—or is it less depraved?—people take a different attitude. As H. Fielding Hall reported from Burma:

> 'To him (the Burmese) men are men, and animals are animals, and men are far the higher. But he does not deduce from this that man's superiority gives him permission to illtreat or kill animals. It is just the reverse. It is because man is so much higher than the animal that he can and must observe towards animals the very greatest care, feel for them the very greatest compassion, be good to them in every way he can. The Burmese's motto should be *noblesse oblige*. He knows the meaning, he knows not the words.'

In *Proverbs* we read that the just man takes care of his beast, but the heart of the wicked is merciless, and St Thomas Aquinas wrote: 'It is evident that if a man practises a compassionate affection for animals, he is all the more disposed to feel compassion for his fellowmen.' No-one ever raised the question of whether they could *afford* to live in accordance with these convictions. At the level of values, of ends-in-themselves, there is no question of 'affording'.

KARL BARTH
Justifiable Killing

[D]oes the lordship of man over the animal consist in his self-evident freedom to take its life in the service of his own ends? Is he permitted and commanded to kill an animal in the same sense in which he fells a tree, whether for the sake of its meat, for its fur, horns, feathers or other useful articles, or even to defend himself against the threat of danger or damage which it offers? Those who know respect for life at the point where it arises in the true and primary sense, namely in the human sphere, will necessarily perceive that there is at least a difference between the two cases. For the killing of animals, in contrast to the harvesting of plants and fruits, is annihilation. This is not a case of participation in the products of a sprouting nexus of life ceaselessly renewed in different forms, but the removing of a single being, a unique creature existing in an individuality which we cannot fathom but also cannot deny. The harvest is not a breach in the peace of creation, nor is the tending and using of animals, but the killing of animals presupposes that the peace of creation is at least threatened and itself constitutes a continuation of this threat. And the nearness of the animal to man irrevocably means that when man kills a beast he does something which is at least very similar to homicide. We must be very clear about this if we maintain that the lordship of man over animals carries with it the freedom to slaughter them. Those who do not hear the prior command to desist have certainly no right to affirm this freedom or cross the frontier disclosed at this point . . .

If there is a freedom of man to kill animals, this signifies in any case the adoption of a qualified and in some sense enhanced responsibility. If that of his lordship over the living beast is serious enough, it takes on a new gravity when he sees himself compelled to express his lordship by depriving it of its life. He obviously cannot do this except under the pressure of necessity. Far less than all the other things

From *Church Dogmatics*, vol. III, part 4, *The Doctrine of Creation*, ET by A. T. Mackay, T. H. L. Parker, H. Knight, H. A. Kennedy, and J. Marks (Edinburgh: T. & T. Clark, 1961), pp. 352–56.

which he dares to do in relation to animals, may this be ventured unthinkingly and as though it were self-evident. He must never treat this need for defensive and offensive action against the animal world as a natural one, nor include it as a normal element in his thinking or conduct. He must always shrink from this possibility even when he makes use of it. It always contains the sharp counter-question: Who are you, man, to claim that you must venture this to maintain, support, enrich and beautify your own life? What is there in your life that you feel compelled to take this aggressive step in its favour? We cannot but be reminded of the perversion from which the whole historical existence of the creature suffers and the guilt of which does not really reside in the beast but ultimately in man himself. The slaying of animals is really possible only as an appeal to God's reconciling grace, as its representation and proclamation. It undoubtedly means making use of the offering of an alien and innocent victim and claiming its life for ours. Man must have good reasons for seriously making such a claim. His real and supposed needs certainly do not justify it. He must be authorised to do so by his acknowledgment of the faithfulness and goodness of God, who in spite of and in his guilt keeps him from falling as He saved Noah's generation from the flood and kept it even though it was no better as a result. Man sins if he does it without his authorisation. He sins if he presumes to do it on his own authority. He is already on his way to homicide if he sins in the killing of animals, if he murders an animal. He must not murder an animal. He can only kill it, knowing that it does not belong to him but to God, and that in killing it he surrenders it to God in order to receive it back from Him as something he needs and desires. The killing of animals in obedience is possible only as a deeply reverential act of repentance, gratitude and praise on the part of the forgiven sinner in face of the One who is the Creator and Lord of man and beast. The killing of animals, when performed with the permission of God and by His command, is a priestly act of eschatalogical character. It can be accomplished with a good conscience only as we glance backward to creation and forward to consummation as the boundaries of the sphere in which alone there can be any question of its necessity. In can be achieved only in recollection of the reconciliation of man by the Man who intercedes for him and for all creation, and in whom God has accomplished the reconciliation of the world with Himself.

This must be the starting-point for all the detailed questions to which we can only allude in the present context. Wherever man exercises his lordship over the animal, and especially across every hunting lodge, abbatoir and vivisection chamber, there should be written in letters of fire the words of St. Paul in Rom. 8:18f . . . concerning the "earnest expectation" (*apokaradokia*) of the creature—for what?—for the "manifestation of the children of God," and therefore for the liberation of those who now keep them imprisoned and even dispatch them from life to death. The creature has become subject to *mataiotēs* [futility], not *hekousa* [of its own will], nor according to its own destiny, but because of man, its subjugator. And it, too, is determined for liberation from the *douleia tēs phthoras* [bondage to decay] together with the liberation of the children of God, so that for the moment it groans and cries with us in the birth-pangs of a new aeon. In this whole sphere what is good is obviously that which can be justified in face of these words, and what is bad that which cannot. A good hunter, honourable butcher and conscientious vivisectionist will differ from the bad in the fact that even as they are engaged in killing animals they hear this groaning and travailing of the creature, and therefore, in comparison with all others who have to do with animals, they are summoned to an intensified, sharpened and deepened diffidence, reserve and carefulness. In this matter they act on the extreme limits where respect for life and callous disregard constantly jostle and may easily pass into one another. On these frontiers, if anywhere, animal protection, care and friendship are quite indispensable.

Yet it is not only understandable but necessary that the affirmation of this whole possibility should always have been accompanied by a radical protest against it. It may well be objected against a vegetarianism which presses in this direction that it represents a wanton anticipation of what is described by Is. 11 and Rom. 8 as existence in the new aeon for which we hope. It may also be true that it aggravates by reason of its inevitable inconsistencies, its sentimentality and its fanaticism. But for all its weaknesses we must be careful not to put ourselves in the wrong in face of it by our own thoughtlessness and hardness of heart.

V. Killing for Food

LEO TOLSTOY
The First Step

Fasting is an indispensable condition of a good life; but in fasting, as in self-control in general, the question arises, what shall we begin with?—How to fast, how often to eat, what to eat, what to avoid eating? And as we can do no work seriously without regarding the necessary order of sequence, so also we cannot fast without knowing where to begin—with what to commence self-control in food.

Fasting! And even an analysis of how to fast and where to begin! The notion seems ridiculous and wild to the majority of men.

I remember how an Evangelical preacher who was attacking monastic asceticism once said to me with pride at his own originality, 'Ours is not a Christianity of fasting and privations, but of beefsteaks.' Christianity, or virtue in general—and beefsteaks!

During a long period of darkness and lack of all guidance, Pagan or Christian, so many wild, immoral ideas have made their way into our life (especially into that lower region of the first steps towards a good life—our relation to food to which no one paid any attention), that it is difficult for us in our days even to understand the audacity and senselessness of upholding Christianity or virtue with beefsteaks.

We are not horrified by this association simply because a strange thing has befallen us. We look and see not: listen and hear not. There

From "The First Step", in *Reeollections and Essays*, ET with an introduction by Aylmer Maude (London: Oxford University Press, 4th ed., 1961), pp. 123–35.

is no bad odour, no sound, no monstrosity, to which man cannot become so accustomed that he ceases to remark what would strike a man unaccustomed to it. And it is precisely the same in the moral region. Christianity and morality with beefsteaks!

A few days ago I visited the slaughter-house in our town of Túla. It is built on the new and improved system practised in large towns, with a view to causing the animals as little suffering as possible. It was on a Friday, two days before Trinity Sunday. There were many cattle there.

Long before this, when reading that excellent book, *The Ethics of Diet*, I had wished to visit a slaughter-house in order to see with my own eyes the reality of the question raised when vegetarianism is discussed. But at first I felt ashamed to do so, as one is always ashamed of going to look at suffering which one knows is about to take place but which one cannot avert; and so I kept putting off my visit.

But a little while ago I met on the road a butcher returning to Túla after a visit to his home. He is not yet an experienced butcher, and his duty is to stab with a knife. I asked him whether he did not feel sorry for the animals that he killed. He gave me the usual answer: 'Why should I feel sorry? It is necessary.' But when I told him that eating flesh is not necessary, but is only a luxury, he agreed; and then he admitted that he was sorry for the animals. 'But what can I do?' he said, 'I must earn my bread. At first I was *afraid* to kill. My father, he never even killed a chicken in all his life.' The majority of Russians cannot kill; they feel pity, and express the feeling by the word '*fear*'. This man had also been 'afraid', but he was so no longer. He told me that most of the work was done on Fridays, when it continues until the evening.

Not long ago I also had a talk with a retired soldier, a butcher, and he too was surprised at my assertion that it was a pity to kill, and said the usual things about its being ordained. But afterwards he agreed with me: 'Especially when they are quiet, tame cattle. They come, poor things! trusting you. It is very pitiful.'

This is dreadful! Not the suffering and death of the animals, but that man suppresses in himself, unnecessarily, the highest spiritual capacity—that of sympathy and pity towards living creatures like himself—and by violating his own feelings becomes cruel. And how deeply seated in the human heart is the injunction not to take life! . . .

We cannot pretend that we do not know this. We are not ostriches, and cannot believe that if we refuse to look at what we do not wish to see, it will not exist. This is especially the case when what we do not wish to see is what we wish to eat. If it were really indispensable, or if not indispensable, at least in some way useful! But it is quite unnecessary,[1] and only serves to develop animal feelings, to excite desire, and to promote fornication and drunkenness . . .

What, then, do I wish to say? That in order to be moral people must cease to eat meat? Not at all.

I only wish to say that for a good life a certain order of good actions is indispensable; that if a man's aspirations toward right living be serious they will inevitably follow one definite sequence; and that in this sequence the first virtue a man will strive after will be self-control, self-restraint. And in seeking for self-control a man will inevitably follow one definite sequence, and in this sequence the first thing will be self-control in food—fasting. And in fasting, if he be really and seriously seeking to live a good life, the first thing from which he will abstain will always be the use of animal food, because, to say nothing of the excitation of the passions caused by such food, its use is simply immoral, as it involves the performance of an act which is contrary to moral feeling—killing; and is called forth only by greediness and the desire for tasty food . . .

But why, if the wrongfulness—i.e. the immorality—of animal food was known to humanity so long ago, have people not yet come to acknowledge this law? will be asked by those who are accustomed to be led by public opinion rather than by reason.

The answer to this question is that the moral progress of humanity—which is the foundation of every other kind of progress—is always slow; but that the sign of true, not casual, progress is its uninterruptedness and its continual acceleration.

And the progress of vegetarianism is of this kind. That progress is expressed . . . in the actual life of mankind, which from many causes is involuntarily passing more and more from carnivorous habits to vegetable food, and is also deliberately following the same path in a movement which shows evident strength, and which is growing larger

---

[1] Let those who doubt this read the numerous books upon the subject, written by scientists and doctors, in which it is proved that flesh is not necessary for the nourishment of man. And let them not listen to those old-fashioned doctors who defend the assertion that flesh is necessary, merely because it has long been so regarded by their predecessors and by themselves; and who defend their opinion with tenacity and malevolence, as all that is old and traditional always is defended.—L. T.

and larger—viz. vegetarianism. That movement has during the last ten years advanced more and more rapidly. More and more books and periodicals on this subject appear every year; one meets more and more people who have given up meat; and abroad, especially in Germany, England, and America, the number of vegetarian hotels and restaurants increases year by year.

This movement should cause especial joy to those whose life lies in the effort to bring about the kingdom of God on earth, not because vegetarianism is in itself an important step towards that kingdom (all true steps are both important and unimportant), but because it is a sign that the aspiration of mankind towards moral perfection is serious and sincere, for it has taken the one unalterable order of succession natural to it, beginning with the first step.

ALEC R. VIDLER

Sermon on Vegetarianism

I was at one time a vegetarian, and I used to read the *Vegetarian News*, but I never succeeded in convincing myself that eating animals is wrong. It may be crude; it may be unaesthetic—I do not see how you can regard a butcher's shop as 'a thing of beauty and a joy for ever'—but it is not wrong. We are right in using the animals for our service and sustenance. The Bible says so quite clearly, but it says no less clearly that God cares for animals, and we must do so too.

We may use the animals for our service and sustenance. In the first chapter of Genesis God says to mankind: 'Have dominion over the fish of the sea, and over the fowl of the air, over every living thing that moveth upon the earth.' Our Lord made use of animals. He rode upon an ass. He ate broiled fish, and he directed his disciples where to fish. St Peter was told in his vision to arise, kill and eat, and we may do so too. St Paul took it for granted that Christians would eat meat. The only question that bothered him was whether they were at liberty to eat meat that had been offered in sacrifice to an idol, as

From "Animals", in *Windsor Sermons* (London: SCM Press, 1962), pp. 173–76.

was the case with much of the meat that was on sale in the markets of Corinth. What was good enough for Peter and Paul is good enough for you and me. So far so good, then.

But that is not what the text is about. 'A righteous man regardeth the life of his beast.' Why does he do so? In the first place, because God cares for the animals. This is brought out again and again by the legislators, by the poets, and by the prophets of Israel. In the Law of Moses the householder is bidden to allow his cattle to enjoy the sabbath rest. The farmer is forbidden to muzzle the ox that treads out the corn so that it too may partake of the fruits of its labours. The passer-by is directed to take care of an ox or an ass that belongs to his enemy. The bird-nester is told not to take the mother bird who has young or eggs. All this means that cruelty to animals is entirely foreign to the nature and the will of God . . .

You have no direct contact, I expect, with the slaughter of animals, but as citizens you are responsible for making sure that it is humanely done. We must ever be on the look out for ways of softening the agonies of animals and for ameliorating their pains. God, who made us, also made them, and has a close regard to the way in which we treat them. I know that women, and men too, can be sentimental and silly about animals, but it is a fact that we are bound up with the animals in God's creation. We depend on them and they depend on us. They are at our mercy. They have no power of changing masters and no means of redressing their wrongs. The very power we have over them entitles them to our care and protection as children are entitled to the care and protection of their parents. As Browning said:

> God made all creatures and gave them our love and our fear,
> To give sign, we and they are his children, one family here.

Kindness to animals brings its own reward, especially with the domesticated animals to whom, just because they are domesticated, we have a special duty. 'With what measure ye mete it shall be measured to you again' is true of the world of animals as well as of the world of men. But that alone would be a low and selfish reason for kindness to animals. It is more worthy of remark that kindness to animals uplifts and ennobles man. It casts out the savagery that lurks in every human heart. It fosters the virtues of gentleness and compassion. Herbert Spencer said in his philosophical manner that 'the behaviour of men to the lower animals, and their behaviour to each other, bear a constant relationship.' I take that to mean, in plainer English, that people who study kindness to animals also study kindness to their fellow-men, and vice versa. As a rule that is true, though there are exceptions to it, alas! Some people who are very fond of cats are very catty to their neighbours.

JOHN CALVIN

The Tyranny of Vegetarianism

[Genesis 9:]3. *Every moving thing that liveth shall be meat for you.* The Lord proceeds further, and grants animals for food to men, that they may eat their flesh. And because Moses now first relates that this right was given to men, nearly all commentators infer, that it was not lawful for man to eat flesh before the deluge, but that the natural fruits of the earth were his only food. But the argument is not sufficiently firm. For I hold to this principle; that God here does not bestow on men more than he had previously given, but only restores what had been taken away, that they might again enter on the possession of those good things from which they had been excluded. For since they had before offered sacrifices to God, and were also permitted to kill wild beasts, from the hides and skins of which, they might make for themselves garments and tents, I do not see what obligation should prevent them from the eating of flesh. But since it is of little consequence what opinion is held, I affirm nothing on the subject.[1] This ought justly to be deemed by us of greater importance, that to eat the flesh

From *Commentaries on the First Book of Moses called Genesis*, vol. I, ET by John King (Edinburgh: Calvin Translation Society, 1847), pp. 291–93.

[1]The question which Calvin here dismisses as one of little importance, has, in modern controversy, assumed a very different position; and most commentators have come to a decision, the reverse of that to which he inclines. His argument appears chargeable with the want of firmness, which he imputes to others. The inference that the flesh of sacrifices was eaten, since otherwise it must have been wasted, is of no force, if we suppose the first sacrifices to have been all *holocausts*, or whole burnt-offerings unto the Lord. The garments or tents referred to as made from the skins of animals were, in all probability, those of the very animals which were thus sacrificed; so that there is no reason hence to conclude, that flesh was eaten before the deluge. But let the reader refer to Magee on the Antonement, Dissertation, No. liii.—*Ed.* [Footnote in the original.—*A.L.*]

of animals is granted to us by the kindness of God; that we do not seize upon what our appetite desires, as robbers do, nor yet tyrannically shed the innocent blood of cattle; but that we only take what is offered to us by the hand of the Lord. We have heard what Paul says, that we are at liberty to eat what we please, only we do it with the assurance of conscience, but that he who imagines anything to be unclean, to him it is unclean, (Rom. xiv. 14.) And whence has this happened to man, that he should eat whatever food he pleased before God, with a tranquil mind, and not with unbridled license, except from his knowing, that it has been divinely delivered into his hand by the right of donation? Wherefore, (the same Paul being witness,) the word of God sanctifies the creatures, that we may purely and lawfully feed on them, (1 Tim. iv. 5.) Let the adage be utterly rejected which says, 'that no one can feed and refresh his body with a morsel of bread, without, at the same time, defiling his soul.' Therefore it is not to be doubted, that the Lord designed to confirm our faith, when he expressly declares by Moses, that he gave to man the free use of flesh, so that we might not eat it with a doubtful and trembling conscience. At the same time, however, he invites us to thanksgiving. On this account also, Paul adds "prayer" to the "word," in defining the method of sanctification in the passage recently cited.

And now we must firmly retain the liberty given us by Lord, which he designed to be recorded as on public tables. For, by this word, he addresses all the posterity of Noah, and renders his gift common to all ages. And why is this done, but that the faithful may boldly assert their right to that which, they know, has proceeded from God as its Author? For it is an insupportable tyranny, when God, the Creator of all things, has laid open to us the earth and the air, in order that we may thence take food as from his storehouse, for these to be shut up from us by mortal man, who is not able to create even a snail or a fly. I do not speak of external prohibition; but I assert, that atrocious injury is done to God, when we give such license to men as to allow them to pronounce that unlawful which God designs to be lawful, and to bind consciences which the word of God sets free, with their fictitious laws.

STEPHEN R. L. CLARK
Empty Gluttony

Of the making of many arguments there is no end . . . I am sure that enough has been said to demonstrate the desperate need for a practical and philosophical reappraisal of our standing in the world. It is no longer enough to fantasize, for example, that dolphins may prove our intellectual equals and be admitted into a new, terrestrial society; it is not enough to tell ourselves stories about those other intelligences who may inhabit other worlds of this galaxy, and speculate on how we may treat each other. There are other sentient creatures all about us, who may lack our verbalizing gifts but who have their lives to live and their own visions of reality to worship. We are not separate from them, and owe them honour. To imagine that their lesser 'intelligence' (whatever that may be) licenses our tyranny is to leave the way open for any human intellectual élite to treat the rest of us as trash. Intelligence is a great gift, certainly, but it is of value only in its service of the multi-millionfold enterprise that is the biosphere, and beyond that, the world . . . Let us try the experiment, you and I, of meaning, when we say 'we', not merely 'we men', but 'we mammals' or 'we animals'. Maybe very few mammals or animals will ever join with you and me in any fully and mutually conscious enterprise: but the same is true even of human beings. And in remembering our solidarity and common ancestry with creatures not of our immediate kind we may come to be kinder to such creatures of our species as are not to our taste. Humanists sought to purchase the welfare of their fellow men by denigrating 'beasts': such antagonisms are counterproductive.

In pursuing the various self-deceptions endemic to man, particularly but not exclusively to civilized man, through the labyrinth of orthodox thought and of my imagination, I have not committed myself to any particular view of the 'facts' or of the nature of 'moral enquiry'. I do not believe that there is any credible account of either which could excuse our present depredations. I am inclined, perhaps unfairly, to

From *The Moral Status of Animals* (Oxford: The Clarendon Press, 1977), pp. 182–83.

think that no-one has any standing in such a discussion who has not taken the simple, minimal step of abandoning flesh-foods. Honourable men may honourably disagree about some details of human treatment of the non-human, but vegetarianism is now as necessary a pledge of moral devotion as was the refusal of emperor-worship in the early Church. Those who have not made that pledge have no authority to speak against the most inanely conceived experiments, nor against hunting, nor against fur-trapping, nor bear-baiting, nor bull-fights, nor pulling the wings off flies. Flesh-eating in our present circumstances is as empty a gluttony as any of these things. Those who still eat flesh when they could do otherwise have no claim to be serious moralists.

This judgement is perhaps unfair: though those who say so should remember that I make it also against my own past self. Nor do I forget that there is no end to human hypocrisy, and that at any stage of our progress we are cosily engaged in practices which at a later date we will consider grievous wrongs—often for their *silliness* as much as for the harm they did. In short, none of us, save some saints or Bodhisattvas, is a decent moral authority. The most that we do is *try*, remembering some of the time to wonder what a decent man *would* do. Such decency is not ours: a decent man would hardly need to think of what to do—he'd act as if the decent thing was the only option, and that an enjoyable one. We struggle to correct our biases, our blindnesses, our secret fears and fantasies, and work out rules that more or less define the sort of life we think we see as proper. But the decent man, the sound man, the reasonable man does what he knows he must.

For Further Reading

Agius, Ambrose, *God's Animals*, foreword by Cardinal Heenan (Catholic Study Circle for Animal Welfare 1970).

Allchin, A. M., *Wholeness and Transfiguration Illustrated in the Lives of St Francis of Assisi and St Seraphim of Sarov* (SLG Press 1974).

Attfield, Robin, *The Ethics of Environmental Concern* (Basil Blackwell 1983).

Black, John, *Man's Dominion: The Search for Ecological Responsibility* (Edinburgh University Press 1970).

Board for Social Responsibility, *Our Responsibility for the Living Environment: A Report of the General Synod Board for Social Responsibility of the Church of England* (Church House Publishing 1986).

Carpenter, Edward et al., *Animals and Ethics* (Watkins 1980).

Clark, Stephen R. L., *The Moral Status of Animals* (The Clarendon Press 1977).

Cobb Jr, John, *Is It Too Late? A Theology of Ecology* (Bruce 1972).

Derr, Thomas Sieger, *Ecology and Human Liberation* (Geneva: WSCF Books 1973).

Frey, R. G., *Interests and Rights: The Case Against Animals* (The Clarendon Press 1980).

——, *Rights, Killing and Suffering: Moral Vegetarianism and Applied Ethics* (Basil Blackwell 1983).

Galloway, A. D., *The Cosmic Christ* (Nisbet & Sons 1951).

Godlovitch, Stanley and Roslind, and Harris, John, (eds.), *Animals, Men and Morals: An Enquiry into the Maltreatment of Non-Humans* (Gollancz 1971).

Griffiths, Richard, *The Human Use of Animals* (Grove Books 1982).

Harrison, Ruth, *Animal Machines* (Vincent Stuart 1964).

Hendry, George S., *Theology of Nature* (Westminister Press 1980).

Hume, C. W., *The Status of Animals in the Christian Religion* (Universities Federation for Animal Welfare 1957).

Jordon, Bill and Ormrod, Stefan, *The Last Great Wild Beast Show: A Discussion on the Failure of British Animal Collections* (Constable 1978).

Lewis, C. S., *The Problem of Pain* (Fontana Books 1967).

Linzey, Andrew, *Animal Rights: A Christian Assessment* (SCM Press 1976).

———, *The Status of Animals in the Christian Tradition* (Woodbrooke College 1985).

———, *Christianity and the Rights of Animals* (SPCK and Crossroad 1987).

Linzey, Andrew and Wexler, Peter J., *Heaven and Earth: Essex Essays in Theology and Ethics* (Churchman Publishing 1986).

Magel, Charles R., *Keyguide to Information Sources in Animal Rights* (Mansell Publishing, 1988).

Mason, James and Singer, Peter, *Animal Factories* (Crown 1980).

McDonagh, Sean, *To Care for the Earth: A Call to a New Theology* (Geoffrey Chapman 1986).

Midgley, Mary, *Beast and Man: The Roots of Human Nature* (Harvester Press 1979).

———, *Animals and Why They Matter: A Journey around the Species Barrier* (Penguin Books 1983).

Miller, H. and Williams, W., (eds.), *Ethics and Animals* (Humana Press 1983).

Moltmann, Jürgen, *God in Creation: An Ecological Doctrine of Creation*, ET Margaret Kohl (SCM Press 1985).

Montefiore, Hugh, (ed.), *Man and Nature* (Collins 1975).

Morris, Richard K. and Fox, Michael W., (eds.), *On the Fifth Day: Animal Rights and Human Ethics* (Acropolis Press 1978).

Moule, C. F. D, *Man and Nature in the New Testament: Some Reflections on Biblical Ecology* (Athlone Press 1964).

Passmore, John, *Man's Responsibility for Nature: Ecological Problems and Western Traditions* (Duckworth 1974).

Paterson, David and Ryder, Richard D., (eds.), *Animals' Rights—A Symposium* (Centaur Press 1979).

Regan, Tom, *All That Dwell Therein: Essays on Animal Rights and Environmental Ethics* (University of California Press 1982).

———, *The Case for Animal Rights* (University of California Press 1983).

———, (ed.), *Animal Sacrifices: Religious Perspectives on the Use of Animals in Science*, introduction by John Bowker (Temple University Press 1986).

Regan, Tom and Singer, Peter, (eds.), *Animal Rights and Human Obligations* (Prentice Hall 1976).

Ryder, Richard D., *Victims of Science: The Use of Animals in Research*, forewords by Richard Adams and Muriel, Lady Dowding (National Anti-Vivisection Society 1983).

Salt, Henry S., *Animals' Rights Considered in Relation to Social Progress*, preface by Peter Singer (Centaur Press 1980).

Santmire, H. Paul, *The Travail of Nature: The Ambiguous Ecological Promise of Christian Theology* (Fortress Press 1985).

Schweitzer, Albert, *My Life and Thought: An Autobiography*, ET C. T. Campion (Allen & Unwin 1933).

——, *Civilization and Ethics*, ET C. T. Campion (A. & C. Black 1967).

——, *Reverence for Life*, ET R. H. Fuller, foreword by D. E. Trueblood (SPCK 1970).

Singer, Peter, *Animal Liberation: A New Ethic for Our Treatment of Animals* (Jonathan Cape 1976).

——, (ed.), *In Defence of Animals* (Basil Blackwell 1986).

Sperlinger, David, (ed.), *Animals in Research* (John Wiley & Sons 1980).

Stewart Jr, Claude Y., *Nature in Grace: A Study in The Theology of Nature*, NABPR Dissertation Series, No. 3 (Mercer University Press 1983).

Thomas, Keith, *Man and the Natural World: Changing Attitudes in England 1500–1800* (Penguin Books 1984).

Torrance, T. F., *Divine and Contingent Order* (Oxford University Press 1981).

Townend, Christine, *Pulling the Wool: A New Look at the Australian Wool Industry* (Sydney: Hale & Iremonger 1985).

Turner, James, *Reckoning with the Beast: Animals, Pain and Humanity in the Victorian Mind* (Johns Hopkins University Press 1980).

Vanstone, W. H., *Love's Endeavour, Love's Expense: The Response of Being to the Love of God*, foreword by H. A. Williams (Darton, Longman & Todd 1977).

Vyvyan, John, *In Pity and in Anger* (Michael Joseph 1964).

——, *The Dark Face of Science* (Michael Joseph 1971).

Ward, Keith, *Rational Theology and the Creativity of God* (Basil Blackwell 1982).

Wynne-Tyson, Jon, (ed.), *The Extended Circle: A Dictionary of Humane Thought* (Centaur Press 1986).

Notes on Contributors

Aquinas, St Thomas (c1225–1274). Great Medieval Doctor of the Church and widely regarded as the greatest Catholic theologian. His most famous and influential works are the *Summa contra Gentiles* (1259–64) and the *Summa Theologica* (1266–73) both of which are systematic expositions of doctrine inspired by Aristotelian philosophy.

Athanasius, St (c296–373). Bishop and Doctor of the Church. A highly influential figure in early debates about doctrine. His work on the incarnation is widely revered in the Catholic world.

Augustine, St (354–430). Bishop of Hippo for 34 years and one of the greatest theologians of the Church. His literary output was vast and included at least 113 books and treatises, 200 letters and 500 sermons.

Baker, John Austin, is Bishop of Salisbury and formerly Chairman of the Doctrine Commission of the Church of England. He is author of *The Foolishness of God* (Darton, Longman and Todd, 1974) and was a member of the *Man and Nature* Working Party set up by Archbishop Michael Ramsey in 1970.

Barth, Karl (1886–1968). Arguably the greatest theologian since St Thomas Aquinas. His magisterial *Church Dogmatics* spans 12 chapter volumes and has been translated throughout the world.

Bonaventure, St (1221–1274). Bishop and Doctor of the Church. Minister-General of the Franciscans in 1257 and Cardinal Bishop of Albano in 1272. His biography of St Francis has become a classic work of spirituality.

Burnaby, John, was Regius Professor of Divinity in the University of Cambridge and Fellow of Trinity College. His *The Belief of Christendom* (SPCK, 1959) is a classic work on the Nicene Creed.

Butler, (Bishop) Joseph (1692–1752). Appointed Bishop of Durham in 1750, after declining an offer of the Primacy in 1747. His *Analogy of Religion* (1736) is a classic work and still widely read. Its defence of animal immortality has been frequently overlooked.

Calvin, John (1509–1564). One of the major Protestant Reformers and arguably the most influential. Among his many commentaries and sermons, *The*

Institutes of the Christian Religion is his most systematic work and still widely read.

Carpenter, Edward F., was recently Dean of Westminster. He is Vice-President of the RSPCA and President of the Anglican Society for the Welfare of Animals. His publications include: *Common Sense About Christian Ethics* (Gollancz, 1964); *Cantuar: The Archbishops in their Office* (Cassell, 1971) and *Animals and Ethics* (Element Books, 1981).

Clark, Stephen R. L., is an Episcopalian, currently Professor of Philosophy at the University of Liverpool. He was formerly Lecturer in Moral Philosophy at the University of Glasgow and Fellow of All Souls, Oxford. His publications include: *The Moral Status of Animals* (Clarendon Press, 1977) and *The Nature of the Beast: Are Animals Moral?* (OUP, 1982).

Davis, Henry, was a member of the Society of Jesus and Professor of Moral and Pastoral Theology at Heythrop College, Oxford. His five-volume *Moral and Pastoral Theology* (Sheed and Ward, 1952) is a major Roman Catholic textbook.

De Sales, St Francis (1567–1622). Catholic Bishop of Geneva. Founder with St Jane de Chantal of the Order of the Visitation. Best known for his two influential works of devotion: *Introduction to the Devout Life* and *The Love of God.*

Descartes, René (1596–1650), sometimes regarded as the father of modern philosophy, has been an enormously influential thinker. His *Meditations* are still widely read and admired.

Farrer, Austin, was an Anglican priest, successively Fellow and Chaplain of Trinity College, Oxford, and Warden of Keble College, Oxford. He wrote many books on the relationship between Christian doctrine and contemporary problems, including *Love Almighty and Ills Unlimited* (Collins, 1962).

Geach, Peter, is a Roman Catholic philosopher and theologian, formerly Professor of Logic at the University of Leeds. His publications include: *Mental Acts: Their Content and their Objects* (Routledge and Kegan Paul, 1957) and *God and the Soul* (Routledge and Kegan Paul, 1969).

Gregorios, Paulos Mar, is Metropolitan of Delhi in the Indian Orthodox Church. He is one of the presidents of the World Council of Churches and he chaired the WCC Conference on Faith, Science and the Future (at M.I.T. in 1979). His publications include: *The Human Presence: An Orthodox View of Nature* (WCC, 1978).

Griffiths, Richard, is an Anglican priest working in the parish of St Matthews, Fulham. He is author of *The Human Use of Animals* (Grove Books, 1982).

Harrison, Ruth, is a well-known member of the Society of Friends (Quakers). She is author of *Animal Machines* (Vincent Stuart, 1964) and was awarded a CBE in 1986 in recognition of her life-long work for the welfare of farm animals. She is a member of the British Government's Farm Animal Welfare Council.

Hick, John, is a Presbyterian minister and is currently Professor of the Philosophy of Religion at Claremont Graduate School, University of California. His many seminal works include: *Evil and the God of Love* (Fontana, 1964), *Death and Eternal Life* (Collins, 1976) and *Philosophy of Religion* (Prentice-Hall, 1973).

Irenaeus of Lyons, St (c130–c202). Bishop of Lyons and theologian. His principal writings against the teaching of the Gnostics (*Adversus haereses*) have been very influential. Believed to have been martyred at Lyons.

Joad, C. E. M., was a distinguished English philosopher and broadcaster. He wrote extensively on the problem of evil, especially animal suffering which he saw as a barrier to theistic belief. His influential works include *God and Evil* (Faber and Faber, 1939) in which he discusses the problem of animal suffering at length and *The Recovery of Belief* (Faber and Faber, 1951) which gives his reasons for returning to Christianity.

John of the Cross, St (1542–1591). Mystical theologian and poet. His chief works are three long poems: *The Dark Night of the Soul, The Spiritual Canticle* and *The Living Flame of Love*. He was named a Doctor of the Church by Pope Pius X1 in 1926.

Kingston, Richard A., is Tutor in Systematic Theology and the Philosophy of Religion at Edgehill College, Belfast. His paper on 'Theodicy and Animal Welfare' (1967) has been widely discussed.

Lewis, C. S. (1898–1963) was Fellow of Magdalen College, Oxford and subsequently Professor of Medieval and Renaissance Literature at the University of Cambridge. He wrote innumerable books on theology, literary criticism, science fiction as well as stories for children. His writings are known to millions of people all over the world in translation.

Linzey, Andrew, is Anglican Chaplain and Director of Studies, Centre for the Study of Theology in the University of Essex. He has written or edited 7 books specialising in Christian ethics including: *Christianity and the Rights of Animals* (SPCK, 1987); *Heaven and Earth* (Churchmans, 1985); *Research on Embryos: Politics, Theology and Law* (Crook Academic, 1988) and *Compassion for Animals* (SPCK, 1988).

Lossky, Vladimir (1903–1958) was a celebrated Orthodox theologian. His books include *The Mystical Theology of the Eastern Church* (James Clarke, 1957) and *In the Image and Likeness of God* (St Vladimir's Seminary Press, 1974).

Manning, Cardinal (1808–1892). Appointed Roman Catholic Archbishop of Westminister in 1865. Well-known for his controversial views on moral issues. He took a leading role in the founding of the first Society for the Protection of Animals from Vivisection serving as one of its Vice-Presidents and speaking at its first meeting in 1876.